How People View Democracy

A *Journal of Democracy* Book

•

Published under the auspices of
the International Forum for Democratic Studies

How People
View Democracy

Edited by
Larry Diamond and Marc F. Plattner

The Johns Hopkins University Press
Baltimore

9 8 7 6 5 4 3 2 1

Chapters in this volume appeared in the following issues of the *Journal of Democracy:* chapter 11, October 2002; chapter 9, October 2004; chapters 4, 6, 8, July 2007; chapter 1, October 2007; chapters 2, 5, 7, 10, January 2008; chapter 3, April 2008. For all reproduction rights, please contact the Johns Hopkins University Press.

The Johns Hopkins University Press
2715 North Charles Street
Baltimore, Maryland 21218-4363
www.press.jhu.edu

Library of Congress Cataloging-in-Publication Data

How people view democracy / edited by Larry Diamond and Marc F. Plattner.
   p. cm. — (A journal of democracy book)
      Includes bibliographical references and index.
      ISBN: 978-0-8018-9060-4 (hardcover : alk. paper)
      ISBN: 978-0-8018-9061-1 (pbk. : alk. paper)
      1. Democracy—Public opinion—Cross-cultural studies. I. Diamond, Larry Jay.
II. Plattner, Marc F., 1945–

 JC423.H7535 2008
 321.8—dc22

2008021269

A catalog record for this book is available from the British Library.

CONTENTS

ACKNOWLEDGMENTS

For the most part, both democracy and public opinion polls were for many years to be found only in the advanced industrial nations of Western Europe and North America. But with the "third wave" spreading democracy to most other regions of the world, public opinion research was soon to follow. Today there is a set of regional "barometers" that monitor attitudes toward democracy in Latin America, Africa, East Asia, South Asia, and even the Arab Middle East (where democracy has yet to take root), as well as a variety of efforts to measure public opinion in the postcommunist countries. A number of members of the Journal of Democracy editorial board—including Michael Bratton, Yun-han Chu, and E. Gyimah Boadi—have played a central role in the creation and management of these enterprises, and the *Journal* has been a pioneer in bringing their findings to a global audience of scholars and practitioners.

We published our first cluster of articles drawn from these surveys in January 2001, and in all we have brought our readers some 20 essays on the subject. In this volume, we gather 11 of these articles, containing the most recent data for each region. They cover postcommunist Europe, Central Asia, East Asia, South Asia, Africa, and Latin America. In addition, the volume opens with two essays that more broadly assess such questions as the role of ordinary people in democratization and the rise of "self-expression values." A third essay is the product of an effort by scholars associated with the regional barometers to draw some global lessons regarding the impact of regime performance on public support for new democracies.

Like our many previous books, this one too would not have been possible without the labor and assistance of many people and organizations—with respect not just to this volume but also to the ongoing work of the *Journal of Democracy*, which is the source of the material published here. Thus we are happy to thank our parent organization, the National Endowment for Democracy, and especially its president, Carl Gershman. We also want to reiterate our thanks to the Lynde and Harry

Bradley Foundation for the assistance that it has provided to the *Journal* over the years. And we wish to express our gratitude to our friends at the Johns Hopkins University Press, both Henry Tom and his colleagues in the books division and Bill Breichner and Carol Hamblen in the journals division. As always, it has been a pleasure to work with them.

The *Journal of Democracy* staff has had to contend with publishing two new books in the summer of 2008, and it has done a magnificent job. The heaviest burden was borne by our managing editor, Sarah Bloxham, who responded with her customary aplomb. Our situation was complicated by her much regretted departure for New York shortly before this volume was completed, but her successor Brent Kallmer did a fine job of stepping in and putting on the finishing touches. Phil Costopoulos and Tracy Brown worked their usual editorial magic, and also benefitted from the assistance of a number of other current and former editors, including Marta Kalabinski, Zerxes Spencer, Sumi Shane, Eric Kramon, and Anja Havedal. We are grateful to them all.

INTRODUCTION

Larry Diamond

Over the past two decades, survey-based public-opinion research on attitudes and values regarding democracy has blossomed along with democracy itself in the developing and postcommunist worlds. Some countries, such as Chile, South Africa, and Taiwan, had relatively long traditions of such survey research. In the 1990s came a new and wider wave of studies that focused far more tightly on how citizens viewed their new democracies. Borrowing questions and approaches from studies of older democracies, particularly in Europe, these fresh research efforts aimed to compile "regional barometers" of opinion through the regular and systematic posing of standardized questions across a number of countries within a given part of the world.

As a result, social scientists began to be able to compare emerging democracies within each region on such vital dimensions as support for democracy, satisfaction with the performance of democracy, confidence in the future of democracy, and trust in democratic institutions. Increasingly in the past decade, the global barometers of attitudes and values toward democracy have borrowed from one another and attempted to develop a common core of standardized questions. In recent years, this has generated a vast new harvest of comparative data telling us how citizens in a diverse array of countries view the principles and institutions of democracy. At the same time, as the World Values Survey (initiated in the early 1980s) spread to more and more countries, it also developed an increasingly explicit concern with democracy.

The *Journal of Democracy* and its readers have been among the beneficiaries of this explosion of social-science research exploring what citizens in new or potential democracies think and feel about democracy and about their own political institutions. Since 1997, the *Journal* has published more than twenty articles examining how people view democracy in every region of the world outside the established democracies. This volume brings together eleven of the most recent articles, which span the cultural and geographic diversity of most of the world.

When it comes to assessing democratic progress in the world, there are few more important sources of data than public opinion. As a system of government that institutionalizes citizen participation and choice, and requires the consent of the governed, democracy stands or falls with citizen commitment to its norms and structures. No democracy can long endure unless it possesses legitimacy in the eyes of its citizens, who must share a broad conviction that democracy is the best form of government for their society, better than any alternative that can be imagined. A critical indicator of democratic consolidation is whether most citizens express a strong belief in the legitimacy of democracy in general and of their particular constitutional system. If most of the public expresses high levels of such "system support" in a robust fashion—across different surveys over time and across different indicators of democratic legitimacy—then strong evidence of democratic consolidation is in hand.[1]

Regional public-opinion "barometers" now cover Latin America, Africa, East Asia, South Asia, postcommunist Europe, and most recently (still in formation) the Arab Middle East, respectively. The articles collected here represent the *Journal*'s first effort to draw together in one volume coverage of the barometers that spans the entire globe save for the industrialized democracies of the West.[2] Using rigorous methods to generate representative samples of national populations (including rural dwellers often ignored by the local mass media and foreign observers) and to achieve consistency in questionnaire wording across the many languages into which the surveys must be translated within a region, the barometers also seek to achieve some degree of global standardization. Borrowing from and interacting with one another, the regional barometers have been refining a shared core of questions that make it easier to compare how people in far-flung parts of the world feel about democracy and their own political systems.

Inevitably, the survey results generate a mixed (and at times, seemingly contradictory) picture of citizen views. But on the whole, they provide a surprisingly hopeful portrait of democratic norms whose reach and vitality are on the rise. In every quarter of the globe, citizen majorities consistently avow their support for democracy as a goal.

Legitimacy: Support for Democracy

As the essays in this book show, there are two revealing approaches to assessing the legitimacy of democracy. One is to determine directly support for democracy as the best system of government. The other is to take what Richard Rose, William Mishler, and Christian Haerpfer call the "Churchillian" approach—by assuming that popular support for democracy may follow the spirit of Winston Churchill's famous dictum that "democracy is the worst form of government, except all those other forms that have been tried from time to time."[3] From this perspective, it may be particularly telling to know the extent to which citizens reject explicit alternatives to democracy, such as rule by the army or by a single party.

One of the most striking findings of the surveys summarized and reviewed in this volume is the strong degree of support that people express over and over again for democracy. One can get a good initial picture of global democratic inclinations by looking at three questions from the World Values Survey. The first probes the extent to which people support democracy by asking whether (and to what degree) they agree or disagree with the statement that "democracy may have its problems, but it's better than any other form of government." The second asks whether people are open to the authoritarian temptation, gauging whether and how strongly they approve or disapprove of "having a strong leader who does not have to bother with parliament and elections." The third question, which asks whether it would be "a good thing" if there were "greater respect for authority" may measure an inclination toward less liberal values.[4]

Strikingly, the belief that democracy is (in principle at least) the best system is overwhelming and universal. While there is a slightly higher preference among the Western industrialized countries, in every region—even the former Soviet Union and the Muslim Middle East—an average of at least 80 percent of people polled say that democracy is best. As we will see shortly, when the question about democratic preference is worded a little differently, people are often much more willing to give a nondemocratic answer. That is also true when concrete regime alternatives are posed. So, for example, the idea of a "strong leader" who would override mechanisms of democratic accountability appeals to nearly half of those in the former Soviet Union, an average of 45 percent of respondents in nine Latin American states, about two in five people on average from eleven Asian states (including China and India), and a little over a third of the public in six Muslim Middle Eastern states. This compares to only a quarter of citizens in 22 Western countries, and a third in the sixteen countries of Central and Eastern Europe. Finally, majorities in every region would like to see greater respect for authority, but here there is no difference between the slight majorities in the West, Asia, and Eastern Europe. Rather, it is in the former Soviet Union, and especially Latin America and the Muslim Middle East, where larger majorities say that more respect for authority is something they desire.

The Afrobarometer's findings are particularly remarkable.[5] In sub-Saharan Africa, the world's poorest region, 62 percent of people surveyed across eighteen countries in 2005 and 2006 said that "democracy is preferable to any other kind of government"—a result they chose even when offered the chance to agree instead that "in some circumstances an authoritarian government can be preferable," or "it doesn't matter."[6] The level of support for democracy reached at least 65 percent in ten of the eighteen countries, and ran as high as 75 percent in Ghana, Kenya, and Senegal. Only in Madagascar and Tanzania did a majority fail to support democracy, and there is evidence from both that the shortfall had more to do with ignorance or apathy than with an active preference for authoritarianism. In fact, in only a few African countries do polls reveal much preference for authoritarian rule, and never does it rise above a fifth of the population. Among those better-informed Africans who are able to volunteer a definition of what democracy means, 75 percent say that democracy is always preferable.

An even higher percentage of Africans on average, 73 percent, reject the option of military rule for their country.[7] Most of the eighteen African publics surveyed in 2005 and 2006 reject military rule overwhelmingly (by margins of 80 percent or more in eight countries). Only in Namibia is the rejection below a majority. These levels represent a modest decline from earlier levels, in 2000 and 2002, when rejection of military rule stood at 82 percent and then 78 percent in the twelve countries surveyed during those earlier years, but the democratic inclination remains strong. Similarly, in 2004, 71 percent of Africans surveyed rejected one-party rule, and 78 percent rejected one-man rule—levels of resistance to renewed authoritarianism that have held steady. Overall, only 39 percent of Africans reject all three authoritarian alternatives *and* say that democracy is always preferable. This is not, however, a true indicator of strong authoritarian sentiment, because in some countries sizeable shares of those surveyed failed to answer one or more of the questions or gave a neutral response. Across the eighteen countries and the three authoritarian-preference items, only one in six Africans on average prefers any particular alternative to democracy.

Africans' support for democracy does not seem to be born of a naïve sense that it will necessarily bring rapid economic progress. When asked to define what democracy means to them, "a majority of Africans interviewed (54 percent) regard it in procedural terms by referring to the protection of civil liberties, participation in decision making, voting in elections, and governance reforms."[8] (Only about one in five says that democracy means a substantive outcome such as economic development or social justice.) As Russell Dalton, Doh C. Shin, and Willy Jou point out in this volume, Africans' penchant for viewing democracy as meaning political freedom (including institutions and procedures meant to secure it) rather than substantive socioeconomic outcomes is shared by their counterparts in Eastern Europe, Asia, and Latin America. No more than about a quarter of the public in any region thinks of democracy mainly in terms of economic or social outcomes. As Dalton, Shin, and Jou conclude, "A basic understanding of democracy has diffused widely around the globe. . . . Instead of assuming that democracy is a Western concept, understood only by affluent and well-educated citizens in established, advanced industrial democracies, these patterns suggest that democracy embodies human values and that most people understand these principles."[9]

In some respects, Africans' appreciation for democracy seems to be deepening. Between 2002 and 2005, the average percentage of respondents in sixteen African countries who agreed that "many political parties are needed" to give voters a real choice grew from 55 to 63 percent. The proportion supporting legislative independence rose from 61 to 66 percent. And the percentage who agreed that their "present system of elected government should be given more time to deal with inherited problems" jumped from 46 percent in 2000 to 56 percent in 2002 and 2005 (and up to three-quarters in Mali, which is one of the world's poorest countries in human-development terms). By 2005, four in five Africans supported open elections and two-thirds backed judicial review (though the latter is a decline from three-quarters in 2002). For a continent on which literacy remains low, these figures bespeak an astonishingly robust commitment to a competitive and fairly liberal conception of democracy. Yet it is altogether in keeping with the substantially liberal and procedural understanding of democracy to which most Africans subscribe.

Latin America and Asia

In Latin America, as measured by the annual Latinobarómetro, the years 1995 to 2007 saw an erosion of support for democracy (as measured by the number of those who told pollsters that "democracy is always preferable"). From an average of about 60 percent in the late 1990s, reports Marta Lagos in the present volume, the level of democratic support across Latin America dipped to 53 percent in 2007 (after spiking up to 58 percent in 2006, perhaps because of good economic performance).[10] All the while, the percentage of Latin Americans preferring authoritarian rule stayed at around 15 percent. In 2005, when Latin Americans were asked if they would "support a military government to replace the democratic government if the situation got very bad," only 30 percent said yes.[11]

Over time, support for democracy as a general preference has been weak and declining in some countries, to levels below 40 percent in Brazil, Guatemala, Honduras, and Paraguay, but each of these countries saw significant improvement in 2006, as did Bolivia, Colombia, and Peru. Venezuela and Argentina have also shown long-term improvement. Thus three-quarters of Latin Americans on average agreed in 2006 that, "democracy may have its problems, but it's the best system of government," while two-thirds agreed that democracy is the only way to become a developed country.[12] Moreover, across time and across most countries, a majority of Latin Americans recognize that democracy cannot exist without a congress (58 percent) and political parties (55 percent).[13]

A new and different regional survey of Latin America, the Latin American Public Opinion Project (LAPOP), has recently found consistently higher levels of public support for democracy in the Americas.[14] Overall, the thirteen-country mean for democratic preference in the 2006 LAPOP survey was 67 percent. The cognate figure from the 2005 Latinobarómetro, by contrast, was only 51 percent. The Latinobarómetro figures may therefore be seen as low-end estimates, and quite possibly underestimates, of democratic support.

Support for democracy varies considerably within East Asia, and not in the direction that might be expected. Although they are the most economically developed and Western-oriented of the new democracies of the region, Taiwan and South Korea both show ambivalence in public commitment to democracy. Support for democracy (as measured by the preference question) rose from 41 to 48 percent in Taiwan between 2001 and 2005, but this is still quite low in comparative terms. In South Korea, support fell from 69 percent just before the East Asian financial crisis of 1997 to 54 percent in 1998 and 45 percent in 2001, before recovering somewhat to 58 percent in 2004.[15] As a result of protracted political polarization and crisis, democratic support in the Philippines fell from 64 percent in 2001 to 51 percent in 2006, and it also fell more modestly in Thailand, but from an exceptionally high level of 83 percent in 2002 to 71 percent in 2006. Japan stood at 67 percent in 2003.

In the five South Asian countries surveyed in 2004, preference for democracy was generally stronger, at 69 percent in India and Bangladesh, 71 percent in Sri Lanka, and 62 percent in Nepal. Pakistan was the outlier, for there only 37 percent of those surveyed said that they preferred democracy over all other forms of government. On average, 62 percent in South Asia prefer democracy, roughly the same proportion as in Africa and East Asia, and slightly higher than in Latin America.

Looking at other dimensions of support for democracy helps us to see that East Asians are much more committed to democracy than they may appear to be at first blush.[16] Majorities in all of the region's democracies think that democracy is "suitable" for their country. This sentiment has risen from 59 to 67 percent in Taiwan (from 2001 to 2005), and from 64 to 79 percent in Korea (from 1997 to 2006), and it remains at or above 80 percent in Thailand and Mongolia. In the Philippines, however, it dropped dramatically between 2001 and 2005, from 80 to 57 percent. Moreover, most East Asians think that democracy can be effective in solving the problems of their respective societies, although the proportions have generally declined in recent years. Most important, large majorities of East Asians reject authoritarian alternatives, and averaging across the six new democracies of East Asia, more than half the public rejects *all* authoritarian alternatives. Seventy to 80 percent (or more) in each country oppose military rule (see Table 2 of the chapter by Chang, Chu, and Park). Over three-quarters of South Koreans, Taiwanese, and Japanese, and substantial majorities as well in the Philippines and Thailand (but in the most recent survey, only a minority of Mongolians) reject a surrender of government to a "strong leader." And large (typically decisive) majorities also reject one-party rule.

Overall, in the first round of surveys, East Asians appeared remarkably similar to Africans: Eight in ten (on average) in the six new democracies opposed military rule, and seven in ten (on average) opposed the options of a strong leader or a one-party state, but only half rejected all four authoritarian options. Encouragingly, as Chang, Chu, and Park show, this propensity to reject authoritarianism has held its own or even strengthened slightly in the most recent surveys (even as some other indicators of support for democracy have weakened). Between 2001 and 2006, resistance to all three forms of authoritarian rule rose sharply in Taiwan (from 56 to 69 percent) and in Thailand (from 46 to 54 percent), while it inched even higher in South Korea (from 69 to 77 percent) but remained low in the Philippines (at 39 percent).

The South Asian pattern is different (or at least it was at the time of the 2004 survey). While support for democracy in principle is strong, resistance to authoritarian rule is not. Only in India does a majority—and even then a surprisingly slim one of just 52 percent—reject the idea of scrapping parliament in favor of a strong leader. Almost half the public feels this way in Pakistan, too, but only a quarter or less in Bangladesh, Nepal, and Sri Lanka. Large proportions in India, Nepal, and Sri Lanka oppose military rule, but only about two in five Bangladeshis and Pakistanis do so.

The Postcommunist Countries

A more striking pattern of divergence is apparent among the former communist countries of Eastern Europe and the former Soviet Union (surveyed in late 2004 and early 2005).[17] There, a line can be drawn distinguishing European Union members from nonmembers. The eight states that acceded to EU membership on 1 May 2004—the Czech Republic, Estonia, Hungary, Latvia, Lithuania, Poland, Slovakia, and Slovenia—reject authoritarian alternatives. In seven of them, this rejection is strong; in Poland, it is weaker. When offered four alternatives to the present democratic system (army rule, communist rule, a dictator, or suspending parliament and elections in favor of "a strong leader who can decide everything quickly"), an average of 61 percent of the public in the eight new EU members rejected all four authoritarian alternatives. The proportions ranged from 72 percent in Hungary to more than 60 percent in Estonia, Slovenia, Lithuania, and the Czech Republic, but only 44 percent in Poland. A stunning 48 percent of the Polish public endorsed (either strongly or "somewhat") the option of rule by a dictator (but this may have come at a highpoint of populist fervor and disaffection that has since abated, as the results of the most recent Polish national election suggest). In most of these countries, suspending parliament and elections was the most popular authoritarian option, enjoying the support of at least a quarter of the public, and a third of the public in the Czech Republic, Latvia, and Poland.

By contrast, the former Soviet countries of Ukraine, Russia, and Belarus were much more welcoming of authoritarian options. Only 45 percent in Ukraine, 27 percent in Russia, and 23 percent in Belarus rejected all authoritarian options. Nearly half of all Russians surveyed said they could support suspension of parliament and elections (and more than 40 percent endorsed a return to communist rule), while nearly two-thirds in Belarus endorsed the option of a dictator (and possibly even the one they have, since 74 percent approve of the current system).

On the conventional measure of democratic preference (democracy is always preferable), the postcommunist states split in a different way. People in the ten new democracies of Eastern Europe show (in the most recent surveys) an average support level of 53 percent (the same as Latin America, according to the Latinobarómetro). Poland stood well below the others, at only 37 percent, but again this may have been a somewhat anomalous political moment. And the low Polish figure was not because of a strong preference for authoritarianism—the proportion backing that option was only one in five, precisely the average for all eight new postcommunist EU members. Rather, the problem appears to be one of sky-high levels of apathy and alienation: Fully 43 percent of all Poles surveyed agreed that "For people like me, it doesn't matter whether we have a democratic or a non-democratic regime."[18] Alone among the thirteen postcommunist countries surveyed, Russia was found to have more than a fifth of its citizens—42 percent, to be exact—saying that authoritarian rule could sometimes be preferable.

As a matter of methodology, it is hazardous to make comparisons over time (or across countries or regions) unless researchers have used precisely the same questions and response structures in all cases. In 1995, Richard Rose and his colleagues posed three authoritarian alternatives: army rule, communist rule, and a "strong leader who can decide everything quickly." Across seven new East European democracies, the mean proportion rejecting all three options was 67 percent.[19] Ten years later, an identical proportion of East European citizens in ten democracies (including now the three Baltic states of Estonia, Latvia, and Lithuania) rejected the same three authoritarian options.[20] On the basis of such consistent evidence, then, we can say that Eastern Europeans have clearly become committed in general to democracy, even if substantial skepticism or hostility lingers across many of the countries that once made up the Soviet Union.

The big picture is clear. Despite democracy's travails and its frequently disappointing performance, panregional majorities in every quarter of the inhabited globe give this form of government their backing and support. Democracy is not yet supported by everyone everywhere, but its levels of support are high enough to let us say that it does appear to be emerging as a universal value. As Nobel laureate Amartya Sen puts it:

> While democracy is not yet universally practiced, nor indeed uniformly accepted, in the general climate of world opinion, democratic governance has now achieved the status of being taken to be generally right. The ball is very much in the court of those who want to rubbish democracy to provide justification for that rejection.[21]

The Middle East

An "Arab Barometer" to measure support for democracy and related attitudes and values in the Arab world is only now in formation. But as Amaney Jamal and Mark Tessler note in this volume, "the evidence . . . from twenty different surveys in nine different Arab countries between 2000 and 2006" shows generally high support for democracy in principle. While the evidence remains preliminary, since the more in-depth democracy-barometer questions had not yet been systematically administered in the Arab world at the time of this writing in May 2008, the portrait of Arab attitudes toward democracy is much more hopeful than is commonly conveyed. Evidence from Algeria, Jordan, Kuwait, Morocco, and Palestine suggests the following generalizations. First, there is broad popular support for democracy in the Arab world. Well over 80 percent of the public in each of these countries (and in Iraq) agrees with the statement that, "despite its problems, democracy is the best form of government." Moreover, most people do not believe that democracy is a Western form of government, incompatible with Islam. And they endorse basic democratic principles of political competition and disagreement, as well as government responsiveness to popular will. In addition, only modest minorities (generally less than a fifth of respondents) favor the regime option of an authoritarian leader.

Arab respondents, however, are much more likely to think of democracy in terms of economic outputs. Jamal and Tessler find that they "attach higher priority to solving economic problems than to securing the political rights and freedoms associated with democracy." Most (83 percent on average) want to see democratic reforms implemented only gradually. More significantly, perhaps, while more religious Muslims are just as likely to support democracy in principle as the less religious, when Arab citizens express support for democracy, it is not necessarily secular democracy that they have in mind. Slightly more than half of those surveyed in these countries so far agree that "men of religion should influence government decisions."

Most of these people favor democracy in principle. It is not yet clear what kind or extent of democracy they have in mind when they endorse this statement, yet Jamal and Tessler's data show that those who favor Islamic democracy in this sense manifest only slightly lower levels of social tolerance than do those Arab-world citizens whose survey responses class them as supporters of secular democracy. Generally, support for an Islamic-oriented democracy seems to be associated with lack of trust in the government and some greater degree of political alienation. But only time (and further research) will tell whether this important segment of Arab public opinion will press for a transition (however gradual) to genuine procedural democracy, or to something that emphasizes Islamic rule as distinguished from democracy as the rest of the world understands it. Reviewing the evidence to date, Jamal and Tessler suggest that the obstacle to democracy in the Arab world stems not from "the alleged antidemocratic impulses of ordinary women and men" but rather from "the structures and manipulations, and perhaps also the supporting external alliances, of a political leadership class that is dedicated to preserving its power and privilege."

Grading Performance

Another important dimension of public opinion regarding democracy is how citizens evaluate the performance of the existing democratic system in their particular country. A common question asks, "How satisfied are you with the way democracy works in [your country]?" In Africa, across the twelve countries surveyed all three times, the overall percentage of respondents who said that they felt satisfied with democracy's workings dipped from 58 percent in 2000 to 45 percent in 2005 (a breakdown of the average shows that satisfaction has declined in eight of the twelve countries). The drop has been starkest in Nigeria, where democratic satisfaction has fallen through the floor, going from 84 percent in 2000 to 26 percent in 2005. In nearby Ghana, where democracy is manifestly working better, satisfaction with it rose from 54 to 70 percent over the same period. Satisfaction is also high (around or above 60 percent) not only in longtime democracy Botswana but also in Mozambique, Namibia, and South Africa. In Mali, the figure tops 50 percent. Madagascar, Malawi, and Tanzania join Nigeria in the 26 percent satisfaction neighborhood, while in Zimbabwe—where there is no democracy—there is also no satisfaction with it (14 percent).

If these figures seem only modest, everything is relative. The Latinobarómetro has found Latin Americans to be persistently dissatisfied with the performance of their democracies: On average, the regional satisfaction level over the last decade has swung between 25 and 40 percent. In 2005, the regional average was less than a third (31 percent). Only in Uruguay and Venezuela were majorities satisfied. Chile and Costa Rica also did better than the rest. In Ecuador, Nicaragua, Paraguay, and Peru, fewer than a fifth of citizens were satisfied. In Mexico and Brazil, the proportion was less than a quarter. Here again, however, the recent LAPOP survey paints a dramatically more positive picture, with a mean level of democratic satisfaction of 48 percent across the thirteen countries surveyed in 2006, compared with a Latinobarómetro finding of 28 percent for the same thirteen countries. In seven of the thirteen, the LAPOP survey found levels of democratic satisfaction more than twice as high as the Latinobarómetro found.

In East Asia between the years 2001 and 2003, about six in ten citizens were satisfied with how democracy was working. This is slightly better than in Europe, where the Eurobarometer finds that satisfaction has tended to oscillate in recent years in the neighborhood of 56 percent, the average level among the EU member states in 2006. (The figure was slightly higher—58 percent—among the former EU fifteen than among the more recently admitted states of Central and Eastern Europe.) In East Asia, Taiwan could boast a 56 percent satisfaction rate by 2005 (up from 45 percent two years earlier), while in Japan fewer than half the respondents (45 percent) felt that Japanese democracy was working in a satisfactory fashion. Satisfaction was highest in Thailand in 2002 at 89 percent, falling only modestly to 78 percent in 2006.[22] In South Asia, democratic satisfaction averaged 64 percent across the five countries, but if one subtracts Pakistan, which has only very recently returned to something approaching a democratic regime (and where only 43 percent were satisfied in the last survey), the proportion jumps to 69 percent.

To the extent that citizens feel dissatisfied with democracy (and even express skepticism regarding its value), perceived shortcomings in democratic performance seem to be the main culprit. While economic performance may play a role, citizens are notably unsettled by the *political* failings that they believe they can detect in their democracies. Citizens expect democracy to deliver accountability and the rule of law. When citizens perceive widespread corruption running rampant instead, they give democracy much lower marks.

As Michael Bratton notes in chapter 8 of this book, figures from the eighteen African countries surveyed around 2005 reveal a significant gap between what Africans want from democracy and what they think they are getting. Four in five want elections that can remove leaders who perform poorly, but fewer than half of respondents (47 percent) judge that they have such elections in their particular country. Two-thirds want their president to be subject to the law, but only 55 percent perceive that he is. Nearly two-thirds want a representative legislature, but only 46 percent think that they have one. On average, Africans think that most of their elected representatives are corrupt—and corruption, Bratton emphatically concludes, "is clearly corrosive to democracy." Africans, he finds, have come to embrace the imperative of honest and free elections, but they also want and need much more: good government between elections, with responsiveness to popular needs and accountability for performance in office.

Latin America offers even more striking data in the same vein. More than nine in ten Latin Americans (most recently, 97 percent in 2001) say that the problem of corruption is serious or very serious. In each of the last few years when the Latinobarómetro has asked the question, overwhelming percentages of respondents (between 75 and 90) have said that corruption has grown worse over the past five years. Fewer than a third of Latin Americans (30 percent in 2005) perceive at least "some" progress in reducing corruption in their country (though the proportions are 40 percent or higher in Chile, Colombia, Uruguay, and Venezuela—all countries where support for democracy has been strong or increasing in recent years). When Latin Americans were asked in 2005 to state what percentage of public officials they thought were corrupt, the average percentage named across the eighteen countries was 68 percent. In sixteen of the eighteen countries, the public thought that at least 60 percent of public officials were corrupt (only in Chile and Uruguay did the average scope of the presumably corrupt fall just below half of all public officials).[23]

Latin Americans also perceive broader problems with the rule of law that diminish the quality of democracy and their commitment to it. Only slightly more than half (54 percent) feel free to "criticize and speak out without restraint" all or most of the time.[24] Seventy percent of citizens (to take Latinobarómetro's 2005 average from across the countries surveyed) see little or no equality before the law in their country (in only two countries, Uruguay and Venezuela, did more than two-fifths of respondents see much equality). Almost four in five Latin Americans think that their fellow citizens are only slightly or not at all "law-abiding." Only one in ten describes the economic situation of the country as fairly or very good.

One result of these perceived failures of performance and accountability is very low trust in politicians and political institutions, as Marta Lagos shows in her chapter in this volume. Some Latin American institutions do enjoy reasonably high levels of trust. Averaging across the eighteen Latin American countries and the years 1995 to 2006, we find, for example, that 72 percent of Latin Americans have expressed confidence in the church and 49 percent in radio (see Table 4 of Lagos). The military, the president, and television all have the trust of slightly over 40 percent of citizens on average in 2006, but the historic average for the military and president is slightly lower. Barely a quarter of Latin Americans over the past decade have expressed trust in congress, however, and only a fifth of citizens trust political parties. Overall, trust in government stood at 36 percent in 2006. The same countries where we detect greater public confidence and support in other respects—Chile, Colombia, the Dominican Republic, Uruguay, and Venezuela—score higher on measures of trust as well, though Costa Rica scores fairly low in relation to its people's strong level of expressed support for democracy.[25] Venezuela represents the paradox of a country slipping out of democracy, yet with the apparent support and approval of a once-excluded and alienated underclass.

There is a striking relationship between trust in political institutions and the perception of progress in reducing corruption in Latin America. Of those with the lowest level of trust in democratic institutions (parties, government, the judiciary, and the congress), half think that there has been no progress in reducing corruption. Of those with the highest level of trust, only 13 percent see no progress, and a third sees a great deal of progress in fighting corruption. In general, the more progress that Latin Americans see in the battle against corruption, the greater their levels of trust in democratic institutions.

Nowhere are levels of trust in parties and representative institutions lower than in the postcommunist states, where citizens had had their fill of "the party" by the time that jubilant East Germans tore down the Berlin Wall. Parties are trusted on average by just 10 percent in the new democracies of the region, and face the active distrust of three out of every four people.[26] Parliament fares not much better (16 percent trust, 63 percent distrust). The courts can count on the confidence of only a quarter of the population, and the distrust of half of it. Only the president is trusted by a majority of the population (barely, 51 percent). These figures stand in sharp contrast to Africa, where, in the typical country, large majorities trust not only the president, the courts, and the military, but also members of parliament. (Since more educated citizens are also more demanding and skeptical, these comparative results are not entirely surprising). The postcommunist malaise is also apparent in the comparison between average democratic satisfaction in the original fifteen EU members (66 percent in 2006) and that in the postcommunist democracies (38 percent across the ten new entrants to the European Union).

If there is this much cynicism about government, why do so many Eastern Europeans accept their democratic systems? Democracy must give the people something. That something is not, as they see it, honest government. Nearly three-quarters of citizens (72 percent) in these ten democracies believe that half or "almost all" of their public officials are corrupt, and roughly the same proportion think that government treats them "definitely" or "somewhat" unfairly. Neither is it economic prosperity. More people in these ten countries approve of the old economic system (69 percent) than the new one (57 percent), and in every country, majorities say that they do not (quite, or definitely) get enough from their main source of income to buy what they need. What people do perceive consistently in large majorities, however, is greater freedom. When asked if they felt freer than before the fall of communism to say what they think, to join any organization, to take an interest in politics or not, and to choose in religious matters, 63 percent answered yes to all four questions. More than half (52 percent) thought the government has some or a lot of respect for human rights (though here there was unusually wide variation, from 76 percent in Hungary to 30 percent in neighboring Romania).

This same recognition of progress with regard to democracy itself appears to account for the durability of democratic support in Africa as well. "By 2005, about two-thirds of Afrobarometer respondents thought they had more freedom of speech (63 percent), more freedom of association (68 percent), and more freedom to vote for the candidate of their choice (68 percent), than they enjoyed 'a few years ago.'"[27] These proportions have declined, on average, since 2000, but only moderately. Moreover, electoral alternation in Africa has made a significant difference, as Michael Bratton shows in chapter 9 of this volume. The perception that one's country has held free and fair elections is one of the most powerful factors accounting for the perceived extent of democracy in Africa. And alternation of parties in power through free and fair elections has a strikingly invigorating effect on support for democracy, as well as on the perception that the "supply" of democracy is adequate. Bratton finds that the passage of time since the last electoral alternation "was negatively related to *every* positive trend in democratic attitudes. . . . In other words, the farther back in the past an electoral alternation (or failing that, a transition to competitive elections) had occurred, the more disillusioned people were with democracy."

Worries and Hopes

Although people in many parts of the world remain ambivalent or even hostile in their attitudes toward democratic institutions and politicians, there are nevertheless some silver linings in the cloudy data presented here. First, majorities in every region support democracy and rate it as *always* preferable to *any* other form of government. In the postcommunist states, Latin America, and Africa, these majorities have held despite difficult economic times and continued or heightened personal economic stress for many citizens. Strong majorities in most of the postcommunist states reject all forms of authoritarian rule, and so do about half those surveyed in Africa and East Asia. In East and South Asia, about three-fifths of the public is satisfied with how democracy is working, though in Africa the cognate figure has declined to less than half, and in Latin America (according to the Latinobarómetro) it has been stuck below 40 percent for quite some time. Levels of trust in democratic actors and institutions are worrisomely low. But at least we have a good indication as to why. Citizens are deeply distressed by what they perceive to be widespread levels of corruption and lawless or self-regarding behavior on the part of politicians.

From listening to the people—something that the barometers enable us to do in a clear, consistent, and globe-spanning manner never available before—it is clear what needs to be done to strengthen and consolidate democracy. In the long run, it remains true that democracy should lead toward the improvement of people's material lives and the advance of economic development. But on the near horizon, what people are saying most clearly is that they want fair, honest, and responsive government—and if they do not get it, at a bare minimum what they demand is the ability to "throw the rascals out" and try again. To the extent that democracy works to provide the political substance that people expect of it—individual freedom, accountability, free and fair elections, the rule of law, and some degree of fairness to all citizens, people will come to value democracy, even if grudgingly at first, and will hold firm against temptations to embrace this or that nondemocratic alternative.

Yet the reverse is also true. By all accounts, citizens lost faith in democracy in Pakistan because of the corruption, lawlessness, and violence that pervade public life there. Hence, they barely resisted or even welcomed General Pervez Musharraf's 1999 military coup.[28] Putin has been able to dismantle democracy in Russia for similar reasons. Many people now worry about Nigeria as well. Most Nigerians say that their country is still a democracy, albeit with major problems. Freedom House is more accurate in judging that gross electoral fraud and abuse of power have pushed Nigeria well below the threshold of electoral democracy. By 2005, public support for democracy had declined only modestly in Nigeria, from 80 to 65 percent, but satisfaction with the way democracy works had collapsed, with 70 percent expressing dissatisfaction. So far, Nigerians still reject alternatives to democracy. In particular, 70 percent reject military rule and 80 percent reject rule by a single party. In 2006, 84 percent of Nigerians opposed an extension of the presidential term (beyond the constitutional two-term limit)—and that public resistance proved crucial in pressuring the National Assembly to say no to the term-extension amendment behind whose passage President Olusegun Obasanjo had mustered all the vast power and wealth that his office could command.

Figures for 2005 show that public patience with democracy was holding steady, with 55 percent of Nigerians willing to give the system more time. But the commitment was not open-ended. The survey revealed a public perception of deep deficits in democratic performance, with only 27 percent willing to say that they trusted their country's electoral institutions. Sadly, the massive rigging of the 2007 national elections—out of which Obasanjo's handpicked successor emerged as the new president—shows how solid is the basis upon which this lack of confidence rests. Nigeria's drama demonstrates that the principal threat to democracy comes not from below but from above. The worry is not that people at large will toss aside democratic aspirations and values. Rather, it is bad and shortsighted political behavior by elites that usually does the crucial damage, as Nancy Bermeo argues in her important book on democratic breakdowns.[29]

In our concluding essay, coauthored by scholars representing most of the regional barometers represented in this volume, we find compelling support for the link between the political performance of regimes on the one hand, and levels of popular support for democracy on the other. As Chu, Bratton, Lagos, Shastri, and Tessler show in their analysis of the pooled data from the African, Latin American, Arab, East Asian, and South Asian barometers, support for democracy is much more closely associated with citizens' evaluations of the political system—such as whether elections have been free and fair, whether citizens have equal rights under the law, and whether key political institutions can be trust-ed—than it is with evaluations of national or family economic circum-stances. Particularly striking is the impact of these political evaluations (now including the control of corruption) on satisfaction with the way democracy works, which is itself the strongest single correlate of sup-port for democracy. In short, while economic performance matters in the consolidation of mass support for democracy, in the near term the provision of political goods matters more. "In a nutshell," the authors conclude, "democracy needs to 'pay its way' by delivering acceptable levels of citizen control and good governance." If these findings are sobering, given the alarmingly high levels of corruption that prevail in so many of the countries surveyed in this volume, there is the hopeful corollary that political reform can indeed produce significant and pos-sibly lasting positive changes in public support for democracy.

There is another hopeful longer-term implication that we would do well to note. As Christian Welzel and Ronald Inglehart show here in their bold analysis of data from the World Values Survey, based on their path-breaking recent book, there are also much deeper developmental forces at work that are very widespread and are generating a culture of democracy. Their long-term effect is to promote the rise of better governed, more liberal and more stable democracies (characterized by what Welzel and Inglehart call "effective democracy") that will be well-suited to control corruption.[30] Economic development, with its increases in personal income and levels of education, gives ordinary citizens more independent resources with which to govern their own lives. At the same time, modernization (even under dictatorial conditions) inelucta-bly gives rise to what the authors call "self-expression values," which motivate people to want to govern their own lives, free of the imposi-tions of an authoritarian state. The generation of these self-expression values (including tolerance, trust, support for equality, and a desire to participate in civic life) is strongly associated with the achievement of democracy—and even more strongly (in fact, overwhelmingly) associated with liberal, "effective" democracy. (While the supporting data are only briefly summarized in their chapter in this volume, they are presented in rigorous and voluminous detail in their book.) Controlling for numerous other factors, such as religion, ethnic fragmentation, and levels of economic development and education, Welzel and Inglehart find that "a society's level of self-expression values emerges as the strongest predictor by far of effective democracy." To the extent that economic development occurs under authoritarian rule, such development will, in the words of Welzel and Inglehart, "emancipate people." In other words, it will give them material and intellectual resources and values of participation, tolerance, and autonomy that will motivate them and enable them to demand democracy. Sooner or later, authoritarianism will give way. As self-expression values grow in society, people are more inclined to demand not just democracy but accountability, freedom, and good governance. This unleashes a virtuous circle in which development and democracy each gradually deepen and advance one another.

Of course, the problem is that so many "developing" countries are anything but that; they are trapped in a vicious cycle of poverty, powerlessness, and bad governance. But the data in this volume provide reason to hope for these countries as well. Even in the world's poorest region—Africa—people are becoming more politically active, demanding, and aware. In roughly half the 48 countries of sub-Saharan Africa, these normative changes have driven or accompanied the rise of electoral democracy. Where democracy is functioning best, as in Botswana, Ghana, and South Africa, economic development is also beginning to take hold. To the extent that more vigilant and aware African populations (and others in the world) are able to hold governments accountable and press for governance reforms, economic growth will accelerate, and self-expression values will grow (possibly even faster than the historical norm). The process is unlikely to be smooth and continuous. But because of the normative changes documented in this volume, it is possible to imagine that it will ultimately lift many more countries out of the poverty trap and onto a path where democratic accountability and economic development gradually reinforce one another in the quest for prosperity, human empowerment, and truly effective democracy.

NOTES

1. Juan J. Linz and Alfred Stepan, *Problems of Democratic Transition and Consolidation: Southern Europe, South America, and Post-Communist Europe* (Baltimore: Johns Hopkins University Press, 1996); Larry Diamond, *Developing Democracy: Toward Consolidation* (Baltimore: Johns Hopkins University Press, 1999).

2. In some cases, these are not the only barometers for the region in question, but each of the barometer projects represented in this volume has developed in interaction with the

others, and in most cases each is either the only regionwide survey of political attitudes and values or the one that focuses most closely on opinions about democracy.

3. Richard Rose, William Mishler, and Christian Haerpfer, *Democracy and Its Alternatives: Understanding Post-Communist Societies* (Baltimore: Johns Hopkins University Press, 1998).

4. The raw data and content of the survey may be found in Ronald Inglehart et al., *Human Beliefs and Values: A Cross-cultural Sourcebook Based on the 1999–2002 Values Surveys* (Mexico City: Siglo XXI, 2004), questions E018, E114, and E123.

5. For documentation of these findings, in addition to the two essays here by Michael Bratton reporting on the Afrobarometer findings, see Michael Bratton, E. Gyimah-Boadi, and Robert Mattes, *Public Opinion, Market Reform, and Democracy in Africa* (Cambridge: Cambridge University Press, 2005), and the papers reporting the third wave of the Afrobarometer findings on *www.afrobarometer.org*.

6. Most of the data presented here from the Afrobarometer are available at *www. afrobarometer.org/publications.html*. See, in particular, "The Status of Democracy, 2005–2006: Findings from Afrobarometer Round 3 for 18 Countries," Afrobarometer Briefing Paper No. 40, June 2006. Some of the data come directly from one of the project's directors, Michael Bratton, and its associate director, Carolyn Logan, both of Michigan State University, and I thank them for their cooperation. Throughout this discussion, the average levels of opinion within a region represent the average of the figures for each of the countries in that region.

7. These Africa-wide figures are not estimates for the total population of Africa, but rather averages of the 23- or 18-country averages.

8. Bratton, Mattes, and Gyimah-Boadi, *Public Opinion, Democracy, and Market Reform in Africa*, 69–70.

9. The preliminary evidence of Amaney Jamal and Mark Tessler, however, shows a larger percentage of Arab respondents (about half) giving an economic rather than a political procedural definition of democracy.

10. *Informe Latinobarómetro 2006* (Santiago de Chile: Corporación Latinobarómetro, 2005), 71. Available at: *www.latinobarometro.org*. See also *Latinóbarometro Report 2005: 1995–2005, A Decade of Public Opinion* (Santiago de Chile: Corporación Latinobarómetro, 2005), 56; and the 2007 annual report of the Latinobarómetro. Available at: *www.latinobarometro.org*.

11. The positive spin, of course, is that 62 percent of Latin Americans reject military government under any circumstance. See *Latinobarómetro Report 2005*, 51.

12. *Informe Latinobarómetro 2006*, 64; *Latinobarómetro Report 2005*, 52.

13. *Informe Latinobarómetro 2006*, 62.

14. This may be owing to a more systematic effort to capture rural respondents in proportion to their actual share of the population, and perhaps also to other differences in sampling and implementation. Rural respondents, LAPOP director Mitchell Seligson argues, are less educated and less critical; they tend to be more supportive of the current system. In this survey, the percentage of Hondurans preferring democracy always is 78 percent rather than 33 percent—a staggering difference. Some other large differences, with the LAPOP survey always showing higher support for democracy than was detected in the Latinobarómetro survey, were noted in Peru (62 versus 40 percent) and Ecuador (69 versus 43 percent). Generally, the differences between the two surveys are more modest, but nevertheless appreciable (in Costa Rica, 86 versus 73 percent; in Chile, 71 versus 59 percent). For further data and explanation, see *www.lapopsurveys.org*, and Mitchell

Seligson, "The Rise of Populism and the Left in Latin America," *Journal of Democracy* 18 (July 2007): 81–95.

15. Doh Chull Shin and Jaechul Lee, "The Korea Democracy Barometer Surveys, 1997–2004," *Korea Observer* 37 (Summer 2006): 237–76.

16. See the essay by Yu-tzung Chang, Yun-han Chu, and Chong-min Park in this volume, and also Yu-tzung Chang, Yun-han Chu, and Min-hua Huang, "The Uneven Growth of Democratic Legitimacy in East Asia," *International Journal of Public Opinion Research* 18 (Summer 2006): 246–55.

17. For additional data beyond those reported in this volume, see Richard Rose, *Insiders and Outsiders: New Europe Barometer 2004* (Glasgow: Centre for the Study of Public Policy, No. 404, 2005).

18. Rose, *Insiders and Outsiders*, 68, question D7.

19. The seven countries were Bulgaria, the Czech Republic, Hungary, Poland, Romania, Slovakia, and Slovenia. See Richard Rose and Christian Haerpfer, *New Democracies Barometer IV: A 10-Nation Survey* (Glasgow: Centre for the Study of Public Policy, No. 262, 1996), 21, 86.

20. The most striking difference is that the proportion of firm democrats in Poland, measured in this way, fell from 63 percent in 1995 to 50 percent in 2004.

21. Amartya Sen, "Democracy as a Universal Value," in Larry Diamond and Marc F. Plattner, eds., *The Global Divergence of Democracies* (Baltimore: Johns Hopkins University Press, 2001), 4–5.

22. The 2006 survey of Thailand was completed before the bloodless military coup that took place in Bangkok on September 19 of that year.

23. *Latinobarómetro Report 2005*, 30.

24. This figure for 2005 was up from 49 percent in 2003.

25. Once again, the LAPOP survey finds a more favorable picture for the region, with much higher levels of trust in congress (43 percent on average in thirteen countries in 2006) and in political parties (36 percent on average). Interestingly, it found about the same level of trust in the church, 69 percent.

26. The methodology for this survey was different than the others in that it provided respondents with a seven-point scale ranging from complete trust to complete distrust, and thus allowed respondents the option of giving a neutral, midpoint answer.

27. Michael Bratton and Wonbin Cho, "Where is Africa Going? View from Below: A Compendium of Trends from 12 African Countries, 1999–2006," Afrobarometer Working Paper No. 60, 2006, *http://www.afrobarometer.org/papers/AfropaperNo60-trends.pdf*.

28. Larry Diamond, "Is Pakistan the (Reverse) Wave of the Future?" *Journal of Democracy* 11 (July 2000): 91–106.

29. Nancy Bermeo, *Ordinary People in Extraordinary Times: The Citizenry and the Breakdown of Democracy* (Princeton: Princeton University Press, 2003).

30. Ronald Inglehart and Christian Welzel, *Modernization, Cultural Change, and Democracy* (New York: Cambridge University Press, 2005).

How People View Democracy

1

HOW PEOPLE UNDERSTAND DEMOCRACY

Russell J. Dalton, Doh C. Shin, and Willy Jou

Russell J. Dalton *is professor of political science at the University of California–Irvine and author of* The Good Citizen: How the Young Are Reshaping American Politics *(2007).* **Doh C. Shin** *is professor of political science at the University of Missouri and director of the Korean Democracy Barometer surveys.* **Willy Jou** *is a doctoral candidate at the University of California–Irvine. This essay originally appeared in the October 2007 issue of the* Journal of Democracy.

The "third wave" of democratization gave rise to Francis Fukuyama's well-known statement that democracy appeared to represent the endpoint of human history.[1] Apparently reaffirming this claim, a new wave of international public-opinion surveys finds striking support for democracy around the globe. World Values Survey data indicate that "in country after country throughout the world, a clear majority of the population endorses democracy,"[2] while opinion surveys in Eastern Europe, Africa, and East Asia also describe broad support for democracy, even in some of the most unlikely places.[3] Indeed, the breadth of democratic support is often amazing, with majorities of the public in nations as diverse as Azerbaijan, Iran, and Vietnam stating that democracy is the best form of government, even if it has its faults.

This public-opinion evidence has generated questions about the substance of popular support for democracy in many developing nations. Some skeptics claim that most residents in such countries are preoccupied with economic needs and have little understanding of democracy. To peasants in Afghanistan or Zimbabwe, democracy may have positive connotations, but their understanding of the concept might be vague or without content. Alternatively, some skeptics suggest that support for democracy signals a desire for Western income levels and living standards, and not for a democratic political system. Still others suggest that rhetorical support for democracy has lost meaning, as democracy is now embraced even by nondemocrats because of the positive image and legitimacy that it enjoys.

So how do ordinary people understand democracy? Do contemporary publics display a reasonable understanding of the meaning of democracy, and what are the contents of their definitions? We draw upon nearly fifty national public-opinion surveys that have recently explored this question in Africa, Asia, Eastern Europe, and Latin America. For a subset of nations, we track how perceptions change after a transition from authoritarianism to democracy. Finally, we discuss the implications of these patterns for the democratization process as well as for programs meant to facilitate democratization.

Defining Democracy

It is rumored that a Chinese student at the 1989 Tiananmen Square democracy rally held a poster that read, "I don't know what democracy means, but I know we need more of it." In fact, democracy is a concept with a variety of potential meanings, and it is not simple to grasp or define.

Thus one might begin by asking whether the average citizen—especially in poor and less democratic nations—can offer a reasonable definition of democracy. Even in advanced industrial democracies, research often highlights the limited political knowledge and sophistication of mass publics. Does a peasant in a developing nation—who often has little schooling and limited access to mass media—have a basis for understanding or evaluating democracy? Some prior surveys suggest that public understanding of democracy is common, but this remains an uncertain pattern across other democratizing nations.[4] The first question, therefore, is what percentage of the public offers any definition of democracy?

For those who offer a definition of democracy, the question turns to which factors they emphasize. The most widely employed scholarly definitions of democracy focus on the *institutions and procedures of democratic governance*. For example, Robert Dahl's seminal writings largely equate democracy with the institutions and processes of representative government.[5] If citizens can participate equally in free and fair elections, and if elections direct the actions of government, then the standards of democracy are met. Indeed, Freedom House rankings and other democracy indicators often treat free and fair elections as a defining element of democracy.

Similarly, the democracy-building activities of governments and international NGOs often focus on democracy's institutional and procedural aspects. Democracy-promotion groups advise governments on constitutional reforms; fund public-education programs to explain the nature of electoral politics and other democratic procedures; monitor elections; and provide aid to create political organizations. Thus we might expect people to think of democracy in institutional and procedural terms, and to cite "free and fair elections," "multiparty competition," and "majority rule" as democracy's defining elements. Indeed, surveys that present respondents with a list of items to define democracy often find that voting, elections, and such procedural choices are common responses.[6]

People might also define democracy in terms of its outcomes. Democracy emphasizes *freedom and liberty* as its essential goals, with democratic institutions as the means to achieve them. This has been part of the political rhetoric of democracy from the preamble of the U.S. Declaration of Independence to Franklin D. Roosevelt's articulation of the four democratic freedoms in his 1941 State of the Union address. Similarly, Larry Diamond lists political liberties, participation rights of citizens, equal justice before the law, and equal rights for women as four of the core democratic values.[7] Even if individuals might not understand the institutional procedures of democracy, their desire for freedom and liberty may generate support for democracy as a means to these goals. In principle, other forms of government might seek to achieve these same goals; in practice, however, it is contradictory for autocratic regimes to protect the freedom and liberties of the citizenry.

Earlier surveys in several developing nations have found that references to freedom, liberties, and rights were the most common answers in defining the meaning of democracy. For instance, Janos Simon found that liberty and basic rights were the first answer given by a majority of the public in four of the five East European nations he studied.[8] References to liberty, freedom, and equality also accounted for the plurality of responses in surveys in Africa and Latin America.[9]

While scholarly definitions of democracy focus on the political, there may also be a third, *social dimension* to public images of democracy—especially in low-income nations. A social-democratic conception of democracy can include such social rights as social services, providing for those in need, and ensuring the general welfare of others. Some proponents of this view argue that the democratic principles of political equality and participation are meaningless unless individuals have sufficient resources to meet their basic social needs. Indeed, even Roosevelt's four freedoms included the freedom from want.

Furthermore, one hears frequent claims that support for democracy in developing nations merely signals a desire for a higher standard of living.[10] To the extent that democracy is identified with affluent, advanced industrial societies, the endorsement of democracy may mean a desire to achieve this same economic—but not necessarily the same political—standard. This orientation would lead people to cite economic improvement, social welfare, and economic security as key elements of democracy. For example, a 1990 survey asked East Europeans to choose

between three political and three economic values that they considered
most important to their country's democratic development; most people
equated democracy with the economic values of prosperity, equality,
and security.[11]

These three broad alternatives—institutions and procedures, freedom and liberties, and social benefits—constitute the primary substantive choices in defining democracy. Certainly people will offer other
responses if asked to define democracy spontaneously. Yet the extent
to which democracy is defined in terms of these three broad choices
provides a framework to assess the high levels of public support for democracy in recent public-opinion surveys and the implications of these
democratic aspirations. Each alternative has different implications for
the interpretation of public opinion toward democracy and the principles
that guide the democratization process.

Measuring Public Understanding of Democracy

How do contemporary publics understand the meaning of democracy? To address this quesion, we assembled the major crossnational surveys that have asked a common open-ended question on the meaning of
democracy.[12] The value of the open-ended format is that it allows (and
requires) respondents to define democracy in their own words. This is a
more rigorous test of democratic understanding than providing a list of
items which respondents rate as important. Our methodology requires
that respondents actively articulate their understanding of democracy.

The Postcommunist Citizen Project adopted a question on democracy's meaning in its surveys of five newly democratized East European nations in the early 1990s. The Afrobarometer, the East Asia Barometer, and the Latinobarómetro adopted a version of this question in
their regional surveys in the early 2000s. The Asia Foundation asked
about the meaning of democracy in Afghanistan and Indonesia, while
the New Soviet Citizens Project surveyed Russian and Ukrainian public
opinion. We expand the breadth of the empirical evidence by merging
these separate projects, which yields results from 49 nations. This includes surveys in four established democracies (Austria, Japan, Spain,
and the United States) to provide a reference point for the developing
nations.[13]

Figure 1 displays the findings grouped into five global regions, with
responses coded into five categories that are averaged across the nations
in the region.[14] The top of each bar displays the percentages who define
democracy in terms of *freedoms, civil liberties, and citizen rights*.[15] This
includes freedom of speech, political liberty, protection of individual
rights, or freedom to participate. The second level presents responses
that involve *democratic institutions* or the *democratic political process,*
which includes such responses as rule by the people, elections, majority

FIGURE 1—THE MEANING OF DEMOCRACY
(PERCENTAGE OF TOTAL RESPONSES)

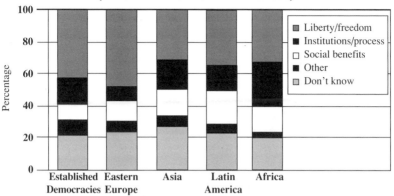

Source: Figure combines results from national surveys in 49 countries.

rule, or open and accountable government. The third category displays responses broadly classified as *social benefits,* which include social and economic development, equality or justice, or peace and stability. The fourth category describes miscellaneous responses that cannot be coded under another heading. Often this category reflects the different coding schemes used in the separate projects, so it becomes a residual category for responses that do not fit the other categories.[16] The bottom part of each bar displays the percentages who do not offer any substantive definition. To those individuals, democracy is a concept largely devoid of meaning.

It is significant that most people in most nations do offer some definition of democracy. In the four established democracies in this set, about a quarter of the public did not provide any definition of democracy (23 percent), illustrating that even in these nations some citizens have limited political knowledge. The percentage of those who provide a definition of democracy in established democracies is not significantly different from the average percentage in the world's other regions. Afrobarometer respondents are actually more likely to offer a definition of democracy than are Spaniards or Japanese, and a large majority in several Asian and Latin American nations also offer definitions. Indeed, even in mainland China—which has very low income levels, a large peasantry, and limited democratic experience—two-thirds of the public can express what democracy means to them. Only in Brazil in 2001 and in Indonesia in 1999 did a majority of the public not offer a response. Several other Latin American nations also score relatively low in democratic awareness, which also appears in other Latinobarómetro surveys.

Awareness of the term "democracy" and a willingness to express a definition are initial indications of the depth of contemporary democratic understanding. More important, of course, is the content of these definitions. Here also the results differ from what many of the skeptics have assumed.

Strikingly, democracy is broadly identified in terms of freedom and civil liberties.[17] In most nations, these democratic outcomes are what most people think of when they define democracy. Definitions referencing elections, majority rule, and other such democratic procedures and institutions are only about half as frequent as those citing freedom and liberty. People seem to understand that electoral and constitutional democracy is not sufficient. To most people, the real meaning of democracy is in what it produces.

The breadth of freedom-and-liberty responses across a wide array of nations is impressive. We might expect such rights consciousness in the United States, and it clearly appears in the U.S. responses. Yet even in poor nations such as Afghanistan and Zambia—which have modest literacy levels, low living standards, and limited access to media and other information sources—the average person primarily cites examples of freedoms and liberties when asked what democracy means to them. It is, perhaps, a testament to the positive attraction of democracy that citizens in even the most unlikely national circumstances understand democracy by its political benefits.

Relatively few people define democracy in terms of social benefits (only about a tenth of respondents do so). This heading includes references to social equality, justice, and equality of opportunities, rather than blatant economic benefits such as employment, social welfare, or economic opportunities. For instance, a relatively large percentage of the public in South Korea, Mongolia, South Africa, and Chile defines democracy in terms of social benefits, but in each case more than three-quarters of these responses involve social justice and equality, and only a small percentage deal with social and economic benefits. These results undercut claims that supporters of democracy really mean they want higher living standards and similar benefits.

A basic understanding of democracy has apparently diffused widely around the globe. Even if one agrees that the depth of understanding has limits, the responses themselves indicate the ideas that contemporary publics associate with democracy.[18] Instead of assuming that democracy is a Western concept, understood only by affluent and well-educated citizens in established, advanced industrial democracies, these patterns suggest that democracy embodies human values and that most people understand these principles.

The Roots of Democratic Understanding

It is surprising that a large proportion of the public in developing nations defines democracy in liberal-democratic terms. Even if these are only "questionnaire democrats"—an interpretation that we reject—it is still remarkable that citizens with limited democratic experience know the "correct" answers.

How can we explain this broad public understanding of democracy? One possibility is a *model of diffusion,* which suggests that democratic norms and aspirations spread across the globe because of their natural appeal as well as from the advocacy of international groups.[19] According to this logic, people are drawn to democracy once they understand its potential benefits. The shopkeeper in Cincinnati, Ohio, knows what it means to have freedom and liberty to live one's own life, and a peasant in China who learns about democracy can also understand this ideal even if it is unrealized in his nation. Moreover, confronting a life without freedom and liberty, the Chinese peasant might be even more aware of the consequences of an autocratic regime, and the potential advantages of democracy in providing basic human rights. If this logic is correct, then public understanding of democracy should be weakly related to national conditions, such as the democratic experience or affluence of the population.

Alternatively, a *logic of learning* suggests that ideas about democracy are learned from democratic experience. For instance, political elites in eastern Germany in the early 1990s expressed as much support for democracy as elites from western Germany, but deeper democratic values such as political tolerance apparently developed from actual democratic experience.[20] Similarly, others have argued that people in emerging democracies generally express democratic aspirations when asked whether they support democracy as a regime form, but that their understanding of democracy's meaning requires some degree of democratic experience.[21] If this logic is correct, then public understanding of democracy should be related to national conditions, such as democratic development.

To examine these rival ideas, we compared the economic and political characteristics of nations to their respective publics' understandings of democracy. Affluent societies with better-educated publics might be more likely to define the concept of democracy, while their level of wealth may also affect the content of democratic definitions. Popular lore presumes that people in less-developed nations are more likely to equate democracy with social benefits and a higher living standard. Similarly, we might expect that a freedoms-and-liberties consciousness is more common in affluent societies. It also seems reasonable to assume that more democratic nations would have citizens who are better able to define democracy, and who would perhaps hold images of democracy that focus on freedoms and liberties and the political process, rather than social benefits.

We examined these ideas with surveys from the 49 nations included in our comparison set. Although one might expect national affluence to correlate with the percentage of the public that gives "don't know"

FIGURE 2—DEMOCRATIC DEVELOPMENT
AND DEFINITIONS OF DEMOCRACY

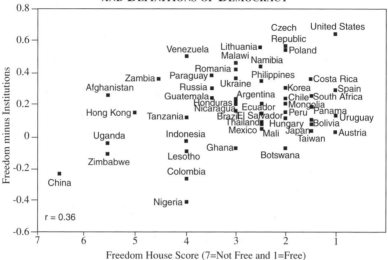

Freedom House Score (7=Not Free and 1=Free)

responses, this relationship is not statistically significant.[22] Respondents in poor nations are almost as likely to express some definition of democracy as affluent publics, and even the content of these definitions varies only slightly according to the level of national affluence. Wealthier publics are slightly less likely to define democracy in terms of its social benefits, but these differences are not statistically significant. Similarly, the level of democratic development—as measured by the Freedom House—is essentially unrelated to the percentage of respondents who give "don't know" responses.

There is, however, some evidence that the content of democratic understanding changes with democratic experience (see Figure 2). Higher levels of democracy are significantly related to a greater emphasis on freedom and liberty (r=0.34), while democratic development is negatively associated with a focus on institutional and procedural definitions of democracy (r=-0.36). People in the least democratic nations—such as China, Uganda, and Zimbabwe—associate democracy with such political processes as majority rule and free and fair elections. With increasing democratic development, however, the emphasis shifts to freedom and liberties. For instance, U.S. respondents were asked only for a single definition of democracy and 68 percent of respondents cited freedom and liberties (the upper-right point in Figure 2), while Chinese, who were asked for three definitions, mentioned freedom and liberties only 23 percent of the time (the lower-left point).

Early studies of political culture and political development often discounted the ability or the willingness of the public in developing nations to understand or embrace democracy.[23] Our results provide a more posi-

FIGURE 3—CHANGES IN MEANING OF DEMOCRACY FOLLOWING A
DEMOCRATIC TRANSITION

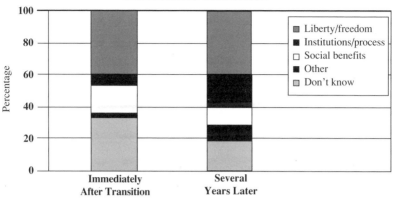

Sources: For Poland, the Czech Republic, Lithuania, and Romania, the Postcommunist Citizens Survey; for Afghanistan, the Asia Foundation Survey, 2004 and 2006; for Indonesia, the Asia Foundation, National Voter Education Survey, 1999, and Democracy in Indonesia—A Survey of the Electorate, 2003.

tive picture of democratic awareness and the breadth of citizen under-standing. Many individuals in these nations may not fully comprehend the exact details of their democratic definitions, but that they cite broad principles of liberal democracy is a notable positive finding. Moreover, the identification of democracy with greater freedom and liberty has broadly diffused across the globe, articulated by publics even in unlikely political and economic circumstances.

Examples of Democratic Learning

According to the logic of democratic learning, people should learn democracy's meaning by experiencing a new democratic order, while new incentives and civic-education efforts may also influence their un-derstanding. Put simply, citizens' democratic understanding should be the sum of their individual experiences.

To test this logic, we assembled time-series trends on public under-standing of democracy from seven nations that had recently undergone a democratizing regime change: Afghanistan, Czechoslovakia, Hungary, Indonesia, Lithuania, Poland, and Romania.[24] Because we can compare responses from the period immediately following democratization with those from a few years thereafter, these nations provide fertile ground for examining whether and how citizens' understanding of democracy shifts in response to a change of regime.

Figure 3 combines results from all seven nations for the first survey after the democratic transition, and a second survey several years lat-er.[25] Citizens' understanding of democracy generally does increase with democratic experience. Except in Poland, where the decline was small, all other countries witnessed significant decreases in the "don't know" responses. The increased awareness of democracy was most salient in Afghanistan, where the share of "don't know" responses dropped 32 percentage points in two years, suggesting that democratic understanding can be learned in a short period of time. Moreover, several of the first surveys were conducted a few years after the democratic transition, which implies that democratic learning might be even greater if we could do true pre- and post-transition comparisons.

In terms of the substance-of-democracy definitions, institutional and political-process definitions increase for this set of nations. This striking phenomenon occurs across all seven countries, and runs contrary to our earlier finding that greater democratic experience leads citizens to emphasize freedom and liberty, rather than the processes of democracy. At the same time, the propensity to define democracy in terms of freedoms and liberties also increases slightly between the two waves of surveys, and this may be understated because of changes in the coding of responses.[26] In the two nations with the same coding methodology in both waves—Afghanistan and Indonesia—definitions based on freedom, liberty, and rights increased by 14 percent between the two waves.

Rates of change appear to differ between countries at different stages of economic development. For instance, the Czech Republic and Hungary saw relatively minor changes over time, while countries ranking lowest on both indices—Afghanistan and Indonesia—witnessed some of the largest changes. It may be that people in more affluent countries are more educated and have more opportunities to receive information about, or even to interact with, democratic societies—which in turn fosters familiarity with the concept (if not the practice) of democracy even before democratic transitions take place. These conditions do not apply to most citizens in less-developed countries that are experiencing democratization.

A comparison of our cross-sectional and time-series results provides an intriguing contrast. The cross-sectional results suggest that perceptions of freedom and liberty grow with democratization, while the cross-temporal results are ambiguous on this point. Democratization may strengthen public emphasis on liberties and rights, but it also may be that democracy finds more fertile ground for development where people are more conscious of the liberties and rights that are embedded in a democratic political order.

Lessons for Democratization

The recent global public-opinion surveys on attitudes toward democracy should reshape our basic images of democracy's popular base. Evidence from the World Values Survey and regional Barometer surveys demonstrates broad public support for democracy as a form of government, even in many undemocratic settings. Our research indicates that support for democracy is more than a hollow expression on behalf of an unknown concept, because most citizens of most developing nations are capable of imputing meaning to democracy in their own words.

Equally important, people most often think of democracy in terms of the freedoms, liberties, and rights that it conveys, rather than in terms of institutional structures and governmental processes. This implies that the popular appeal of democracy lies not in its procedures for elections and governance, but rather in the freedom and liberty that democracy provides. Even in less-developed nations, relatively few people equate democracy with such social benefits as a higher living standard, secure employment, or personal security.

These different definitions of democracy also shape citizen attitudes toward democracy. According to Michael Bratton and his associates, Africans' ability to define democracy has a significant and independent effect on their demand or support for democracy. As Bratton and his team explain, "understanding of democracy is a top-ranked element explaining why some Africans demand democracy and others do not."[27]

Generally, our findings suggest that the broad popular support for democracy displayed in contemporary public-opinion surveys is legitimate, as endorsements of democracy are typically paired with reasonable definitions of democracy's meaning. We should be cautious about reading too much into public definitions of democracy, because democracy requires more than an understanding of the term. Yet the extent of liberal understandings of democracy indicates a level of political awareness that previous research on the political culture of developing nations did not recognize. Indeed, these patterns suggest that democratic aspirations reflect deeper human values for control over one's life and individual freedom that are readily understood by people across the world.[28]

The popular emphasis on freedom and liberty also holds implications for democracy-promotion efforts. Governments and international agencies often focus their democracy-building activities on the institutional elements of democracy. These are important parts of the democratic process. Yet people are naturally drawn to the freedoms, liberties, and rights that democracy can provide, which suggests that public-education efforts might more consciously link democratic procedures to their potential to produce the freedoms that people desire. Put simply, the respondents in these surveys are telling us that democracy is more than a form of government, and these political benefits are most salient to them.

Our findings also suggest that our previous thinking about citizens in developing nations has not done them justice. Most often, analysts have described these publics as passive subjects, often tolerating or endorsing various forms of autocratic government.[29] To paraphrase Adlai Stevenson, research suggested that people get the type of political system they deserve—so less democratic nations must have less democratic publics. Now that we can finally systematically study public opinion in the developing world, the democratic potential among the citizenry is greater than previously presumed. It should not be surprising that people want freedom, liberty, and control over their lives—and that they see democracy as a means of achieving these goals.

We realize that one must be cautious in placing too much emphasis on broad categories of responses coded from open-ended questions, and some caution is warranted. One expects that when an American or an Austrian discusses the meaning of democracy, that person draws upon greater understanding and experience than is available to residents in a newly democratizing nation. Yet there is a surprising awareness of democracy even in unexpected places, and respondents' emphasis on freedom and liberty suggests that democracy's worth is readily recognized by those who value such principles.

NOTES

We presented a previous version of this paper at the 2007 annual meeting of the Midwest Political Science Association in Chicago, Illinois. We want to thank Samuel Barnes, Michael Bratton, Dieter Fuchs, Hans-Dieter Klingemann, Tim Meisberger, Andrew Nathan, Edeltraud Roller, and George Varughese for their assistance.

1. Francis Fukuyama, *The End of History and the Last Man* (New York: Free Press, 1992).

2. Ronald Inglehart, "How Solid Is Mass Support for Democracy—and How Can We Measure It?" *PS: Political Science & Politics* 36 (March 2003): 51.

3. Doh Chull Shin, "Democratization: Perspectives from Global Citizenries," in Russell Dalton and Han-Dieter Klingemann, eds. *Oxford Handbook of Political Behavior* (Oxford: Oxford University Press, 2007); Russell Dalton and Doh Chull Shin, eds., *Citizens, Democracy and Markets around the Pacific Rim* (Oxford: Oxford University Press, 2006); Michael Bratton, Robert Mattes, and E. Gyimah-Boadi, *Public Opinion, Democracy, and Market Reform in Africa* (Cambridge: Cambridge University Press, 2004); and Richard Rose, William Mishler, and Christian Haerpfer, *Democracy and Its Alternatives: Understanding Post-communist Societies* (Baltimore: Johns Hopkins University Press, 1998).

4. Bratton, Mattes, and Gyimah-Boadi, *Public Opinion, Democracy, and Market Reform in Africa*; and Roderic Camp, ed., *Citizen Views of Democracy in Latin America* (Pittsburgh: University of Pittsburgh Press, 2001).

5. Robert Dahl, *Polyarchy: Participation and Opposition* (New Haven: Yale University Press, 1971).

6. Dieter Fuchs and Edeltraud Roller, "Learned Democracy? Support for Democracy in Central and Eastern Europe," *International Journal of Sociology* 36 (Fall 2006): 70–96.

7. Larry Diamond, *Developing Democracy: Toward Consolidation* (Baltimore: Johns Hopkins University Press, 1999).

8. Janos Simon, "Popular Conceptions of Democracy in Postcommunist Europe," in Samuel H. Barnes and Janos Simon, eds., *The Postcommunist Citizen* (Budapest: Erasmus Foundation, 1998).

9. Bratton, Mattes, and Gyimah-Boadi, *Public Opinion, Democracy, and Market Reform in Africa*; and Camp, ed., *Citizen Views of Democracy in Latin America,* 17.

10. We hear this comment frequently when presenting findings on the remarkable level of support for democracy in many autocratic or transitional political systems. For instance, when 72 percent of the Vietnamese public (in the World Values Survey) say that democracy is the best form of government, the critics claim that this means they want to have the higher standard of living that they identify with the United States but not the U.S. system of government.

11. Mary McIntosh and Martha Abele, "The Meaning of Democracy in a Redefined Europe," paper presented at the Annual Meeting of the American Association for Public Opinion, St. Charles, Illinois, 1993. In contrast, the same study found that citizens in Britain, France, and West Germany emphasized the political values of political freedom, party competition, and a fair justice system.

12. *The Postcommunist Citizen* survey was conducted in 1990; it asked: "There is considerable argument concerning the meaning of democracy. What is your opinion about this question? What is for you the meaning of democracy?" This dataset does not include the open-ended responses; we received these marginals from Hans-Dieter Klingemann. The 2000–2001 Afrobarometer question reads: "What, if anything, do you understand by the word 'democracy?' What comes to mind when you hear the word?" *(www.afrobarometer. org)*. The East Asia Barometer used two different questions that overlap with other studies: "To you, what does 'democracy' mean? What else?" or "What for you is the meaning of the word 'democracy?' What else?" (EAB website: *eacsurvey.law.ntu.edu.tw*). The 2001 Latinobarómetro asked "To you, what does 'democracy' mean? What else?" *(www. latinobarometro.org)*. The U.S. results are from Camp, ed., *Citizen Views of Democracy in Latin America.* The Spanish and Austrian results are from Simon, "Popular Conceptions of Democracy in Postcommunist Europe." The Russian and Ukraine surveys are from the New Soviet Citizen Project (Inter-university Consortium for Political and Social Research ICPSR 6521). The Asia Foundation collected the Afghan and Indonesia surveys *(www. asiafoundation.org)*. We appreciate access to all these surveys, and the analyses presented below are the responsibility of the authors.

13. Before presenting the results, we want to acknowledge the limitations. Comparing responses given to open-ended questions across nations presents a methodological challenge. Even in established democracies, there is an active debate about the political knowledge and sophistication of mass publics. Furthermore, it is difficult to ask open-ended questions in a comparable manner, because they are subject to different interpretations by respondents and answers are often imprecise and must be transcribed by interviewers. Question-order effects may influence open-ended responses, especially when combining different survey projects. The administration of the interview by different survey-research firms can affect the extensiveness of responses and the number of responses to open-ended questions. Then, coders identify the meaning, which can add further variability into the data. In our case, the stem question was similar—but not identical—across nations. Each project then independently coded the responses. Therefore, we used the available coding to construct comparability between these different coding systems. The resulting cross-national evidence is admittedly imprecise (although they are probably more comparable within projects than between projects). Yet this evidence provides valuable insights into public thinking, and the results do present a surprisingly consistent view of how ordinary people think about the meaning of democracy. We therefore focus on broad crossregional patterns rather than the specific percentages in any single nation.

14. The full country-by-country results are presented in Russell Dalton, Doh Chull Shin, and Willy Jou, "Popular Conceptions of the Meaning of Democracy: Democratic Understanding in Unlikely Places," available at *http://repositories.cdlib.org/csd/07-03/*. The number of nations in each group is as follows: established democracies (4); Eastern Europe (7); Asia (9); Latin America (17); and Africa (12).

15. Each project used its own categories in coding responses. To the best of our ability, we generated comparable broad categories from the specific codes. Using the Afrobarometer as an illustration, "freedom and liberties" includes civil liberties, personal

freedoms, group rights, and group freedoms; "institutions and governmental processes" includes voting, electoral choice, multiparty competition, government by the people, government effectiveness and accountability, majority rule; and "social benefits" includes socioeconomic development, personal security, equality and justice, peace, and unity. Other responses, such as general positive or negative comments about democracy, were coded as "other."

16. For instance, the East Asian Barometer and Latinobarómetro included categories of "other positive terms" and "other negative terms." Without further information we included these in the "other" category. In addition, "other" included miscellaneous responses such as "national independence," "change government," and references to individual politicians or political parties.

17. Most of the surveys coded up to three responses to the open-ended question. In some nations, however, only one or two responses were coded. To adjust for this difference, we compare substantive responses in Figure 1 as a percentage of all the total responses. Thus if 59.3 percent of Koreans mentioned freedom and civil liberties, this is divided by the total responses (158.3 percent), so that 37.4 percent of the total Korean responses deal with freedom or liberties. Thus the percentages in Figure 1 sum to 100 percent in each column, but the percentage that cites each of the three substantive categories is generally higher when multiple responses are counted.

18. Previous research on advanced industrial democracies debates the sophistication of contemporary publics, and the average citizen's political information and knowledge is limited. Thus we are not implying that responses citing freedom or liberties reflect a full philosophical understanding of these terms. We are suggesting that citizens in developing nations have an understanding of the key tenets of democracy that is greater than previous research has presumed, and the patterns are not dramatically different from the responses offered by citizens in established democracies.

19. Robert Rohrschneider, *Learning Democracy: Democratic and Economic Values in Unified Germany* (Oxford: Oxford University Press, 1999); on the diffusion of international norms, see Wayne Sandholtz and Mark Gray, "International Integration and National Corruption," *International Organization* 57 (Fall 2003): 761–800.

20. Rohrschneider, *Learning Democracy*.

21. Rose, Mishler, and Haerpfer, *Democracy and Its Alternatives*; and Robert Mattes and Michael Bratton, "Learning about Democracy in Africa: Awareness, Performance, and Experience," *American Journal of Political Science* 51 (January 2007): 192–217.

22. GNP per capita is positively correlated with freedom and liberty responses (.27), and negatively related to "don't know" (-.17), institutions (-.19), and social-benefits responses (-.12). Freedom House democracy scores are positively related to freedom and liberty (.34) and social-benefits responses (.24), and negatively related to "don't know" (-.18) and institutions (-.36) responses.

23. Gabriel Almond and Sidney Verba, *The Civic Culture* (Princeton: Princeton University Press, 1963); and Lucian Pye and Sidney Verba, eds., *Political Culture and Political Development* (Princeton: Princeton University Press, 1965).

24. The Afghanistan (2004 and 2006) and Indonesia (1999 and 2004) surveys were conducted by the Asia Foundation. The five East European nations were included in the first wave of the Postcommunist Citizen Project and a second wave conducted around 2000.

25. The full country-by-country results are presented in Dalton, Shin, and Jou, "Popular Conceptions of the Meaning of Democracy." Figures for the Czech Republic at the second timepoint may not be entirely comparable with the Czechoslovak responses at the

first timepoint, since the early survey combined the Czech Republic and Slovakia. We could not correct for this because we do not have access to the original surveys.

26. In the five Central and East European countries, the first wave of the survey contained a "rights" category, but the second wave did not. Between 6 percent and 17 percent of respondents were coded as giving a rights response in the first survey. The lack of this category may lower the percentage of "freedom and liberties"–focused responses at the second timepoint.

27. Bratton, Mattes, and Gyimah-Boadi, *Public Opinion, Democracy, and Market Reform in Africa,* 274.

28. Amartya Sen, "Democracy as a Universal Value," *Journal of Democracy* 10 (July 1999): 3–17; and Inglehart and Welzel, *Modernization, Cultural Change, and Democracy.*

29. Almond and Verba, *The Civic Culture*; and Pye and Verba, *Political Culture and Political Development.*

2

THE ROLE OF ORDINARY PEOPLE IN DEMOCRATIZATION

Christian Welzel and Ronald Inglehart

Christian Welzel *is professor of political science at Jacobs University in Bremen, Germany, and is a member of the World Values Survey Executive Committee. He is also an affiliated faculty member of the Center for the Study of Democracy at the University of California–Irvine.* ***Ronald Inglehart*** *is professor of political science at the University of Michigan. He directs the World Values Surveys and his books include* Modernization, Cultural Change, and Democracy *(with Christian Welzel, 2005). This essay originally appeared in the January 2008 issue of the* Journal of Democracy.

Human empowerment is becoming an increasingly important driving force behind democratization. Although elite bargaining was central when representative democracy first emerged and still plays an important role, the development of "effective democracy" reflects the acquisition by ordinary people of resources and values that enable them effectively to pressure elites. The importance of this process, called "human empowerment," is generally underestimated.

There is a tension between two different conceptions of democracy. The narrow concept hinges on suffrage and considers any regime that holds competitive, free, fair, and regular elections to be a democracy.[1] In this scenario, elite agreement is key and mass preferences matter little. Advocates of this position argue that certain requisites of democracy such as social mobilization are unimportant. This construct is often labeled "electoral democracy."[2]

Critics of this view charge that it accepts even the most elite-manipulated societies as democratic as long as they hold competitive elections, and ignores the principle that genuine democracy is government by the people in which mass preferences shape public policy. Advocates of this broader concept contend that true democracy goes far beyond the right to vote. "Liberal democracy," as opposed to electoral democracy, is based on mass voice in self-governance.[3] The emergence and survival of democracy therefore depends on social preconditions such as the wide distribution of participatory resources and a trusting, tolerant public that prizes free choice.[4]

Which of these contending views is correct? Is democracy simply a product of elite agreements and concessions, or should it reflect the orientations of the general public? If the first, narrow view is correct, then the emergence and survival of democracy are independent of socio-economic development. If the broader view is correct, however, then the emergence and survival of democracy are indeed linked to development. Both views of course hold true, depending on the definition of democracy being used.

During the "third wave" of democratization, which began in 1974 and peaked in the late 1980s and early 1990s, electoral democracy spread rapidly across large parts of the world. Strategic elite agreements played an important role. Additionally, the international environment, transformed by the end of the Cold War, facilitated democratization—especially in countries where the threat of Soviet military intervention had blocked it, or where Western support had long propped up anticommunist autocracies. A number of these same countries today, however, could not meet the requirements of the broader definition.

Again, when we use the narrow electoral definition of democracy, the correlation between democracy and socioeconomic development is relatively weak, but it becomes much stronger when we apply broader measures. For example, when the Polity Project's narrowly institutional "autocracy-democracy index"[5] is used to measure democracy, the UN's Human Development Index (HDI)—based on measurements of life expectancy, Gross Domestic Product per capita (GDPpc), and literacy—explains only 35 percent of the cross-national variation in levels of democracy (N=114). This is a substantial share of the variance and clearly undermines the view that social requisites are unimportant—but it does leave the door open to the claim that elite actions might explain most of the variance. If we apply Freedom House's somewhat broader measure of democracy, which takes civil liberties into account, the HDI explains a larger share of the variance (41 percent).[6] Although this suggests that development is important, it remains compatible with the view that elite agreements are the major force in establishing democracy—that is, if we focus solely on electoral democracy.[7]

The picture changes dramatically when we analyze the preconditions for effective democracy. Many scholars argue that a number of the new democracies are plagued by massive corruption and lack the rule of law that makes democracy effective. A growing literature, therefore, emphasizes the inadequacy of "electoral democracy," "hybrid democracy," "authoritarian democracy," and other forms of sham democracy in which mass preferences, rather than having a decisive influence on government decisions as democratic theory implies, can be largely ignored by political elites. Thus it is crucial to distinguish between effective democracies on the one hand, and ineffective or pseudodemocracies on the other.[8]

What Is "Effective" Democracy?

The essence of democracy is that it empowers ordinary citizens. But holding elections alone will not accomplish this. It takes more than simply passing laws that formally establish political rights to empower the people; those laws must be implemented.

In order to measure effective democracy, then, we must measure not only the extent to which civil and political rights exist on paper, but also the degree to which officeholders actually respect these rights. Freedom House scores measure the first of these two components. If a country holds free, fair, and competitive elections, Freedom House tends to rate it as Free, giving it scores at or near the top of their scales. Thus the new democracies in Eastern Europe receive scores as high as those of the established democracies of Western Europe, although in-depth analyses indicate that widespread corruption makes these new democracies far less responsive to their citizens' choices than the Freedom House scores would indicate.[9] Meanwhile, the World Bank's "good governance" data, especially its "control of corruption" scores, provide the best available measure of the degree to which those in power abide by the law.[10]

To determine the level of effective democracy, we first take the Freedom House combined scale of political rights and civil liberties (with 14 being the worst and 2 being the best), invert its direction, and standardize it into a 0 to 100 scale, with 100 being the most free. We multiply these scores by the World Bank's anticorruption scores (standardized on a scale from 0 to 1.0, with 1.0 measuring the least corruption) to produce an index of effective democracy. Effective democracy is thus the product of formal democracy and elite integrity.[11] The standard for effective democracy is obviously considerably more demanding than the standard for electoral democracy. Using the inverted Freedom House scale alone, the average country score increased from 51 in 1985 to 72 in 2000. But the level of effective democracy, which weights that freedom score for elite integrity, only improved from 37 to 44 during the same period.

Effective democracy is closely linked to a society's level of development. Thus, the HDI explains fully 60 percent of the variation in effective democracy. In other words, the HDI explains almost twice as much of the variance in effective democracy as it does in electoral democracy. Developmental factors thus clearly play a dominant role in the emer-

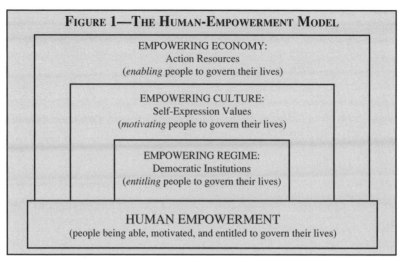

FIGURE 1—THE HUMAN-EMPOWERMENT MODEL

EMPOWERING ECONOMY:
Action Resources
(*enabling* people to govern their lives)

EMPOWERING CULTURE:
Self-Expression Values
(*motivating* people to govern their lives)

EMPOWERING REGIME:
Democratic Institutions
(*entitling* people to govern their lives)

HUMAN EMPOWERMENT
(people being able, motivated, and entitled to govern their lives)

gence and survival of effective democracy. By contrast, one can establish electoral democracy almost anywhere, but it may not be deep-rooted or long-lasting if it does not transfer power from the elites to the people. Effective democracy is most likely to exist in states with a relatively developed societal infrastructure, which includes not only economic resources but also widespread participatory habits and an emphasis on autonomy among the public.

The Human-Empowerment Triad

Democracy can be effective only if power is vested in the people. We have identified a human-empowerment sequence that consists of three elements: action resources, self-expression values, and democratic institutions (see Figure 1). Each of these components empowers people on a different level.

Action resources include both material resources and cognitive resources, such as education and skills, which help people to govern their own lives. Modernization not only increases people's economic resources, it also brings rising educational levels and moves people into occupations that require independent thinking, making them more articulate and better equipped to participate in politics.

Mass values and attitudes also play an important role. Factor analysis of national-level World Values Survey data from scores of societies reveals that two main dimensions account for well over half the cross-national variance across a wide range of values concerning political, economic, and social life.[12] The first dimension reflects the transition from agrarian to industrial society. The second dimension, called "survival versus self-expression values," is linked to the rise of postindustrial society. Societies that emphasize self-expression values give high priority to self-expression; have participatory orientations toward society and politics; support gender equality; are relatively tolerant of foreigners, homosexuals, and other out-groups; and rank high on interpersonal trust. Societies that emphasize survival values, on the other hand, tend to have the opposite preferences in each of these areas. A growing emphasis on self-expression values increases the demand for civil and political liberties, gender equality, and responsive government, thereby helping to establish and sustain democratic institutions. These values play an important role in democratization because they give high priority to free choice in leading one's life.[13]

Democratic institutions provide the civil and political rights that allow people to shape public life as well as their private lives. Together these elements make human empowerment possible. Consequently, effective democracy tends to be found in societies with strong self-expression values and abundant action resources. Rising levels of resources increase people's ability to place pressure on elites. Abundant resources also generate a greater emphasis on self-expression values, leading publics to put greater emphasis on free choice in politics—thereby making it increasingly difficult for elites to resist effective democratization.

The human-empowerment sequence is based on two causal linkages. First, economic development increases ordinary people's resources, leading to the emergence of self-expression values. Virtually everyone wants freedom and autonomy, but people's priorities reflect their socioeconomic conditions, and they therefore place the highest subjective value on their most pressing needs. Since material sustenance and physical security are the first requirements for survival, people assign them top priority under conditions of scarcity; with growing prosperity, people become more likely to emphasize autonomy and self-expression values. Moreover, people tend to adjust their aspirations to their capabilities, making democratic freedoms more imperative when people have the resources needed to practice them. Thus a society's level of resources explains 77 percent of the variation in how strongly a country's people emphasize self-expression values.[14]

Second, effective democratic institutions emerge in societies that emphasize self-expression values. In response to survey questions about whether democracy is desirable, strong majorities endorse democracy, even in countries where self-expression values are weak—but in such cases, both the priority placed on self-expression and the propensity to engage in political action are relatively weak, leaving the elites safe to ignore mass preferences. This does not necessarily prevent elites from adopting democratic institutions; pressures from external actors might prompt them to do so. But if elites are not under strong domestic pressure to make these institutions effective, they are likely to corrupt them, rendering democracy ineffective. Again, the empirical evidence supports this claim. Although the extent to which a given public endorses democracy explains only 20 percent of the variance in effective democracy, the extent to which a public emphasized self-expression values in the 1990s explains 81 percent of the cross-national variation in effective democracy during the period from 2000 to 2002.[15]

Conceivably, the linkage between self-expression values and democratic institutions might be spurious. But in regression analyses controlling for the impact of endorsement of democracy, confidence in state institutions, participation in voluntary institutions, and the length of time a society has lived under democratic institutions, we have found that self-expression values explain far more of the variance in effective democracy than do any of these other variables.[16] Similarly, in regression analyses controlling for the impact of a society's level of economic development, income inequality, educational level, ethnolinguistic factionalization, and religious tradition, a society's level of self-expression values emerges as the strongest predictor by far of effective democracy.[17]

The relationship between self-expression values and democratic institutions does not seem to result from democratic institutions causing self-expression values to emerge. The length of time a society has lived under democratic institutions in fact shows no impact on self-expression values when we control for a society's level of economic development. Economic development tends to make self-expression values increasingly widespread, regardless of whether people live in democracies or authoritarian societies.

These findings help to explain why economic development is linked with democracy: Development increases people's resources, giving rise to self-expression values, which give high priority to freedom of choice. Since democratic institutions provide the broadest latitude for free choice, people with self-expression values tend to seek democracy. In regression analysis, a society's level of action resources by itself explains about 75 percent of the variation in effective democracy; but if one includes the strength of self-expression values in the regression, the explanatory power of action resources drops to 35 percent, while self-expression values by themselves account for 45 percent of the variance in effective democracy. Growing resources contribute to effective democracy mainly insofar as they engender self-expression values. Effective democracy does not emerge because elites choose in a vacuum to adopt democracy. As publics become increasingly articulate, well-organized, and motivated to demand democracy, elites have less choice in the matter.

The Role of Self-Expression Values

The literature on political culture has always assumed that certain mass attitudes are conducive to democracy, but until recently this assumption remained an act of faith. Almond and Verba's influential 1963 work *The Civic Culture* study covered only five countries and could not perform statistically reliable tests of whether certain individual-level attitudes were linked with democracy, which exists only at the societal level.[18] Today, the World Values Surveys cover more than eighty countries containing almost 90 percent of the world's population, making it possible to measure whether countries in which certain attitudes are relatively widespread actually *are* more democratic than other countries.

The findings demonstrate that certain mass attitudes are very strongly linked to democracy, but face-validity is an unreliable guide in terms of which attitudes have the greatest impact. A good deal of recent research is based on the assumption that societies in which the public says favorable things about democracy are most likely to be democratic. This presumption seems perfectly plausible—until one discovers that the percentages expressing favorable attitudes toward democracy are higher in Albania and Azerbaijan than they are in Sweden or Switzerland. At this point in history, most people are ready to pay lip service to democracy, and strong majorities in most countries tell opinion pollsters that democracy is the best form of government. But this does not necessarily indicate deep-rooted orientations or strong motivations. In some cases, it simply reflects social-desirability effects.

Globally, explicit mass-level endorsement of democracy shows a fairly strong and statistically significant correlation with the existence of democracy at the societal level. But, surprising as it may seem, self-expression values—which do not directly refer to democracy—are a much stronger predictor of democracy than is explicit support for democracy.[19] Endorsement of democracy is not necessarily accompanied by the interpersonal trust, tolerance of other groups, and political activism that are the core components of self-expression values, and empirical analysis demonstrates that these are far more important to the emergence and survival of democratic institutions than is mere lip service.[20] This is true in part because self-expression values are much more conducive to prodemocratic mass actions.[21] These values give high priority to freedom and autonomy as goods in and of themselves. Explicit endorsement of democracy, on the other hand, may reflect a variety of other motivations. Thus answers to survey questions concerning whether democracy is preferable to authoritarian alternatives are substantially weaker than self-expression values as predictors of whether democratic institutions are actually present at the societal level.

The Emergence of Self-Expression Values

There is a remarkably strong empirical correlation between self-expression values and effective democracy. The evidence indicates that the causal linkage is mainly from self-expression values to democracy rather than the other way around, and that democratic institutions need not be in place for self-expression values to emerge. World Values Surveys data indicate that in the years preceding the most recent wave of democratization, self-expression values had emerged through a process of intergenerational value change not only in Western democracies, but also in authoritarian societies.[22]

By 1990, the people of East Germany and Czechoslovakia, who lived under two of the most authoritarian regimes in the world, had developed high levels of self-expression values. The crucial factor was not the political system; it was that these countries were among the most economically advanced in the communist world, with sophisticated educational and social-welfare systems. Thus when the threat of Soviet military intervention was removed, they moved swiftly toward democracy.

Self-expression values emerge when a large share of the population grows up taking survival for granted. As action resources develop, this worldview tends to materialize even under the most repressive political regimes, as people become more economically secure, more intellectually independent, more articulate, and more socially connected. This emancipates people, giving them more choice about how to spend time and money, what to believe, and with whom to connect. Even repressive regimes find it difficult to check these tendencies, for they are intimately linked with modernization, and repressing them tends to block the emergence of an effective knowledge sector.

By increasing people's material means, cognitive skills, and social connections—in other words, their action resources—modernization transforms people's values and widens their action repertoire. And people tend to use this expanding repertoire because free choice and individual autonomy have a profound psychological payoff: They increase people's subjective well-being, in accordance with what seems to be a universal psychological tendency.[23]

There is no guarantee, of course, that economic development and modernization will occur. Some countries with authoritarian regimes may develop and others may not. But to the extent that these countries do modernize, they tend to experience the liberating effects of modernization, which their rulers can stamp out only by renouncing development itself. Although fascism and communism remained viable alternatives for much of the twentieth century, the urbanization, mass education, and economic development that accompanied industrialization made representative democracy possible. With the rise of the knowledge-based or postindustrial society, the proliferation of liberal democracies becomes more likely.

In knowledge societies, people grow accustomed to exercising their own initiative and judgment in their daily lives. As a result, they become more likely to question rigid, hierarchical authority. If the idea of democracy were not already known, it would probably be invented wherever self-expression values became widespread, because free choice and autonomy are universal aspirations. They may be subordinated to the needs for subsistence and order when survival is precarious, but they tend to take higher priority as survival becomes more secure. The specific institutional manifestations of democracy that have emerged over the past two-hundred years are largely a product of Western political history. But the basic impetus for democracy—the human desire for free choice—is the natural product of an environment in which expanding action resources give rise to self-expression values.

Elites almost always prefer to retain as much power as possible. Accordingly, democratic institutions have generally emerged because people struggled for them, from the liberal revolutions of the eighteenth century to the democratic revolutions of the late-twentieth century. People's motivations and values played an important role in the past and are playing an ever more important role today, since values based on self-expression have been on the rise in most parts of the world. Does this mean that authoritarian systems will inevitably crumble? Not necessarily. While self-expression values tend to erode the legitimacy of authoritarian systems, as long as determined elites control the armies and police services, they may be able to repress prodemocratic forces. Fortunately, people do not struggle for democracy for instrumental reasons alone. If they did, it would be relatively easy to buy off the leaders of democratic movements. The most dedicated activists in the struggle are those who value freedom intrinsically.

Modernization tends to bring both cognitive mobilization and growing emphasis on self-expression values. This in turn motivates ever more people to demand democratic institutions and enables them to be effective in doing so as elites watch the costs of repression mount. Finally, with intergenerational replacement, the elites themselves may become less authoritarian and repressive if their younger cohorts are raised in societies that value self-expression. Social change is not deterministic, but modernization increases the probability that democratic institutions will emerge.

Democracy and the Redistribution of Wealth

Recent influential works by Carles Boix and by Daron Acemoglu and his coauthors interpret democracy as resulting from a struggle between propertied elites and impoverished masses, in which both sides are motivated by conflicting interests as regards economic redistribution.[24] The masses want widespread suffrage in order to vote in the redistribution of wealth, while the elites oppose such suffrage precisely because they fear such a result. Consequently, elites will concede widespread suffrage only if they believe that it will not lead to extensive redistribution. These analyses use narrow definitions of democracy; they are analyzing how elections emerge, not how effective democracy emerges. As we have argued, elections and effective democracy are not the same thing.

FIGURE 2—THE CHAIN OF PROCESSES PROMOTING HUMAN EMPOWERMENT					
EXPANDING ACTION RESOURCES					
⇩		⇩		⇩	
Economic growth and the welfare state increase people's *material* means.		Rising levels of education, expanding mass communication, and more knowledge-intensive work widen people's *intellectual* skills.		Growing social complexity widens and diversifies people's *social* opportunities.	
⇩		⇩		⇩	
Material Autonomy		Intellectual Autonomy		Social Autonomy	
⇩		⇩		⇩	
People get a sense of human autonomy, which leads them to question unlimited and uncontrolled authority over people and makes them receptive to the ideas of individual freedom and equality.					
⇩					
RISING SELF-EXPRESSION VALUES					
in nondemocracies			in democracies		
⇩	⇩	⇩	⇩	⇩	⇩
growing number of civil and political rights activists	growing mass support for civil and political rights movements	growing number of liberal reformers among elites	growing number of equal opportunity activists	growing mass support for equal opportunity movements	increasingly mass-responsive elites
⇩	⇩	⇩	⇩	⇩	⇩
Formal adoption of democratic institutions			Increasing efficiency of democratic institutions		
⇩			⇩		
STRENGTHENING DEMOCRATIC INSTITUTIONS					

Boix's version of this model postulates that the elites' fear of redistribution diminishes if income distribution becomes more equal, reducing the number of people who stand to gain a great deal by radical redistribution. Similarly, as capital mobility increases, the elites have less fear of being dispossessed, since they can move their capital out of reach. This model assumes that the masses are always in favor of democracy; being a constant factor, then, mass demands for democracy do not affect democratization. Likewise, this model ignores the possibility that processes such as social and cognitive mobilization will enhance the general population's ability to intervene effectively in politics; this, too, is implicitly constant. It is solely in the hands of the elites to decide whether to repress mass demands for democracy or to expand the franchise. Modernization influences the likelihood of democracy only insofar as it brings rising income equality and capital mobility, making universal suffrage more acceptable to the elites.

These assumptions are highly questionable. Empirically, we find tremendous variation in the degree to which certain publics give high priority to obtaining democratic institutions and in their ability to struggle for them, since both action resources and mass emphasis on self-expression values vary greatly from one society to another. The decision to expand political rights remains exclusively an elite choice only while the average person's action resources are meager. But economic development dramatically changes this scenario. Greater material and cognitive resources enable the people to mount more powerful collective actions and to put effective pressure on elites.

Accordingly, the survival of authoritarian regimes is not simply a question of whether elites choose to repress the masses. Rather, it reflects the balance of forces between the elites and the masses, and this balance changes over time. The most recent wave of democratization was, in large part, a story of effective mass mobilization, motivated by a strong emphasis on self-expression values among people who had become increasingly articulate and good at organizing mass movements. The major effect of modernization is not that it makes democracy more acceptable to elites, but that it increases ordinary people's capabilities and willingness to struggle for democratic institutions.

Boix has developed a parsimonious and well-argued theoretical model that interprets democratization as emerging when relatively high levels of income equality and high levels of capital mobility are present. Under these conditions, the political elites feel relatively safe in granting universal suffrage. His theoretical argument is persuasive, and we have little doubt that such conditions are among the factors that sometimes contribute to democratization.

But Boix's empirical attempt to demonstrate that this *alone* is the whole story is unconvincing. In particular, his indicators of capital mobility are inadequate to prove his thesis. They include the relative size of the agricultural sector, which is a standard indicator of modernization; indeed, the transition from agrarian to industrial production is at the very core of the modernization process. But the transition from agriculture to industry is not a specific indicator of capital mobility and is linked with it only in the general sense that modernization tends to increase capital mobility along with many other things. Boix also uses a society's average years of schooling as an indicator of capital mobility. Here again, he is using one of the central indicators of modernization, but it could be better used to support the social-mobilization thesis that rising levels of mass education enable people to participate in politics more effectively. Far from being an indicator of how secure the elites feel in their struggle to prevent income redistribution, mass education is actually an indicator of how effective the people are becoming in their struggle for political rights. Boix has simply relabeled standard indicators of modernization as indicators of capital mobility—and in demonstrating that they are linked with the emergence of democracy, his empirical analysis gives more support to various versions of modernization theory than to his own model of the conditions under which elites feel safe in granting political rights.

Acemoglu and his coauthors, meanwhile, explore why wealthy countries are more likely to be democratic than poor ones and in doing so discover some new insights. Using a massive historical data set, Acemoglu and his colleagues probe far back in time to see if increasing wealth preceded increasing democracy. Only when they push their analysis back fully five-hundred years do they find a positive correlation between changes in income and changes in democracy—a correlation that weakens or disappears when they control for fixed country effects. They conclude that both economic development and the rise of democracy are strongly path-dependent and that five centuries ago certain European countries and their colonists embarked on a development path linked with both democracy and high economic growth, while other countries moved on a path that led to political repression and lower economic growth.

Although the authors emphasize elite bargaining, their findings indicate that cultural factors also play a decisive role. While their analysis indicates the importance of nation-specific effects, they do little to clarify the nature of these effects. The nation-specificity and astonishing durability of these effects suggest that they are deeply rooted cultural factors similar to those uncovered by Robert D. Putnam in his analysis of the differences between the political cultures of northern and southern Italy, which he too traced back to patterns that have persisted for centuries.[25]

Acemoglu and his coauthors are right: Economic development alone does not bring democracy. It does so only in combination with certain cultural factors. But these factors are not necessarily unique to certain European countries and the lands that they colonized. Evidence from the World Values Surveys indicates that in recent years these cultural factors have been spreading throughout much of the world.

Neither the Boix model nor the Acemoglu model treats mass values and skills as having an autonomous impact on democratization. Rather, these values and skills are implicitly held to be constants, and mass protest is simply viewed as something that happens when economic inequality is high. These assumptions may fit historical data fairly well, but they cannot adequately explain the most recent wave of democratization. Political motivations have in fact substantially shifted, and the propensity to participate in demonstrations in postindustrial societies has more than doubled since 1974.[26] In keeping with this, we see that from 1987 to 1995 historically unprecedented numbers of demonstrators provided the impetus for outbreaks of democratization from Seoul and Manila to Moscow and East Berlin. Moreover, the struggle was not primarily about economic redistribution but about political liberty. Indeed, democratization in the former communist countries was not motivated by mass pressures for greater economic equality; instead it shifted political power away from an elite class that strongly emphasized economic equality and gave more of such power to the wider populace, which emphasized economic equality less.

Democracy does not emerge simply from an interest in universal suffrage and the redistribution of wealth. It emerges from a struggle for democratic freedoms that go far beyond the right to vote. Throughout most of human history, despotism and autocracy have prevailed. This was not simply because elites were able to repress the masses. Rather, until the modern era, the masses lacked the resources and organizational skills needed to seize democratic institutions, and obtaining them was not their top priority. To understand how democracy emerges, it is insufficient to focus solely on elites—increasingly, one must also study mass-level developments.

Although economic development correlates positively with effective democracy, development's impact stems primarily from its tendency to encourage self-expression values. Modernization is a process centered on industrialization, which brings mass education, a modern occupational structure, and higher levels of existential security—all of which eventually lead ordinary people to place increasing emphasis on democracy. Oil-exporting states have accumulated massive wealth without following this trajectory, and to the extent that their people have not shown themselves motivated to seek democracy, such states have not become democratic.

It is not the have-nots who desire democracy most strongly, as some political economists assume. Instead, when people have relatively ample economic and cognitive resources, and move from emphasizing survival values toward emphasizing self-expression values, they strive most strongly for democratic institutions. Self-expression values reflect a synthesis of interpersonal trust, tolerance, and political activism that plays a crucial role in the emergence and survival of democracy.

Democracy can be defined narrowly or broadly, and if we use the minimalist definition of electoral democracy, the characteristics of the people *are* relatively unimportant—elections, after all, can be held almost anywhere. But generally accepted standards of what constitutes democracy have become more demanding over time. When representative democracy first emerged, property qualifications and the disenfranchisement of women and slaves were considered perfectly compatible with a democratic state; today, virtually no one would accept that definition. Scholars are likewise becoming more critical of narrow electoral definitions of democracy. If we view democratization as a process by which political power moves into the hands of ordinary citizens, then a broader definition of democracy is required, and with such a definition we find that the orientations of ordinary citizens play a central role in democratization.

NOTES

1. Electoral definitions go back to Joseph Schumpeter and are used by Adam Przeworski and Fernando Limongi, "Modernization: Theories and Facts," *World Politics* 49 (January 1997):155–83.

2. The notion that democracy emerges as a product of strategic elite agreements is advanced by Guillermo O'Donnell and Phillippe C. Schmitter in *Transitions from Authoritarian Rule: Tentative Conclusions About Uncertain Democracies* (Baltimore: Johns Hopkins University Press, 1986).

3. The liberal notion of democracy, which considers a wide set of civil and political rights to be an integral part of democracy, is proposed by Robert A. Dahl in *Polyarchy: Participation and Opposition* (New Haven: Yale University Press, 1971).

4. The argument that democracy emerges and survives in a setting of widespread participatory resources and self-expression values, supported by empirical evidence from more than seventy societies, is made by Ronald Inglehart and Christian Welzel, *Modernization, Cultural Change, and Democracy* (New York: Cambridge University Press, 2005).

5. The Polity Index measures democracy in terms of constitutional limitations on executive power and channels of popular participation.

6. The Freedom House ratings are based on expert ratings of civil liberties and political rights.

7. Since they include a Civil Liberties scale, one might think that Freedom House's freedom ratings would measure liberal democracy rather than mere electoral democracy. But Freedom House's dichotomous distinction between "electoral democracies" and "non-democracies" shows a .88 correlation with its 13-point freedom ratings. As they are actually coded, these ratings do not go much beyond electoral democracy.

8. David Collier and Steven Levitsky emphasize the distinction between effective democracy and deficient democracy in "Democracy with Adjectives: Conceptual Innovation in Comparative Research," *World Politics* 49 (April 1997): 430–51; Larry Diamond also emphasizes the importance of this distinction in "Thinking About Hybrid Regimes," *Journal of Democracy* 13 (April 2002): 21–35.

9. See Richard Rose, "A Diverging Europe," *Journal of Democracy* 12 (January 2001): 93–106.

10. See Daniel Kaufmann, Aart Kraay, and Massimo Mastruzzi, "Governance Matters III: Governance Indicators for 1996–2002," World Bank Policy Research Working Paper 3106.

11. For a detailed discussion of this index of effective democracy, see Inglehart and Welzel, *Modernization, Cultural Change, and Democracy*, ch. 7.

12. Ronald Inglehart, *Modernization and Postmodernization* (Princeton: Princeton University Press, 1997); Ronald Inglehart and Wayne Baker, "Modernization, Cultural Change, and the Persistence of Traditional Values," *American Sociological Review* 65 (February, 2000): 19–51; Inglehart and Welzel, *Modernization, Cultural Change, and Democracy*.

13. Inglehart and Welzel, *Modernization, Cultural Change, and Democracy*; chapter 2 explains how self-expression values are measured.

14. Inglehart and Welzel, *Modernization, Cultural Change, and Democracy*, 150.

15. Inglehart and Welzel, 155.

16. Inglehart and Welzel, 249–58.

17. Inglehart and Welzel, 196–208.

18. Gabriel A. Almond and Sidney Verba, *The Civic Culture: Political Attitudes and Democracy in Five Nations* (Newbury Park, Calif.: Sage, 1989).

19. Ronald Inglehart, "How Solid Is Mass Support for Democracy—And How Do We Measure It?" *PS: Political Science and Politics* 36 (January 2003): 51–57. This finding is confirmed in Inglehart and Welzel, *Modernization, Cultural Change, and Democracy*, ch. 11, and draws further support from Christian Welzel, "Are Levels of Democracy Influenced by Mass Attitudes?" *International Political Science Review* 28 (September 2007): 397–424.

20. For further support of this claim, see Christian Welzel, "Democratization as an Emancipative Process," *European Journal of Political Research* 45 (October 2006): 871–896.

21. Welzel, "Are Levels of Democracy Influenced by Mass Attitudes?" 418. A multi-level analysis of World Values Survey data, which includes 250,000 respondents from the full range of societies—from plainly authoritarian to fully democratic, finds that self-expression values do lead people to participate in elite-challenging mass actions, regardless of how undemocratic a given regime may be.

22. Inglehart and Welzel, *Modernization, Cultural Change, and Democracy*, chs. 8 and 9.

23. The cross-culturally virtually universal impact that a sense of free choice has on life satisfaction is demonstrated in Inglehart and Welzel, *Modernization, Cultural Change, and Democracy*, 140.

24. Carles Boix, *Democracy and Redistribution* (New York: Cambridge University Press, 2003); Daron Acemoglu and James A. Robinson, *Economic Origins of Dictatorship and Democracy* (New York: Cambridge University Press, 2005); and Daron Acemoglu, Simon Johnson, James A. Robinson and Pierre Yared, "Income and Democracy," NBER Working Paper No. W11205 (2005), *http://papers.ssrn.com/sol3/papers.cfm?abstract_id=689386*.

25. Robert D. Putnam, *Making Democracy Work: Civic Traditions in Modern Italy* (Princeton: Princeton University Press, 1993).

26. For evidence, see Inglehart and Welzel, *Modernization, Cultural Change, and Democracy*, 118–26 and 224–27.

3

PUBLIC OPINION AND DEMOCRATIC LEGITIMACY

Yun-han Chu, Michael Bratton, Marta Lagos,
Sandeep Shastri, and Mark Tessler

Yun-han Chu is distinguished research fellow of the Institute of Po-
litical Science at Academia Sinica, Taiwan, and director of the Asian
Barometer. ***Michael Bratton*** *is University Distinguished Professor of*
Political Science and African Studies at Michigan State University, East
Lansing, and a codirector of Afrobarometer. ***Marta Lagos*** *is the found-*
ing director of Latinobarómetro Corporation. ***Sandeep Shastri*** *is direc-*
tor of the International Academy for Creative Teaching, Bangalore, and
a founding member of the State of Democracy in South Asia Project.
Mark Tessler *is Samuel J. Eldersveld Collegiate Professor of Political*
Science at the University of Michigan, Ann Arbor, and director of the
Arab Barometer. This essay originally appeared in the April 2008 issue
of the Journal of Democracy.

Why does popular support for democracy vary from one country to another? Is it because of economic factors, or does politics matter more? Those who favor the first kind of explanation argue that democracy must earn its legitimacy mainly by "delivering the goods"—if people see a net improvement in their material welfare under democracy, this reasoning goes, they will support it. Those who lean toward political explanations caution against economic reductionism and claim that citizens' sense of commitment to democracy may be less a function of how they think the market is working than of how they experience democracy itself.

This debate is important not only theoretically, but for practical reasons as well. All other things being equal, a strong coupling between economic performance and popular commitment to democratic governance is not conducive to the consolidation of young democracies. A country's economic condition is always subject to numerous contingencies, and can fluctuate sharply from one year to another. This is particularly so in the age of globalization, as supranational economic forces increasingly hamper the ability of democratically elected governments to manage their respective nations' economies and protect their citizens' material well-being.

Just how important is it, then, for young democracies to deliver economic growth and material well-being to their citizens? Casting our eyes over the globe, we have found an encouraging pattern that clearly shows economic factors to be relatively *un*important in explaining levels of popular support for democracy. A glaring exception to this encouraging picture comes from East Asia, where a number of high-income countries yield figures which suggest that publics there expect democratic regimes to keep up the kind of miraculous economic growth that took place under earlier and more authoritarian forms of governance.

Earlier research on experiences of political transition in postcommunist Central and Eastern Europe suggested that, of the many factors influencing citizens' support for democracy, perceptions of change in individual or national economic circumstances are the most important.[1] Writing about how citizens respond to and form attitudes about democratic transition, Adam Przeworski similarly stressed that the most relevant factor is the gap between subjective expectations and real economic experiences. Consequently, if citizens believe that democracy improves their personal economic situation and that of the nation, then popular support for democracy increases.[2] Russell Dalton also discovered that citizens' attitudes toward democracy in the former East Germany are strongly linked to their evaluations of the national economy.[3]

These findings emphasizing the economic basis of popular support for democracy came under challenge from Geoffrey Evans and Stephen Whitefield, who analyzed survey data from eight postcommunist countries in the early 1990s. Evans and Whitefield found that there is very little link from economic experience to support for democracy when the perceived responsiveness of the electoral system and support for marketization are controlled for.[4] Richard Rose, William Mishler, and Christian Haerpfer studied public opinion in nine former East Bloc countries, and also warned against reductionist theories "that treat all political attitudes as if they were simply derivative of economic conditions." They found that both economic and political factors determine levels of popular support for democracy, but politics matters more.[5]

Subsequently, researchers studying other regions have also called into question the conventional wisdom that governments in new democracies legitimize themselves mainly through economic performance. Robert Mattes and Michael Bratton found that Africans support democracy even while being discontented with its achievements in both the political and the economic realms. This implies a measure of intrinsic support that supersedes instrumental considerations. Mattes and Bratton also found that approval of democracy remains performance-driven, though approval hinges less on the delivery of economic goods than on the government's record of securing basic political rights.[6]

Analyzing data from the multiyear Latinobarómetro survey, Marta Lagos found that when many Latin American countries were hit by severe economic crises around the turn of the millennium, satisfaction with market-based policies and the actual workings of democratically chosen governments began to drop even as support for democracy as a regime type went up. This suggests that Latin Americans are learning to distinguish between democracy as a system and this or that democratic government which they may like or dislike.[7] Working with the same data, Carol Graham and Sandip Sukhtankar later corroborated Lagos's findings.[8]

This good news about citizens' readiness to "decouple" their view of democracy in general from the economic record of particular democratic governments needs a major qualification, however. In the latest Asian Barometer survey of seven East Asian countries, citizens' evaluations of both their nation's and their household's economic condition emerge as one of the stronger predictors of support for democracy when the cross-national survey data are pooled together. This suggests that analyses restricted to the level of individual countries—where the data show people judging democracy more by its provision of political "goods" such as accountability, equal rights, and citizen empowerment than by national or household income—are missing significant cross-national patterns.[9]

What is causing this discrepancy between the regional and country-level patterns in East Asia? The answer may be that variation in people's perception of economic performance across countries tends to be much greater than within one country. Within a single country, people's economic evaluation tends to move in one direction at a time: thumbs-up during booms, thumbs-down during busts. This built-in convergence is likely to attenuate the observed causal relationship between people's economic evaluation and the level of support that they express for democracy. Therefore, country-by-country analyses cannot be conclusive because they might be missing some significant cross-national pattern of causality. Any analysis based on a single world region will likewise suffer because it may fail to capture a significant cross-regional pattern. Since national economic cycles within a single region often move in synchronized fashion, this is a legitimate concern. Unfortunately, virtually all the existing empirical studies on the issue have been confined to survey data collected in a few countries or at most one geographical region.

We are trying to offer the first systematic global investigation of the relative importance of citizens' economic evaluations to their support for a democratic form of government. Our effort relies on a newly available cross-regional merged data set created under the auspices of the Globalbarometer. This set pools all identical (or at least functionally equivalent) indicators from four regional surveys, namely Latinobarómetro, the Afrobarometer, the Asian Barometer (which covers both East and South Asia), and the newly launched Arab Barometer.[10] Together, the pooled set covers more than 54 countries spread over four continents.[11] Since our capacious data set maximizes cross-national variation and minimizes the risk of underestimating the economic factors' impact on support for democracy, our scope of analysis puts the claim that "economic factors matter more" to an eminently fair (and even favorable) test.

We base our analysis on a survey item that is widely used to gauge popular support for democracy as a preferred political system. Typically, respondents are asked to choose among three statements: "Democracy is always preferable to any other kind of government"; "Under some circumstances, an authoritarian government can be preferable to a democratic one"; and "For people like me, it does not matter whether we have a democratic or a nondemocratic regime."[12] This has been the most widely used item due not only to its face validity, but also to the way in which it facilitates meaningful comparisons.

We use comparable measurements to examine the impact of both the "sociotropic" consideration (how people think their country's economy is doing) and the immediate "pocketbook" effect (how their own household is doing).[13] The goal is to find out whether there is a discernible global relationship between economic performance and democratic legitimacy, and whether or how each region deviates from this global pattern. We also break up the four regions and reclassify countries into four groups depending on whether their national income is low, lower-middle, upper-middle, or high.[14] This regrouping will allow us to learn if economic performance is less important to popular support for democracy in richer rather than poorer countries or vice-versa.

In the Figure, we plot a country's level of popular support for democracy against its mean scores on the evaluation of economic condition. For simplicity's sake, we combine the measure for evaluating national economic conditions with that of personal economic conditions to yield a single indicator of perceived economic performance.[15] The horizontal axis marks the average score of people's evaluation of economic condition with a maximum range of 1 (very bad) to 5 (very good). On the vertical axis, 0.6 means that 60 percent of the respondents in a given country believe that democracy is the best form of government for their society, while 0.4 means that 40 percent do so, and so on.[16]

As the scatterplot in the Figure shows, many third-wave democracies must cope with substandard legitimacy. Fewer than half the emerging democracies that we survey have reached the two-thirds level that may be taken as a minimum threshold of mass support for democracy in a consolidated regime.[17] Many countries, such as Brazil, Ecuador, Mongolia, Pakistan, Paraguay, South Korea, and Taiwan, have dipped below 0.5, meaning that (according to this measure) less than half the population in those places unconditionally embraces democracy.

FIGURE—SUPPORT FOR DEMOCRACY VERSUS EVALUATION OF CURRENT ECONOMIC CONDITION

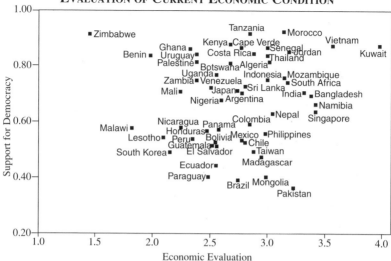

Africa: Benin, Botswana, Cape Verde, Ghana, Kenya, Lesotho, Madagascar, Malawi, Mali, Mozambique, Namibia, Nigeria, Senegal, South Africa, Tanzania, Uganda, Zambia, Zimbabwe
Arab world: Algeria, Jordan, Kuwait, Morocco, Palestine
Asia: Bangladesh, India, Indonesia, Japan, Mongolia, Nepal, Pakistan, Philippines, Singapore, South Korea, Sri Lanka, Taiwan, Thailand, Vietnam
Latin America: Argentina, Bolivia, Brazil, Chile, Colombia, Costa Rica, Ecuador, El Salvador, Guatemala, Honduras, Mexico, Nicaragua, Panama, Paraguay, Peru, Uruguay, Venezuela

Next, we examine the scatterplot for any clues it may hold regarding any cross-national pattern featuring a linear relationship between perceived economic performance and the strength of citizens' commitment to democracy at the aggregate level. We see no linear relationship between people's perception of current economic conditions and the extent to which publics believe that democracy is the best form of government for their society. Countries where citizens take a dim view of current economic conditions can vary greatly as regards levels of popular commitment to democracy as the only legitimate form of government. Notable examples are Benin and Paraguay. At the same time, many countries that register relatively high popular support for democracy vary significantly in terms of how their citizens evaluate economic conditions. The figure's three outliers (Kuwait, Vietnam, and Zimbabwe) occupy the two polar ends on the horizontal axis. Both Vietnamese and Kuwaitis are extraordinarily upbeat about their respective national economies while Zimbabweans feel very down about theirs, but all three publics register very high levels of popular yearning for democracy.[18]

To further substantiate the claim that economic performance plays a secondary role in shaping attitudes toward democracy, we apply correlation analysis to our merged data so that the strength of their linear association at the individual level can be more precisely gauged.[19] To assess

TABLE 1—SOURCES OF POPULAR SUPPORT FOR DEMOCRACY: CORRELATION ANALYSIS

	GLOBAL	By GEOGRAPHICAL REGION				By PER-CAPITA INCOME			
		AFRICA	ARAB WORLD	ASIA	LATIN AMERICA	LOW INCOME COUNTRIES	LOWER MIDDLE-INCOME COUNTRIES	UPPER MIDDLE-INCOME COUNTRIES	HIGH INCOME COUNTRIES
Current country economic evaluation	0.07	0.04	0.07	0.10	0.02	0.01*	0.11	0.03	0.20
Current personal economic evaluation	0.02	0.02	0.07	0.04	-0.01*	-0.01*	0.05	0.02*	0.17
Trust in political parties	0.12	0.07	0.02*	0.14	0.04	0.12	0.10	0.09	0.07
Trust in parliament	0.13	0.07	0.02*	0.15	0.05	0.09	0.12	0.09	0.11
Trust in the courts	0.13	0.03	0.07	0.16	0.04	0.09	0.13	0.09	0.19
Citizen empowerment	0.08	0.02	0.01*	0.08	0.15	0.01*	0.09	0.16	0.09
Free and fair elections	0.06	0.06	0.01*	0.09	NA	0.08	-0.02*	0.13	0.04
Equal rights	0.06	-0.03	NA	0.12	0.04	0.05	0.06	0.01*	0.07
Satisfaction with democracy	0.18	0.18	0.03*	0.13	0.21	0.14	0.19	0.22	0.05
N	44270	14068	4082	10782	15337	14792	16858	8311	4308

Note: Most of our correlation coefficients are statistically significant due to the sheer fact that our sample sizes are very big. Coefficients that are not significant are marked with an asterisk (*). Sample sizes may vary from one row to another due to pair-wise deletion of missing cases. The reported N in the bottom row indicates the number of valid cases for estimating the correlation coefficients in the first row, in essence between support for democracy and evaluation of a country's current economic conditions.

the relative importance of economic performance in explaining people's normative commitment to democracy, we also include measures of how many people believe that democracy of an acceptable quality is being supplied in their country. Our comparative survey contains three sets of indicators that reveal essentials regarding how the political system looks in citizens' eyes. The first set gauges how much people trust the key institutions of parliament, the courts, and political parties.[20] The second set comprises indicators that measure the extent to which the political system fulfills such minimal requirements of liberal democracy as empowering the people to change a government they dislike,[21] holding free and fair elections,[22] and guaranteeing equal rights under law.[23] The third set gathers data regarding citizens' overall satisfaction with the way that democracy works in their particular country.[24]

In Table 1, we juxtapose the correlation coefficients between support for democracy and the two economic indicators with each of the seven political indicators. The left-most column reports the correlation coefficients indicating the strength of linear association based on the entire global pool of our survey data.[25] The next four columns report the results of correlation analysis based on the pooled survey data from each of the four regions. The last four columns show the strength of linear association for each of the four income groups, from low-income countries to high-income countries.

The correlation coefficients are not strong for any of the nine explanatory variables. This is not surprising: The indicator that we use to measure support for democracy is very limited. Its binary scale tends to attenuate correlation coefficients, and thus underestimates the underlying strength of linear relationships. So we should pay more attention to the relative strength of each variable's linear relationship with support for democracy. The left-most column shows that, across all four continents, how respondents perceive overall national economic conditions matters more than how they evaluate their personal economic circumstances. But neither exerts the kind of influence on attitudes toward democracy that most of our political factors do. The levels of trust that people feel toward parliament, parties, and courts, as well as respondents' sense that citizens are politically empowered, far outweigh judgments of national or personal economic weal or woe. Among all the political indicators, satisfaction with democracy exerts the strongest influence on people's normative commitment to democracy. Since such satisfaction is a catch-all measure, it might well carry the cumulative impact of all the factors listed above.

When we move down to the regional level, this pattern continues to hold. Among Africans, levels of trust in parliament, the courts, and free and fair elections matter more than does the perception of national economic conditions—and much more than does the perception of personal economic conditions. Again, the impact of overall satisfaction with democracy, which arguably enjoys the closest causal proximity to support for democracy, surges to the top. Among Latin Americans, evaluations of national and personal economic conditions are the two least important factors in shaping people's sense of democracy's legitimacy. For Asians, belief in the preferablility of democracy hinges more on trust in parliament and the courts, plus overall satisfaction with democracy and the sense that rights are receiving equal protection.

The five Arab-majority countries surveyed differ from this emerging pattern on two scores. First, no factor, economic or political, explains the positive orientation toward democracy with much power, for no correlation coefficient exceeds 0.07. The correlations may be low because of the limited variance on the item that gauges support for democracy across the Arab world. The level of aggregate support in all five countries—Algeria, Jordan, Kuwait, Morocco, and Palestine—exceeds 0.80, putting each of these lands well above the global mean of 0.67 (see the Figure on p. 35). Support for democracy in the Arab world, in other words, is very high (perhaps because people there, having never experienced democracy, can think of it as an ideal to which they aspire rather than as a system of governance whose ups and downs they have actually had to deal with). Moreover, among the few factors that exert some meager impact, the two economic-conditions indicators come out stronger. Indeed, they surpass all political indicators except trust in courts.

Of all four regions, the one where perceptions of national economic condition make the strongest impact is clearly Asia. This is probably because many East Asian countries have traveled along a distinctive trajectory of regime transition. Most of today's East Asian democracies are the successors of growth-friendly, market-conforming, soft-authoritarian regimes. Moreover, a great majority of East Asia's citizens have seen an extraordinary socioeconomic transformation unfold within their lifetimes. They live in a region replete with authoritarian regimes, such as China's and Vietnam's, that have attained a high degree of economic success, and their own countries must live with constant competitive pressure from precisely those rising (authoritarian) economic powers. As a result, East Asians who live under democracy tend to apply much higher standards of success when they assess how their governments are performing economically. East Asians also place more emphasis on economic success, seeing it as a pillar of national pride, self-esteem, and security. This value priority is especially salient among the most socioeconomically advanced East Asian countries.[26]

In the four right-most columns, we report the correlation coefficients calculated on the basis of pooled survey data from countries with different levels of per-capita annual income. Contrary to the received view that a rising level of economic development promotes "self-expression values" such as freedom of speech and participation in the decision-making process,[27] we found that people's economic evaluations had the strongest impact on support for democracy in the high-income countries, and the weakest impact in the low-income countries. In the low-income lands, citizens' assessments of their own and their countries' economic circumstances had no impact at all. What mattered instead was trust in key democratic institutions—parliament, the parties, and the courts—plus the political system's perceived adeptness at delivering free and fair elections and equal rights.

The pattern of linear relationship observed among people living in high-income countries is just the opposite. There, citizens' evaluations of national and personal economic conditions are, respectively, the most important and third-most important factors explaining their normative commitment to democracy. While political factors (especially trust in courts) still matter, they rank behind economic factors. Reinforcing our argument about the high priority that people living in advanced East Asian countries give to economic development is the observation that four of the five high-income countries (Japan, Singapore, South Korea, and Taiwan) are East Asian. The fifth, Kuwait, is the only one from outside the region.

In the countries belonging to the upper part of the middle-income range, trust in democratic institutions, citizen empowerment, and free and fair elections all carry much more weight than economic performance in shaping orientations toward democracy. In countries in the lower part of that range, evaluations of national economic conditions carry more weight in explaining the level of legitimacy that democracy enjoys, but political factors such as trust in parliament and the courts weigh heavier still.

Across the four income groups, to the extent that bad economic performance can erode people's support for democracy, assessments of the national economy loom larger than do evaluations of personal economic circumstances. People outside the five high-income countries mostly neither credit nor blame democracy for their personal economic fortunes.

In the bulk of cases, the single most important factor in accounting for people's normative commitment to democracy is their level of overall satisfaction with the way democracy works. This calls for further exploration. In Table 2, we run a parallel correlation analysis in order to identify which factors shape people's satisfaction with democracy's overall performance. This analysis not only helps us to sort out the various ingredients that make up democratic satisfaction, but also aids our effort to learn whether this catchall approval rating serves as an important intermediary variable between perceived economic performance on the one hand and support for democracy on the other.

The combination of a weak (but still statistically meaningful) association between economic performance and support for democracy with a much stronger linear relationship between economic evaluation and democratic satisfaction suggests that economic evaluation exerts no direct impact on people's belief in democratic legitimacy. Rather, eco-

TABLE 2—SOURCES OF POPULAR SATISFACTION WITH DEMOCRACY: CORRELATION ANALYSIS

	GLOBAL	By Geographical Region				By Per Capita Income			
		AFRICA	ARAB WORLD	ASIA	LATIN AMERICA	LOW INCOME COUNTRIES	LOWER MIDDLE-INCOME COUNTRIES	UPPER MIDDLE-INCOME COUNTRIES	HIGH INCOME COUNTRIES
Current country economic evaluation	0.29	0.29	0.20	0.35	0.20	0.32	0.31	0.26	0.17
Current personal economic evaluation	0.14	0.18	0.10	0.18	0.13	0.18	0.15	0.13	0.08
Trust in political parties	0.34	0.30	0.20	0.34	0.16	0.31	0.34	0.28	0.22
Trust in parliament	0.39	0.36	0.37	0.38	0.19	0.40	0.37	0.31	0.25
Trust in the courts	0.32	0.23	0.29	0.32	0.19	0.26	0.34	0.29	0.24
Citizen empowerment	0.14	0.20	0.12	0.10	0.10	0.22	0.12	0.11	0.00*
Free and fair elections	0.37	0.41	0.30	0.34	NA	0.39	0.34	0.36	0.32
Equal rights	0.11	-0.20	NA	0.30	0.16	-0.04*	0.19	0.06	0.32
Controlling corruption	0.25	0.21	0.20	0.32	NA	0.23	0.29	0.19	0.25
N	44733	14476	4346	9852	16058	13993	17606	8543	4590

Note: Sample sizes vary from one row to another due to pair-wise deletion of missing data. Coefficients that are not significant are marked with an asterisk (*). The reported N at the bottom row indicates the number of valid cases for estimating the correlation coefficients in the first row, in essence between support for democracy and evaluation of country's current economic conditions.

nomic evaluation exerts only an indirect effect that is mediated through people's satisfaction with the overall performance of democracy. If the linear association between perceived economic performance and support for democracy is stronger than that between democratic satisfaction and democratic support, we can confidently infer that perceived economic performance exerts at least some direct impact on people's normative commitment to democracy. The same logic can be extended to the theoretical standing of political factors as well.

Globally speaking, all factors under investigation are important to people's evaluation of the overall performance of the democratic regime. Trust in democratic institutions and the free and fair voting process does the most to encourage popular approval of the way that democracy works. People's evaluation of national economic conditions also matters, and its impact lags only slightly behind that of the various political indicators (see the left-most column of Table 2). This global pattern holds up well among Africans, Asians, and Arabs. In Latin America, by contrast, perceived national economic conditions matter more than political factors, but not by much. Across the four regions, how people assess the national economy appears to affect democratic satisfaction the most strongly in Asia.

Comparing the first row of Table 2 with its counterpart from Table 1, we see that for all four regions the impact of perceived national economic condition on democratic satisfaction is much stronger than its influence on democratic support. This implies that economic performance exerts only an indirect influence over people's normative commitment to democracy, acting mainly through its impact on popular approval of the way that democracy is actually working in a given country.

This pattern also holds across the three income groups below the high-income countries. The glaring exception, in fact, is the high-income group, where the impact (at 0.17) of perceived national economic conditions on democratic satisfaction is actually slightly weaker than its influence (at 0.2) over support for democracy. (It is well to bear in mind that for citizens of high-income countries, their perception of national economic conditions ranks highest as a shaper of belief in democratic legitimacy, while satisfaction with democracy ranks almost at the bottom.) Putting all these together, an inescapable conclusion emerges: In high-income countries, economic performance is an important ingredient of popular support for democracy. People's perceptions of how their national economies are faring have a significant and direct impact on how committed they feel toward democracy.[28] This is a phenomenon peculiar to high-income countries, and especially the affluent East Asian countries that make up four-fifths of our high-income group.

Our global survey underscores three important points: First, the success of third-wave democratization is not yet a foregone conclusion. Many third-wave democracies have experienced slow and uneven growth in democratic legitimacy, with substantial portions of their citizenries harboring reservations about democracy. Building a robust foundation of legitimacy remains a daunting challenge for most third-wave democracies.

Second, citizens of most new democracies can distinguish between the political and economic dimensions of regime performance. Many of them come to value democracy for the political goods that it produces even when its economic performance is perceived to be poor in the short term. More specifically, people's acceptance of democracy as legitimate hinges mostly on whether certain key political institutions command citizen trust, and on the political system's ability to meet such basic requirements of liberal democracy as free and fair elections, the provision of equal rights under law, and the empowerment of citizens to make changes of government by lawful means. In a nutshell, democracy needs to "pay its way" by delivering acceptable levels of citizen control and good governance.

Third, we cannot entirely write off economic performance as a factor in democratic consolidation. Democracies that have inherited records of stunning economic success from nondemocratic predecessors are under pressure to live up to high citizen expectations regarding continued economic excellence. Furthermore, all emerging democracies are subject to the harsh likelihood that protracted economic stagnation will sap popular support for democracy by destroying that sense of satisfaction with democracy's performance that is essential to democracy's legitimation.

NOTES

1. Herbert Kitschelt, "The Formation of Party Systems in East Central Europe," *Politics and Society* 20 (March 1992): 7–50.

2. Adam Przeworski, *Democracy and the Market: Political and Economic Reforms in Eastern Europe and Latin America* (Cambridge: Cambridge University Press, 1991).

3. Russell Dalton, "Communists and Democrats: Democratic Attitudes in the Two Germanies," *British Journal of Political Science* 24 (October 1994): 469–93.

4. Geoffrey Evans and Stephen Whitefield, "The Politics and Economics of Democratic Commitment: Support for Democracy in Transition Societies," *British Journal of Political Science* 25 (October 1995): 485–514.

5. Richard Rose, William Mishler, and Christian Haerpfer, *Democracy and Its Alternatives: Understanding Post-Communist Societies* (Baltimore: Johns Hopkins University Press, 1998), 157 and 174.

6. Robert Mattes and Michael Bratton, "Support for Democracy in Africa: Intrinsic or Instrumental?" *British Journal of Political Science* 31 (July 2001): 447–74; and Robert Mattes and Michael Bratton, "Learning About Democracy in Africa: Awareness, Performance, and Experience," *American Journal of Political Science* 51 (January 2007): 192–217.

7. Marta Lagos, "Latin America's Lost Illusions: A Road with No Return?" *Journal of Democracy* 14 (April 2003): 163–73.

8. Carol Graham and Sandip Sukhtankar, "Does Economic Crisis Reduce Support for Markets and Democracy in Latin America? Some Evidence from Surveys of Public Opinion and Well Being," *Journal of Latin American Studies* 36 (May 2004): 349–77.

9. Huo-yan Shyu, "Does Economic Performance Matter? Economic Evaluations and Support for Democracy in Seven Asian Countries," paper presented at an Asian Barometer international conference on "Why Asians Support Democracy and Why Not?" 9–10 August 2007, Taipei.

10. For more information about the four regional barometers, visit *www.globalbarometer.net, www.afrobarometer.org, www.arabbarometer.org, www.asianbarometer.org,* or *www.latinobarometro.org.* The Asian Barometer is a federation of two independent survey projects, East Asia Barometer and the State of Democracy in South Asia Project *(www.lokniti.org).*

11. The data included in the merged file include eighteen countries from the third-wave Afrobarometer (2005–2006); five countries from the first-wave Arab Barometer (2006–2007); five countries from the first-wave State of Democracy in South Asia Project (2004–2005); nine countries from the second-wave East Asia Barometer (2006–2007); and seventeen countries from Latinobarómetro (2003).

12. This is the exact wording of the item used in Afrobarometer, Asian Barometer, and Latinobarómetro. The item used in the Arab Barometer, although somewhat different, is arguably functionally equivalent. The respondents were asked if they agreed or disagreed with the statement, "Democracy may have its problems but is better than any other form of government."

13. Regarding the current conditions of national economies, we asked our respondents, "How would you rate the overall economic condition of our country today? Very good? Good? So-so (not good, not bad)? Bad? Very bad?" Regarding the current personal economic conditions, we asked, "As for your own family, how do you rate your economic situation today? Very good? Good? So-so (not good, not bad)? Bad? Very bad?" For both items, the five-point response grid was converted to a numerical scale (2, 1, 0, -1, or -2) for the sake of statistical analysis. The exact wording of the response categories varied slightly from one region to another.

14. We follow the World Bank's classification, which divides national economies into income groups according to 2005 Gross National Income per capita, calculated using the World Bank Atlas method. The groups are: low income (LIC), $875 or less; lower middle income (LMC), $876–3,465; upper middle income (UMC), $3,466–10,725; and high income, $10,726 or more. See the Bank's *World Development Report, 2007* (Washington, D.C.: World Bank, 2008), 287.

15. The correlation between the two measures is sufficiently large (0.5) to justify our collapsing the two into one.

16. This indicator is coded as a binary, with 1 meaning believing democracy is the best form of government and 0 not believing so.

17. This threshold was suggested by Larry Diamond in his *Developing Democracy: Toward Consolidation* (Baltimore: Johns Hopkins University Press, 1999), 179.

18. It would be wise not to read too much into the extraordinarily high levels of popular support for democracy in the three outliers, however. All three countries are still under authoritarian rule, and their peoples' understanding of democracy might be quite different from the understanding of democracy that prevails elsewhere.

19. We also evaluated the relative importance of each explanatory variable in multivariate context with logistic regression, which is methodologically more conclusive, to

buttress our simple bivariate analysis. For the sake of space, these additional findings are not reported here.

20. In order to measure institutional trust, we read the following statement to our respondents: "I am going to name a number of institutions. For each one, could you tell me how much trust you have in it? Is it a great deal of trust, some trust, not very much trust or none at all?" For the sake of statistical analysis, we converted the four-point response grid for each item into a numerical scale comprising values of 2, 1, -1, or -2.

21. To gauge the extent of citizen empowerment, Afrobarometer asked its respondents the following question: "Think about how elections work in practice in this country. How well do elections enable voters to remove from office leaders who do not do what the people want? Very well? Well? Not very well? Not at all well?" The question used in other regional surveys follows essentially the same design, though each survey has its own nuances.

22. We asked our respondents: "On the whole, how would you rate the freeness and fairness of the last national election, held in [year]? Completely free and fair? Free and fair but with minor problems? Free and fair but with major problems? Not free or fair?"

23. In order to gauge whether people think that the rights of all are equally protected, Asian Barometer employed the following item: "Everyone is treated equally by the government. Strongly agree, somewhat agree, somewhat disagree, or strongly disagree." Questions used in other barometer surveys slightly deviated one way or another from this, but all adopted a four-point response grid. For instance, Afrobarometer asked, "Are people treated unequally under the law? Always? Often? Rarely? Never?"

24. To measure satisfaction with democracy, we asked our respondents: "On the whole, how satisfied or dissatisfied are you with the way democracy works in [country]? Very satisfied? Fairly satisfied? Not very satisfied? Not at all satisfied?" This four-point response grid was converted to a numerical scale, ranging from 2 to -2, for the sake of statistical analysis.

25. We use a weighting variable to fix each country's sample size to 1,000 cases so that any country happening to have a large sample would nonetheless not dominate the statistical results.

26. This is consistent with the findings that we reported earlier.

27. For instance, see Ronald Inglehart, *Modernization and Postmodernization: Cultural, Economic, and Political Change in 43 Societies* (Princeton: Princeton University Press, 1997).

28. This direct causal relationship is further confirmed by our analysis within the framework of the structural-equation model. Explaining this model, however, would involve a great deal of technical material that we omit here for brevity's sake.

4

LEARNING TO SUPPORT NEW REGIMES IN EUROPE

Richard Rose

Richard Rose *is director of the Centre for the Study of Public Policy at the University of Aberdeen, Scotland, and creator of the New Europe Barometer surveys of mass response to transformation in postcommunist countries. His latest book, coauthored with William Mishler and Neil Munro, is* Understanding Transformation: From Unstable to Stable European States *(2009). This essay originally appeared in the July 2007 issue of the* Journal of Democracy.

The fall of the Berlin Wall in November 1989 radically altered the way in which hundreds of millions of Europeans could learn about democracy. Across Central and Eastern Europe and the Baltic states, new regimes replaced the communist systems that had been aligned with the Soviet Union. With these sweeping changes, citizens could begin to learn the meaning of democracy for themselves rather than vicariously through clandestine radio broadcasts from the West. When the first free elections were held in 1990, people had high hopes as well as fears regarding democracy and the economic and social transformations that would accompany it.

How do people born in a communist regime now evaluate their postcommunist regime? In order to give meaningful support to democracy, people must learn what democracy actually means in practice. Inexperienced leaders need to learn that governing is different from leading protest demonstrations, and citizens need to learn which of their hopes and fears may be justified. It has now been more than a decade and a half since the Wall fell, and citizens in affected countries have had plenty of time to see how their new regime actually works and to judge it for what it is. Some postcommunist regimes have succeeded in being accepted as democracies, while others have not.

In Central and Eastern Europe, politicians quickly adapted to electoral competition, and citizens have used the right to vote to turn out of office their government of the day. The rejection of Soviet rule was complemented by a desire to "return to Europe." Institutionally, this meant gaining admission to the European Union (EU). In principle, the EU is prepared to accept member states from all over Europe, and between its founding in 1957 and the fall of the Berlin Wall in 1989 it had grown from six to fifteen members. But acceptance as an EU member requires applicant countries to be democratically governed, respect the rule of law, and have a functioning market economy. By 2004, eight former communist countries—the Czech Republic, Estonia, Hungary, Latvia, Lithuania, Poland, Slovakia, and Slovenia—were admitted to the EU, and in 2007 Bulgaria and Romania were also admitted, although with reservations.[1]

In post-Soviet states, the pattern has been different: Unfree or unfair elections have been the rule in Belarus, Ukraine, Russia, and across Central Asia. In Belarus, Alyaksandr Lukashenka has established a dictatorship behind an electoral façade. In Ukraine, elections have been competitive, but governments have been quarrelsome at best and brutal and corrupt at worst. In Russia, President Vladimir Putin replaced the unpredictability of the late Boris Yeltsin's rule (1991–99) with an order that restricts civil and political liberties. Freedom House characterizes the bulk of Soviet successor states as Partly Free or Not Free.

The democratic ideal is that a new government will consolidate popular support by delivering what voters want. Some theories of political culture explain the persistence of nondemocratic regimes as showing that authoritarian cultural norms cause some people to want a nondemocratic regime, and Russian history is cited in support of this view. Winston Churchill's realist explanation for a government's survival offers an alternative view: A new regime is supported, notwithstanding its faults, so long as it is viewed as a lesser evil. Thus a nondemocratic regime may receive resigned acceptance from people who would ideally prefer a democracy on the grounds that the available alternatives are worse or simply because people do not see any alternative at all.

To find out how much support there is for the no-longer-new regimes of Central and Eastern Europe and the former Soviet Union, we need public-opinion surveys taken over a period of time from the early 1990s to EU enlargement in 2004. To see to what extent people give resigned acceptance to nondemocratic regimes, we need public-opinion evidence from both democratic and nondemocratic political systems.

The New Europe Barometer (NEB) provides the data we need to investigate popular support for new political systems. Since 1991, the Centre for the Study of Public Policy has been surveying mass response to transformation in Central and Eastern Europe and the former Soviet Union, and has conducted more than a hundred surveys in the region. Because the NEB has repeated the same key questions in each round of surveys, there is copious data to measure trends in public opinion.[2] In this analysis, we draw especially on the latest NEB survey, conducted in the winter of 2004–2005. It covered ten countries that are now democratic member states of the EU: the Czech Republic, Estonia, Hungary, Latvia, Lithuania, Poland, Slovakia, Slovenia, Bulgaria, and Romania. The survey also covers three post-Soviet states that are not EU members: Russia, Belarus, and Ukraine.[3]

Evaluating Alternative Regimes

When asked what democracy means, people born in countries that were formerly part of the communist bloc emphasize three themes: the freedom to do and say what you want; the choice of government by competitive elections; and a welfare state.[4] The first two elements are found in almost every definition of democracy. The addition of welfare policies, such as universal health care and a guaranteed minimum income, differs from the association of political freedom and the free market espoused by former U.S. president Ronald Reagan and former British prime minister Margaret Thatcher, while being consistent with European ideas of a social-demo-cratic or social-market state.

Throughout the thirteen countries listed above, most adults today have lived for a longer time under communist rule than under democratic rule, if they have experienced the latter at all. Thus the competition for political support in a postcommunist country is less between political parties than between alternative systems of governance. To ascertain whether people who learned to accept dictatorship would like to live in a democracy, the NEB asks people where they would like their political system to be on a scale that ranges from complete democracy (10) to complete dictatorship (1).

Democracy as an ideal is positively endorsed in all thirteen countries; altogether, 82 percent of those surveyed give it a favorable rating, 7 percent favor a dictatorship, and 11 percent appear to endorse something midway between the two. Moreover, the largest group, 35 percent of respondents, gives democracy the highest possible rating (10). The only difference is in the size of the majority endorsing democracy as an ideal. In new EU member countries, the mean score is 8.1, with more than half of Hungarians and Romanians surveyed giving a complete democracy the highest possible score. By contrast, in post-Soviet countries the mean score is 7.5, and in Russia it falls to 6.6, the lowest of all thirteen countries surveyed.

We also find that a decade and a half after the fall of the Berlin Wall, postcommunist regimes have not, or at least have not yet, provided the political institutions that their citizens desire. Citizens do not see these systems as close to complete democracy. When they are asked to evaluate their current regime, the mean rating is only 5.6, almost exactly halfway between being a complete dictatorship and a complete democracy. The average score is slightly higher in new EU member states (5.8) than in post-Soviet countries (5.3). People who give three cheers for democracy as an ideal are often not even willing to give two cheers for the way it operates today, and a significant fraction point their thumbs downward.

There is a substantial gap in ratings between what citizens would like their new system of government to be and what they think it actually is. The gap is greatest in Romania (3.5 points) because of the high value that most Romanians place on democracy as an ideal (8.6) and the low rating that they give the system that they have actually experienced (5.1). The gap is least in Russia (1.1), because of the low rating that many Russians give to democracy as an ideal (6.6).

Dissatisfaction with the new regime discourages people from voting and encourages cynicism about politics as well as a high degree of distrust toward parties and politicians. This does not mean, however, that citizens want to replace their imperfect regime with a nondemocratic alternative. To test this, the NEB survey offers a variety of alternatives that are historically relevant in the region, ranging from rule by the army to a return to communist rule.

A majority of citizens in every country almost always rejects each nondemocratic alternative; the only difference between countries is in the size of the majority that disapproves. As the Figure shows, in both the new EU member states and the post-Soviet states, there is very little support for turning to military rule. Even though NEB surveys find that the army is more trusted than most institutions in postcommunist societies and that many worry about disorder and crime, more than 90 percent of postcommunist citizens do not want to be subject to a military dictatorship. This is consistent with the self-image of the military, which was subordinate to the old communist ruling parties before the Soviet bloc collapsed, and in most countries today is outwardly oriented toward the opportunities offered by integration into NATO.

There is a tendency for new EU member states to be less inclined toward strongman rule than people in post-Soviet states. In the Czech Republic, Hungary, Slovakia, and Slovenia, more than three-quarters of those surveyed reject dictatorship, as do three-quarters in Romania, which experienced the most despotic communist regime. It would be a mistake to infer from Putin's popularity that Russians want to be ruled by a dictator; 63 percent say that they do not. In Belarus, however, 63 percent endorse the statement that it is better to get rid of parliament and elections and have a strong leader who can quickly decide everything. Large minorities in Poland (48 percent) and Ukraine (42 percent) also agree with this statement.

Survey evidence of the popularity of the communist era reflects nostalgia for a past that is gone rather than a demand for communist rule in the future.[5] When NEB respondents are asked to evaluate the former communist regime, an average of 57 percent give a positive reply, and the proportion doing so is as high as 71 percent in Russia. Yet when asked whether they would like to see the communist regime return, most people who speak favorably of the old regime do not want it back. Altogether, 80 percent reject a return to communism. Where a communist regime

FIGURE—SUPPORT FOR NONDEMOCRATIC ALTERNATIVES
(MEAN PERCENTAGE ENDORSING)

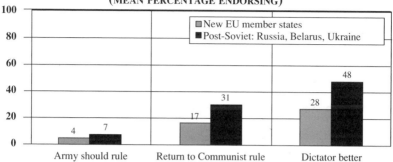

Question: "Our present system of government is not the only one that this country has had. Some people say that we would be better off if the country was governed differently. What do you think? a) Army should rule; b) Return to Communist rule; c) Strong man better."
Source: Centre for the Study of Public Policy, New Europe Barometer surveys, October 2004–February 2005. Total number of respondents: 15,354. Details at *www.abdn.ac.uk/cspp.*

was imposed by the force of the Soviet army, there is the lowest support for a return to communism. In the Baltic states, where ethnic Russians form a substantial minority, more than four-fifths of ethnic Russians reject the idea of returning to communist rule. In Russia, even though a substantial minority of 42 percent endorses a return to communist rule, there remains a majority against it—and an even larger majority that does not vote for the Communist Party in elections.

In the ten new EU member states, 67 percent on average—and as many as 75 percent in Hungary—reject all three nondemocratic alternatives. The pattern is different in post-Soviet countries. Fully 74 percent of Belarusians and 58 percent of Russians endorse at least one nondemocratic alternative. The political impact of those attracted to nondemocratic alternatives tends to be dispersed, however, since there is no agreement about which alternative should replace the current regime. Even among those favoring a dictatorship in principle, there is unlikely to be agreement among the political elite or the general public about who would make the best dictator. In sum, while citizens are critical about the democratic achievements of their new regime, nondemocratic alternatives have limited appeal.

To measure support for the current regime, NEB surveys do not ask about satisfaction with how democracy is working, since the political system is nondemocratic in some countries where people are interviewed. Instead, immediately after asking for an evaluation of the old regime, people are asked to evaluate "the current system of governing" on a thermometer scale running from +100 to -100. The overall mean of +11 across all the NEB countries is not far from the middle of the 201-point scale. In Russia, Bulgaria, and Slovakia, the mean is exactly 0, and it is no more than three points higher in Latvia, Poland, and Romania. While opinions vary within each country, most tend to fall within a moderate range. Relatively few respondents rate their regime near the top of the scale, and fewer still rate it near the bottom.

Across the region as a whole, 61 percent are positive about their new regime and an additional 9 percent are neutral, while less than one-third are negative. A striking feature is that those who favor the new regime make up a slightly larger share of the populace in the three post-Soviet countries (63 percent) than in the new EU member states (61 percent). Further evidence that endorsement of the new regime is not based on its democratic credentials is the presence of higher support levels in Belarus and Ukraine than in most new EU member states.

In order to gauge attitudes toward regime change, NEB respondents are asked if they would "approve or disapprove if parliament was closed down and parties abolished." In new EU member states, an average of 74 percent reject getting rid of infirm representative institutions, and in each country surveyed a majority holds this view. This result is striking, since distrust of representative institutions is widespread. Across the region, only 11 percent express trust in parties and only 17 percent express trust in parliament. Yet even though citizens do not trust these political institutions, they want them to remain in place in the belief that even bad elected representatives are better than no elected representatives.

The Path of Change

The logic of democratic consolidation is that trends over time are crucial. Whatever the initial support for a new regime, it should increase as the persistence of a new regime leads to popular acceptance of it as the "only game in town."[6] Theories of democratic consolidation also imply that support for nondemocratic alternatives should fall—yet this does not necessarily happen. For example, after a decade or so, citizens may take for granted the freedom that was immediately gained after the collapse of a nondemocratic regime, thereby depriving the new regime of the advantage of being a lesser evil compared to its predecessor.

In postcommunist regimes, the benefits and costs of transition did not come all at once. First came the political benefits. The collapse of communist regimes removed the repressive constraints that had been put on individual freedoms. In the 1993 NEB survey, people were asked to compare their freedom to voice their thoughts under the new regime with what was the case under the old regime. In the ten countries that are now EU members, an average of 84 percent said that they felt freer with communism gone, and very few felt less free. In the three post-Soviet countries surveyed, an average of 72 percent felt freer than before. This gain in freedom has been an important factor in maintaining support for the new regimes, whatever their weaknesses.

There were also great costs to the changes in governing systems. Immediately after the first free elections in 1990, people learned that they not only would reap the benefits of freedom from state repression, but would have to bear the costs of moving from a bureaucratic planned economy to a market economy. Economic theories of political behavior fueled predictions that such transition costs would spur mass protests and topple elected governments, after which a reborn communism or some other form of dictatorship would arise. Other theories less beholden to the "dismal science" pointed to the advantages that the new regimes enjoyed by virtue of having replaced a repressive and often foreign-imposed communist system. Shortly after the transitions, the economies of these countries did shrink severely, and many citizens suffered. Yet in defiance of notions about politics drawn from economics, material hardship did not provoke citizens to repudiate their new governments.

People learned how to be patient after living for years within the communist bloc. Moreover, people who had endured the pathologies of a nonmarket economy could blame the old regime for the economic problems that beset life under the new regime. The immediate costs of transition were offset by the hope that benefits would follow at some uncertain time in the future. That patience has been rewarded. Since the mid-1990s, economies that at first had contracted severely have been growing at rates several times higher than those characteristic of the United States or Western Europe. The benefits of transition are visible in the well-stocked shops and in the spread of consumer goods into many households. Entry into the EU has expanded opportunities for education and employment that were inconceivable in the days when these countries lay behind the Iron Curtain. Even so, people's idealism about democracy has dissipated because of the rancorous conflicts between political parties, the raw opportunism of certain politicians, and persistent corruption.

Russia exemplifies both the positive and negative trends. Official statistics record that the Russian economy contracted by 43 percent between 1990 and 1998, but grew by more than two-thirds between 1998 and 2006. Yet the Putin administration has not eliminated the corruption that financed President Yeltsin's election campaigns; instead, it has reallocated benefits by bending laws to its own advantage. In the new EU member states, economic turnarounds have been faster and often more dramatic. After a controversial dose of economic "shock therapy," the Polish economy began to show signs of sustained growth in 1994, and official statistics show that its Gross Domestic Product in 2005 had become more than two-thirds greater than it was at the end of the nonmarket communist system. Of the ten new EU members, only Bulgaria and Latvia continue to be plagued by the rising unemployment and inflation that marred the first years of economic transition.

Most citizens of the new EU member states now respond positively when asked to evaluate the regime under which they live, although as Table 1 shows, trajectories of support have varied. Since the transitions from communist rule in the early 1990s, support for the postcommunist systems of

TABLE 1—CHANGES IN SUPPORT FOR THE CURRENT REGIME
(PERCENTAGE GIVING POSITIVE SUPPORT)

	EARLY 1990s	CURRENT	CHANGE
NEW EU MEMBERS			
Estonia	55	75	20
Lithuania	47	71	24
Slovenia	49	70	21
Czech Republic	71	70	-1
Hungary	57	65	8
Poland	52	53	1
Slovakia	50	52	2
Latvia	41	52	11
Bulgaria	64	51	-13
Romania	69	51	-18
Mean	55	61	6
POST-SOVIET			
Ukraine	25	70	45
Belarus	35	74	39
Russia	14	69	55
Mean	25	71	46

Question: "Here is a scale for ranking how our system of government works. The top, plus 100, is the best; the bottom, minus 100, the worst. Where on this scale would you put our current system of governing with free elections and many parties?"
Source: New Europe Barometer surveys, Centre for the Study of Public Policy, *www.abdn.ac.uk/cspp*. Results from the early 1990s were found in the following years: seven EU countries (new EU members minus the Baltic states), 1991; Belarus and Ukraine, 1992; Baltic states, 1993; and Russia, 1994.

government has risen substantially in just over half the NEB countries. Support has risen by as much as 24 percent in Lithuania and 21 percent in Slovenia and has remained steady and high in the Czech Republic and Hungary, whereas it has been steady but only just above 50 percent in Poland and Slovakia. By contrast, in Bulgaria and Romania, support has fallen significantly since the early 1990s by 13 and 18 percent, respectively.

The biggest gains in regime support have occurred in post-Soviet states, where democracy has not made strong headway. In Russia, the regime had very little popular support when the first NEB survey was launched in January 1992 (14 percent), the first month of the new regime there. From that very low starting point, the regime has made fluctuating gains. Support shot up from 39 percent in 2000 (just after Putin took office) to as high as 69 percent as President Putin approached the end of his term of office in April 2007. From 1992 to 2004, support for the new regime more than doubled in Belarus too, underlining the point that people can adapt to nondemocratic as well as to democratic regimes. In Ukraine, support for the regime increased, temporarily at least, as a consequence of the Orange Revolution, which followed the courts declaring the initial presidential ballot illegal in the autumn of 2004.

A sense of greater freedom is strong throughout the postcommunist region, including in nondemocratic states such as Russia and Belarus, and citizens continue to feel freer than they did in the early 1990s. What might account for the strong support that regimes such as those in Russia and Belarus enjoy? The greater freedom felt by Russians, notwithstanding the Putin government's use of security services to constrict the freedoms of opposition elites, reflects the Kremlin's tolerance of the views of the "unimportant" public and the public's lack of empathy with Putin's billionaire critics.

Across the region as a whole, there is a downward trend in the proportion of citizens who favor abandoning the parliamentary system and halting elections in favor of dictatorship. Among the new EU member states, the early 1990s were a time when as many as a third of NEB respondents said that they would prefer dictatorship. By the 2004–2005 NEB survey, approval of dictatorship had fallen in nine out of these ten countries by an average of 11 percentage points, and by as many as 33 points in Lithuania and 28 points in Bulgaria. Poland is the only country where the minority that supports dictatorship has been consistently high, reaching almost half in 2004, the year before the Kaczyński twins won power as leaders of the populist Law and Justice party. In each of the three post-Soviet states, endorsement of dictatorship has fallen by 10 percentage points or more, although this support remains above the levels found in new EU member states.

Future Expectations

The consolidation of popular support is a process that can take a decade or longer, as it did in Germany after the Second World War and in Spain after the death of Francisco Franco. Political attitudes reflect both current circumstances and expectations about the future. In the early 1990s, when citizens had no experience with their postcommunist systems, political judgments could have reflected either hopes for the future or abhorrence of the past and fears that it might return.[7] People have since learned about their new systems' strengths and faults, and because most regimes have plenty of both, keeping expectations for the future positive remains important as a means of encouraging people to accept the systems' continuing shortcomings.

Popular expectations about the political future are invariably more positive than evaluations of the present. Across the new EU member states, 75 percent of citizens express a positive view of what they expect their regime to be like in five years, compared to the 61 percent who feel positive about the regime as it is today. Optimism runs high not only in well-governed states such as Slovenia and Estonia, but also in those where governance has been full of faults—in Romania, for example, just over three-quarters of those polled feel optimistic about the future, even though only half feel positive about today.

Optimism is also high in the post-Soviet states. In Ukraine immediately after the Orange Revolution, 89 percent of citizens polled said that they felt positive about the future, including a majority of ethnic Russians as well as ethnic Ukrainians. In Belarus—which has experienced nothing like the Orange Revolution—the percentage of citizens who feel positive about their country's political future is almost as high, at 82 percent. By April 2007, 75 percent of Russians were optimistic about what their regime would be like in five years, and only 17 percent negative, with the remainder uncertain.

As time passes, the previous regime becomes a fading memory and the new one increasingly appears as a matter of fact. People can learn to adapt to what they have, whatever may have been their hopes at the time of transition, and each new generation is socialized to support a system that can now be seen as a given. Adaptation does not require a new regime to deliver a high level of economic growth. Popular acceptance of a regime is a reflection of the demonstrated capacity of its institutions to persist—whether they are democratic or not.

Today, the great majority of people who lived through the transformation of a communist to a noncommunist regime do not expect another change of regimes. In order to probe the extent to which people think that their regime is secure against overthrow, the NEB asks respondents how likely or unlikely they think it is that their country's parliament will be shut and opposition parties abolished (results are in Table 2). When the question was initially asked in the early 1990s, in what are now EU member states an average of 36 percent thought that a change in regime might happen, and in Poland as many as 55 percent thought this possible.

Since the early 1990s, the proportion of citizens who expect that regime change might occur has fallen sharply. In new EU member states, only 13 percent think that representative institutions could be abolished. In no country did even one-fifth of those surveyed see regime change as a possibility, and in Hungary only 3 percent thought so. Moreover, those who consider regime change to be a possibility are fewer than those who want it to happen. In the new EU member states, 18 percent are frustrated fascists; they would like to get rid of parliament and abolish parties but do not think that this will happen. By contrast, only 9 percent are optimistic authoritarians who would like to see an end to representative institutions and believe that this could occur.

Citizens of post-Soviet states also expect parliament and competing parties to stay, even though these institutions are less important than in the democratic states of the EU. Under certain conditions opposition groups can use them to effect political change, as recent events in Ukraine show. In Russia, as parliament and parties have weakened, the possibility of these

TABLE 2—LOW EXPECTATION OF REGIME COLLAPSING
(PERCENTAGE SAYING LIKELY OR MIGHT HAPPEN)

	EARLY 1990S	CURRENT	CHANGE
NEW EU MEMBERS			
Estonia	41	13	-28
Lithuania	36	9	-27
Slovenia	29	14	-15
Czech Republic	39	10	-29
Hungary	25	3	-22
Poland	55	19	-36
Slovakia	47	16	-31
Latvia	28	19	-9
Bulgaria	30	13	-17
Romania	32	15	-17
Mean	36	13	-23
POST-SOVIET			
Ukraine	40	22	-18
Belarus	43	18	-25
Russia	61	21	-40
Mean	48	20	-28

Question: "Some people think this country would be better governed if parliament was closed down and all parties were abolished. How likely do you think this is to happen in the next few years?"
Source: New Europe Barometer surveys, Centre for the Study of Public Policy, *www.abdn.ac.uk/cspp.* Results from the early 1990s were found in the following years: seven EU countries (new EU members minus the Baltic states), 1991; Belarus and Ukraine, 1992; Baltic states, 1993; and Russia, 1994.

institutions being abolished has diminished substantially. In October 1993, President Yeltsin used troops and gunfire to subdue his opponents in the Russian parliament and 61 percent thought that something like this could happen again. By April 2007, the percentage thinking that the Duma (the lower house of the national legislature) and parties could be shut down had dropped to 21 percent. Moreover, the proportion of frustrated fascists who would like to see the Duma abolished but do not think it will happen now outnumbers the 14 percent of Russians who are optimistic authoritarians, thinking that the Kremlin could get rid of the Duma and political parties.

In new EU member states, there is an expectation that regimes with many shortcomings will become more democratic within five years. When people in these countries are asked to place the current regime on a scale in which 1 is a complete dictatorship and 10 a complete democracy, the mean score is 5.8, which is close to the midpoint. Yet when asked what they expect the regime to be like in five years, large majorities expect it to be substantially democratic, as reflected in the higher mean score of 7.0. Moreover, popular expectations that the regime will become more democratic are increasing faster in Bulgaria and Romania, where shortcomings have been particularly evident, than the average for the new EU member states as a whole. Citizen expectations are thus consistent with the theory, so firmly held in Brussels, that EU admission will aid the consolidation of a new member's democratic institutions.

By contrast, in Belarus and Russia people do not believe that democratization will advance. Very little change is expected from the current situation, which people see as a kind of halfway zone between democracy and full-blown dictatorship. Most Belarusians believe that in five years their country's regime will still fall between these alternatives, with a mean score of 5.8 on the 10-point scale compared with 5.0 for current practices. Russians on average place the current regime at the arithmetic midpoint between dictatorship and democracy, 5.5, while showing signs of optimism about the future, giving the regime in five years a mean score of 7.0 in the April 2007 survey. After the Orange Revolution and Viktor Yushchenko's accession to the presidency, Ukrainians professed themselves optimistic that their country's regime would move toward democracy. They gave their regime a mean rating of 5.3 for the present but 7.2 for five years in the future. Yet events in Ukraine since 2005—including rancorous and tangled political confrontations between the president and the prime minister—make it appear unlikely that such a pronounced move toward democracy will occur.

Consolidation, for Better or Worse

A new regime consolidates when people accept it as the only system of government that they can expect to have in the future. Thus the longer a new regime persists, the more realistic it is for consolidation to occur as citizens, for a variety of reasons, come to accept that the regime is there to stay. In new EU member states, citizens accept the system because they are positive about the current regime and, although aware of its faults, they remain confident that it will become more democratic in the future. If these expectations become reality, the process of democratic consolidation will become complete.

In the post-Soviet states, some citizens not only approve of their new regime but also expect it to improve—though not to become more democratic. Others offer only resigned acceptance of the current regime. Many post-Soviet citizens regard democracy as the ideal form of government and do not see their current regime as a democracy. They do not, however, expect it to give way to any alternative system. The gap between the popular endorsement of democracy as an ideal and the reality of the regime today has not led to mass frustration that would ignite explosive rebellion, as some political scientists would theorize.[8] Instead, people believe that leaders will ignore demands for reforms or harass anyone demanding political change.

Russians have had to adapt to the mixed consequences of political and economic transition, but because the consequences have been mixed, they can focus selectively on the benefits gained rather than on the difficulties encountered. Communism's collapse gave Russians more freedom from the state in their everyday lives, and this is an important influence encouraging support for the new regime. The well-publicized attacks on media moguls and political dissidents are of little concern to ordinary people. Furthermore, Putin has had better luck than did Soviet ruler Leonid Brezhnev (1964–82) at building support through a policy of "welfare-state authoritarianism." Whereas the Soviet Union's planned economy could not deliver the consumer goods that Russians sought, Putin's good fortune is that the introduction of a market economy has made consumer goods available in abundance, and that an economic boom based on the worldwide rise in oil and gas prices has made more of these goods affordable.

The immediate challenge to the current Russian regime lies in the term-limits law that requires Putin to hand the presidency to a successor in the spring of 2008. A thorough analysis of the NEB surveys leads to the conclusion that popular support for the regime owes far more to political inertia and the passage of time than it does to Putin's personal appeal. This suggests that as long as Russia's political elites manage to agree on a successor to Putin, a quiescent public will likely go along.[9] Should the political insiders split ranks and begin fighting over who is to be the next president, however, the resulting conflict could change the regime's character.

The longer a nondemocratic regime remains in place, the more pressure its subjects will feel to learn to live with it rather than to accept the risks that come with protest or rebellion. People who have lived much of their lives under communist regimes have experience with accepting the powers that be, and may exploit weaknesses in the system when opportunities arise. Reasons for accepting the regime can also be found in the lesser-evil principle. Instead of having the current regime, for example, the country could be engaged in a bloody civil war or be under the control of a totalitarian party that exercises absolute control over the lives of its subjects.

When the Levada Centre surveyed Russians in 1998 about whether they had adapted to the major changes that had happened in their society, only 29 percent said that they had done so, while 26 percent said that they were trying, and 45 percent said that they would never adapt. When it asked the same question in March 2007, a 60 percent majority said that they had adapted to the new system and 18 percent expected to do so in the near future, while the share of those who said that they would never adapt had been halved to 22 percent.

A consolidated regime, whether democratic or nondemocratic, can be described as being in equilibrium so long as the response of its citizens is consistent with the institutions that the country's elites supply. But sooner or later its leaders will face a challenge from unexpected and unwelcome domestic developments or from forces abroad. With respect to democratic systems, Robert A. Dahl argues that every actual polity falls short of the democratic ideal, which is a goal to be striven for but which can never be completely achieved. The gap between popular aspirations for a complete democracy and popular evaluations of new regimes found in many postcommunist countries can be interpreted as evidence of democratic realism. This gap may also prove to be a positive stimulus for reformers, spurring them to demand changes that would make their system more democratic.

NOTES

1. Olli Rehn, *Europe's Next Frontiers* (Baden-Baden: Nomos and Center for Applied Policy Research, 2006), 14.

2. Richard Rose, *Diverging Paths of Post-Communist Countries: New Europe Barometer Trends Since 1991* (Aberdeen: Centre for the Study of Public Policy No. 418, 2006) and *www.abdn.ac.uk/cspp.*

3. NEB interviewing started in October 2004, five months after eight countries that had once belonged to the communist bloc became EU members and their citizens became eligible to vote in the election of the European Parliament. Bulgaria and Romania were subsequently admitted in January 2007. The Ukraine survey was carried out in February 2005, shortly after opposition presidential candidate Viktor Yushchenko was elected but before the March 2006 parliamentary election was won by the party of his opponent during the presidential race, Viktor Yanukovich. See Richard Rose, *Insiders and Outsiders: New Europe Barometer 2004* (Glasgow: Centre for the Study of Public Policy No. 404, 2005). In a few instances, current Russian public opinion is cited from a New Russia Barometer survey carried out in April 2007. The surveys have been funded over the years by many institutions, starting with the Austrian Ministry of Science and Research and the Austrian National Bank in cooperation with the Paul Lazarsfeld Society, Vienna. Most recent surveys have been principally funded by the British Economic and Social Research Council RES 062 23 0341.

4. Janos Simon, *Popular Conceptions of Democracy in Post-Communist Europe* (Glasgow: Centre for the Study of Public Policy No. 273, 1996).

5. Neil Munro, "Russia's Persistent Communist Legacy: Nostalgia, Reaction, and Reactionary Expectations," *Post-Soviet Affairs* 22 (October–December 2006): 289–313.

6. Juan J. Linz, "Transitions to Democracy," *Washington Quarterly* (Summer 1990): 143–64.

7. Indeed, in the years just after the fall of the Berlin Wall, there was no assurance that new states would survive. The breakup of Yugoslavia beginning in 1991 and the bloody fighting that lasted for years was a palpable reminder that even state boundaries were up for grabs. The 1993 breakup of Czechoslovakia was completely peaceful and the Baltic states regained independence with only a dozen lives lost. From Moldova to the Caucasus, however, there is continuing evidence of force being used to decide state boundaries.

8. Ted R. Gurr, *Why Men Rebel* (Princeton: Princeton University Press, 1970).

9. See Richard Rose, William Mishler, and Neil Munro, *Russia Transformed: Developing Popular Support for a New Regime* (New York: Cambridge University Press, 2006), ch. 9.

5

LATIN AMERICA'S DIVERSITY OF VIEWS

Marta Lagos

Marta Lagos is managing director of MORI (Market and Opinion Research International), Chile, and founding director of the Latinobarómetro, a yearly survey of public opinion that covers eighteen Latin American countries. This essay originally appeared in the January 2008 issue of the Journal of Democracy.

In the twelve years since the inception of the Latinobarómetro, Latin American societies have evolved politically and economically, sometimes considerably, but they have not been transformed.[1] Levels of public support for democracy, underlying attitudes toward the democratic regimes in the region, and individual feelings and anxieties about politics and governance have changed in some countries, but only very gradually and unevenly in the region overall. While there are some signs of democratic progress and hope, more striking is the perception of democracy as being unresponsive and elite-dominated. In general, democratization in the region has been slow and heterogeneous; although citizens recognize some positive changes, so far these have been insufficient to achieve the kind of transformation in governance or social and economic structures that would help consolidate democracy.

According to our findings, Latin Americans on the whole do not feel that they have a functioning democracy in their countries yet, at least not according to their own understanding of what democracy should be. Instead what people see is the superficial framework of a political regime that is not what it says it is. On average (during the period from 1996 to 2000), about eight in ten Latin Americans say that there are still things to be done for democracy to be established, and on a scale from 1 to 10 depicting how democratic their country is, Latin Americans in 2006 placed their country at an average of 5.8—precisely the same average as in 1997.[2] The data on this are abundant and fairly consistent; for example, averaging across the different countries and years, slightly over half

TABLE 1—SUPPORT FOR DEMOCRACY BY EDUCATION, AGE, AND SEX, 1995–2006

		DEMOCRACY IS ALWAYS PREFERABLE	SOMETIMES AN AUTHORITARIAN REGIME
Education	Primary	51	20
	Secondary	59	18
	Higher	67	13
Age	16–25	53	21
	26–39	56	19
	41–60	58	17
	61 and over	60	14
Sex	Male	59	17
	Female	54	19
Total		57	17

Figures represent averages for the 176,447 interviews conducted in eighteen countries by the Latinobarómetro, 1995–2006.

(54 percent) of Latin Americans say that democracy in their countries has major problems, and only 4 percent say that there is full democracy.

As a result, support for democracy is limited to a modest majority of the public, and it has failed to rise above the average of a decade ago. In 2006, averaging across the eighteen Latin American countries surveyed, only 58 percent said that "democracy is always preferable," while 17 percent felt that "under some circumstances an authoritarian government can be preferable," and 8 percent said, "for people like me, it doesn't matter." As regional averages, these figures have oscillated only within narrow bands, and in 2006 they returned to the exact levels of 1995. Among the more than 176,000 Latin Americans interviewed during the eleven Latinobarómetro surveys conducted during this period, we find a pattern in which older and more-educated people show higher degrees of support for democracy, while the younger generations and the less educated are less inclined to think that democracy is always preferable. Men also show more support than women (see Table 1).

Among the eighteen countries surveyed, there has been a general pattern throughout this period: Two of the most liberal and well-established democracies, Uruguay and Costa Rica, have consistently exhibited the highest levels of support for democracy, while the lowest levels of support have generally been found in countries with the weakest or most tenuous democracies, such as Paraguay and Guatemala. In recent years, support for democracy has improved noticeably over the historical average of the preceding decade in Argentina, the Dominican Republic, Bolivia, Ecuador, and Brazil. This returned democracy in Argentina to the high level of support (74 percent) that it enjoyed during the late 1990s, before the country's economic and political crisis at the end of the Menem years; but it brought Brazil up only modestly, to what is still one of the lowest levels of support (46 percent).

Many observers are confused when they try to apply to Latin America old categories such as "left" and "right," whose meanings are no longer as clear as they were during the Cold War years. They are likewise puzzled by the fact that in Latin America, despite the large degree of cultural homogeneity, there is much less political or historical similarity among countries. So while there is a temptation among analysts to speak of "Latin America" as a coherent region, the Latinobarómetro data show that Latin America itself is not the proper unit of analysis—its individual countries are. Few common traits can be adequately analyzed or summarized at the regional level. Rather, attitudes, opinions, and behavior must be viewed in the context of each country in order to find the determinants of beliefs and behavior. In fact, far more crucial than culture or position along the left-right spectrum are the unique social and political settings in which they rest, as well as the historical experience of each country.

Left, Right, or Center: Who Are the Democrats?

Who are the democrats in Latin America, and how has the political profile of support for democracy changed over time? While older and especially better-educated citizens are generally more likely to support democracy in Latin America, it is not possible to generalize across countries with respect to the ideological sources of support for democracy. Depending on the country and—crucially—the historical moment, people on both the left and the right may have "democratic" or "undemocratic attitudes," as manifested in their ability or inability to embrace democracy as always preferable.[3]

Patterns of support do not depend on ideology in any fixed way. Only in Chile do we find a significant correlation over time between attitudes toward democracy and position on the left-right scale, although in Chile too this is beginning to change. A comparison between historical averages (from 1995 to 2005) and 2006 levels of support for democracy and authoritarianism in each country[4] shows that in Argentina, Chile, Ecuador, Mexico, and Uruguay, the left has tended to be more democratic than the right, while in Guatemala, Honduras, Nicaragua, Paraguay, Peru, the Dominican Republic, El Salvador, and Venezuela, the right historically has been more supportive of democracy than the left. In the remaining countries—Bolivia, Brazil, Colombia, and Panama—the most democratic element on the political spectrum has been the center (see Table 2 on p. 63).

Democracy is about the asymmetric history of power in each country, and this is a significant determinant of whether the left or right is more democratic. Likewise, the history and political culture of each country are also significant determinants of democracy: Uruguay is the most democratic country in the region, and there the left and right are both substantially democratic. In Paraguay, the most authoritarian country, the left and right as well as the center have all harbored substantial levels of support for authoritarianism.

On a hopeful note, we see in Table 2 that after the wave of elections in 2006, virtually every country surveyed either increased its support for democracy over the historical average[5] or remained substantially the same; only Panama suffered a decline of more than three percentage points (from an average of 60 percent support to 55 percent in 2006). No definite conclusion can be drawn, however, since the 2007 data register a decline in support for democracy in thirteen countries between 2006 and 2007, with an increase in only five: Ecuador, Nicaragua, Costa Rica, Panama, and Bolivia. Apparently, the 2006 post-election boost in democratic support was short-lived.

When comparing the historical averages of preference for an authoritarian regime by country with the 2006 data, we find seven countries in which there is essentially no change in preference—Argentina, Bolivia, Brazil, Colombia, Costa Rica, Honduras, and Uruguay; five in which it has declined modestly or dramatically—Chile, Ecuador, Mexico, Paraguay, and Venezuela; and six in which it has increased—El Salvador, Guatemala, Nicaragua, Panama, Peru, and the Dominican Republic, with Guatemala in particular registering a striking increase (from 19 to 35 percent).

When we examine the ideological patterns of support for democracy over the last decade, a number of interesting findings emerge. The most striking case is the dismantling of the authoritarian attitudes of the right in Chile. Support for the authoritarian option—the belief that sometimes an authoritarian government can be preferable—has collapsed on the political right in Chile, plunging from a historical average of 39 percent to only 12 percent in 2006. There is also no longer a correlation between support for democracy and the political left.[6] In fact, it is the center in Chile that is now the principal reservoir of support for democracy, while among those on the left—unsatisfied with what democracy has delivered—support has plummeted from a historical average of 71 percent to 43 percent in 2006 (with the authoritarian preference increasing from 8 to 14 percent).

The presidency of Ricardo Lagos (2000–2006), who was of the Socialist Party but governed with more moderate (and economically successful) policies than the right had expected, has laid to rest most of the right's apprehensions about democracy.[7] At the same time, the election of Chile's first female president, Michelle Bachelet, and the failure of the governing Coalition of Parties for Democracy to bring about a more radical socioeconomic transformation after four successive governments have led to the sharp decline in support for democracy on the left. President Bachelet's government has so far produced a 10-point decline in support for democracy in 2007, down to 46 percent.

TABLE 2—CHANGE IN SUPPORT FOR DEMOCRACY BY LEFT-RIGHT SCALE* (COMPARISON BETWEEN HISTORICAL AVERAGE AND 2006)

		LEFT		CENTER		RIGHT		TOTAL		TOTAL
		HA	2006	HA	2006	HA	2006	HA	2006	2007
LEFT DEMOCRATIC										
Argentina	Dem.	73	74	72	78	66	72	68	73	63
	Auth.	15	14	16	19	20	15	16	16	20
Chile	Dem.	71	43	61	71	31	59	53	56	46
	Auth.	8	14	14	10	39	12	16	13	21
Ecuador	Dem.	50	43	51	63	45	57	47	54	65
	Auth.	22	13	22	22	24	29	21	17	13
Mexico	Dem.	56	48	54	50	52	64	52	54	48
	Auth.	22	11	23	16	26	16	23	15	14
Uruguay	Dem.	84	60	81	80	78	83	80	77	75
	Auth.	7	14	9	8	10	5	9	10	10
CENTER DEMOCRATIC										
Bolivia	Dem.	55	50	58	62	56	67	54	62	67
	Auth.	20	4	19	22	20	16	18	18	14
Colombia	Dem.	44	45	58	43	52	55	50	53	47
	Auth.	18	13	17	18	14	17	15	15	12
Brazil	Dem.	40	33	46	42	41	52	40	46	43
	Auth.	21	9	21	24	19	18	19	18	17
Panama	Dem.	60	54	62	50	60	52	60	55	62
	Auth.	14	12	15	22	14	23	14	19	13
RIGHT DEMOCRATIC										
Costa Rica	Dem.	67	78	75	67	82	75	75	75	83
	Auth.	12	5	11	8	6	12	9	9	5
El Salvador	Dem.	54	36	61	48	57	53	53	52	38
	Auth.	16	16	10	21	10	14	11	15	20
Guatemala	Dem.	40	36	45	42	47	38	41	40	32
	Auth.	22	25	25	33	19	44	19	35	33
Honduras	Dem.	47	49	53	47	58	52	52	51	38
	Auth.	17	7	15	23	12	13	12	12	17
Nicaragua	Dem.	51	48	61	54	62	63	57	57	61
	Auth.	16	13	15	15	12	15	12	14	10
Paraguay	Dem.	43	26	42	37	49	46	43	41	33
	Auth.	36	31	40	32	37	28	38	30	36
Peru	Dem.	51	30	59	52	59	60	55	55	47
	Auth.	20	10	18	22	16	18	17	20	22
Dominican Republic	Dem.	53	68	64	62	70	66	62	71	64
	Auth.	15	15	14	27	12	25	13	20	21
Venezuela	Dem.	61	62	64	65	71	73	65	70	67
	Auth.	22	9	20	15	15	11	15	11	14

* Left-right self-placement scale 0 to 10: 1–3 Left, 4–6 Center, 7–10 Right.
Note: HA is the historical average during the period from 1995 through 2005. This provides a more meaningful baseline against which to measure change in 2006, as it neutralizes the fluctuations over preceding years.

Similarly in Brazil, where overall support for democracy increased from a historical average of 40 percent to 46 percent in 2006, the shift has been especially significant on the right—increasing from a historical average of 41 percent to 52 percent in 2006. Support on the left, however, decreased during this period from 40 percent to 33 percent. The reasons are similar to those in Chile—namely, a leftist government (headed by President Luiz Inácio "Lula" da Silva of the Workers' Party, who was elected in 2002 and reelected in 2006) that has managed the economy more prudently than expected while leaving the left unsatisfied. Lula's success, ironically, has democratized the right in Brazil, just as the success of Lagos did in Chile.

In Mexico, by contrast, the modest success of a moderate right-of-center president, Vicente Fox, dramatically increased support for democracy on the right (from 52 to 64 percent) but lowered it on the left (from 56 to 48 percent). Even more striking in Mexico has been the dramatic decline in support for the authoritarian option in all three ideological groups. In fact, overall support for authoritarian rule has fallen from a historical average of 23 percent in Mexico to 15 percent in 2006.

The election of populist Evo Morales, the first Bolivian president from the country's indigenous majority, has democratized both the left and the right in Bolivia—increasing support for democracy from a historical average of 54 percent to 67 percent in 2007, while eroding the preference for authoritarian rule on the right and the left. This decline was sharpest on the left, however, where support for the authoritarian option plunged from a historical average of 20 percent to 4 percent in 2006. Among those who do not identify themselves as left or right, however, support for authoritarianism increased slightly in Bolivia, and thus the overall national average remained the same (18 percent). This shows how much national averages can hide changes and reveals the limited relevance of the left-right spectrum in assessing the evolution of attitudes toward democracy.

In Chile, Brazil, and Bolivia, the political success of the left has had the paradoxical and unexpected effect of strengthening support for democracy on the right. In fact, in Chile and Brazil in particular (and perhaps in the long run even in Bolivia), the rule of a democratic left, more than anything else, has strengthened democracy. From this perspective, the rule of a moderate, competent, and democratically committed left is a very powerful political good. On the other hand, the left is now unhappy with democracy because, in spite of leftist governments being in power, the desired economic and social changes (in reducing poverty and inequality, for example) have not come about with the expected speed and scope.

Support for democracy on the left has decreased from the historical average in nine countries: Chile, Ecuador, Mexico, Uruguay, Brazil, El Salvador, Guatemala, Nicaragua, and Paraguay. Even in Uruguay, the most democratic country in the region, support for democracy was down

24 points (from 84 to 60 percent) on the left after the 2005 election of President Tabaré Ramón Vázquez Rosas, the first leftist to win the presidency in seventy years. As in Chile, Brazil, and Bolivia, the victory of the left seems to have strengthened support for democracy on the right in Uruguay, but this gain was overtaken by the erosion of support for democracy on the left, which had begun several years earlier. As a result, the overall support for democracy in Uruguay in 2006 showed a modest decline from the historical average of 80 percent. The 2007 results reinforce this trend, as overall support for democracy declined from 56 to 46 percent in Chile, from 46 to 43 percent in Brazil, and from 77 to 75 percent in Uruguay (see Table 2).

Chile is a good example of the left's disillusionment. Chileans are more dissatisfied with President Bachelet's socialist government than with any administration since the transition to democracy, with 50 percent of respondents saying that the country is going in the wrong direction.[8] Democratization and socioeconomic transformation have been slow, and social mobility has not increased. As a result, dissatisfaction with the performance of democracy comes disproportionately from those who are excluded, discriminated against, and lacking in opportunities—not necessarily from the poor in general (who are eligible for subsidies).

Context, country, and historical experience determine attitudes toward democracy more than ideology or demographic characteristics in the abstract. It is difficult to generalize across Latin America about who supports democracy and why; we must understand the politics and historical trajectories of individual countries. Likewise, averages are not necessarily indicative of the shifts in support for democracy along the left-right political spectrum. While some aspects are evolving, no major or definite transformation in attitudes toward democracy has yet taken place, except perhaps in Bolivia. The structural changes that Bolivia is undertaking suggest that major changes are essential for democracy to consolidate. It may even be argued that in Bolivia, after five-hundred years of extreme exclusion of the majority indigenous population, some degree of political conflict and instability will be an unavoidable component of democratization.

What Does Democracy Mean?

The meaning of democracy comprises three elements: the demand for liberty; the power of elections; and the right to satisfaction of basic needs. In the Latinobarómetro, two questions—one open-ended and one closed—aim to capture the meaning of democracy in the minds of the people.[9] When analyzing the findings per country per year, we find no significant changes in how people rank these elements, although there has been some increase in certain items.

The findings do vary by country, however. For example, elections hold more prominence in some countries than in others. By enabling people to replace their leaders and ruling parties, and thus to hold leaders accountable, elections have brought some measure of political dignity to the region. But elections are seen more as a tool to implement democracy than as the embodiment of it. Economic dignity and the fair distribution of wealth likewise carry different weight in different countries. Latin America has faced the triple challenge of simultaneously addressing the need for social, political, and economic change, and this is reflected in the weight given to the different elements of the meaning of democracy by different sociodemographic groups.

Over the years, the Latinobarómetro has tested the consistency of people's answers on the meaning of democracy by placing the question at the very beginning and at the very end of the questionnaire in different years. In 2006, the open-ended question "What does democracy mean to you?" was the last of a hundred. The 2006 results for that question do not differ significantly from those obtained in the three other years in which the question had been asked very early or in the middle of the survey, suggesting that the preceding 99 questions (many of them about democracy) did not influence the responses. The meaning of democracy can thus be interpreted as a robust and deeply rooted value that is not subject to change by the design of the survey.

As Ronald Inglehart of the World Values Survey has reported, values change from generation to generation, so the key driver is socialization. The population of Latin America is indeed showing that socialization through experience changes attitudes toward democracy. Experience of life under democracy is thus an important route to the democratization of people's values. The 2007 data show the impact of the experience of five years of continuous economic growth for the first time in the last 25 years. These "five virtuous years" have shown that economic growth in itself is not a democratizing agent.

Russell Dalton, Doh Shin, and Willy Jou analyze only the open-ended question about the meaning of democracy at only one point in time, and I believe this leads them to a flawed conclusion—that the economic component has little significance in people's conception of democracy.[10] When we consider the responses to all questions, both open and closed, about the meaning of democracy over the years, we see a rather different picture. When the same results for different questions at different points in time appear repeatedly, strong conclusions can be drawn.[11] One measurement on one question is not sufficient to produce conclusive results. Based on Latinobarómetro data, conclusions drawn from single questionnaire items often do not hold up to testing with different variables in different years. Democracy is a historically defined concept. Time is a key component of the analysis, and it is particularly relevant in consolidating democracies.

If we examine how the different meanings of democracy are related to the major status variables (education, age, and sex), one principal

TABLE 3—How Latin Americans Understand the
Meaning of Democracy (in percentages)

		LIBERTY	ELECTIONS	AN ECONOMY THAT ENSURES A FAIR INCOME
Education	Primary	30	25	17
	Secondary	38	28	18
	Higher	43	27	18
Age	16–25	30	25	19
	26–39	36	27	19
	41–60	37	27	19
	61 and over	32	27	17
Sex	Male	36	27	19
	Female	32	27	19
Total		34	27	19

Figures represent averages for the 176,447 interviews conducted in eighteen countries by the Latinobaró-metro, 1995–2006.

finding stands out. The emphasis on liberty as the meaning of democracy—which could also be interpreted as a "demand" for liberty—increases with education and age. In addition, men stress liberty somewhat more than women. This is the same precise pattern we find in support for democracy. The understanding of democracy as the holding of elections or the demand for a fair income, on the other hand, does not seem to vary by sex, age, or education (see Table 3).

The demand for liberty is part of the demand for democratization. Latin Americans desire greater freedom of expression: 51 percent of respondents state that they can always, or almost always, say what they think, but the other half believe that they cannot always voice their opinions. When the question is restricted to politics, however, only 34 percent feel that they can openly state their political views. There is a long way to go with respect to freedom of expression in the region.

The exercise of freedom of expression depends in part on political equality—on all citizens having the same political and civil rights. Yet for most Latin Americans, voting on election day is the only circumstance in which they experience the democratic promise of equality before the law. To be sure, Latin America has achieved something of great significance in the past two decades, as county after country has replaced violence and authoritarian rule with democratic elections as the means for choosing and replacing leaders. The high voter turnout in the 2006 elections across numerous states in the region (averaging over 70 percent) gives vivid testimony to the motivating power of competitive elections—even though only about one in five citizens believes that a full range of options is available on election day.

The biggest problem, however, is that few Latin Americans perceive there to be political equality in any real sense. Only about a quarter of Latin Americans (26 percent in 2005) say that everybody is equal before the law; only 19 percent say that people abide by the law; and only 31 percent say that people are conscious of their obligations. None of these figures (all for 2005) have shown any significant change over the past decade. Once Latin Americans look beyond the basic level of democracy that is provided through electoral choice, they see no significant increase in their exercise of liberty or equality.

Perceptions of Economic Fairness

A fair salary is the third most important meaning of democracy in the minds of Latin Americans. There has been a great deal of speculation regarding Latin American attitudes toward the market economy, with many observers interpreting the lack of support for a market economy as a choice for another type of system. The fear of regression away from the market economy, along with the fear of authoritarian regression, has haunted speculations about the region's future. Rather than upholding the conservative credo that government is part of the problem rather than the solution, the 2007 data show that the region instead wants more state and less market, as the market has proven, despite economic growth, to be ineffective in bringing balanced prosperity to the majority of the population.

People's perception of the economic system has many dimensions. One is the fairness and efficiency of the state in collecting taxes. There is an overwhelming perception (72 percent) that people manage to pay less tax than they should—or, put more precisely, that those who have more pay less than they should. Tax evasion is one more indicator of the general unfairness of the political and social system and of the entrenched inequality before the law. A second dimension concerns corruption, which Latin Americans perceive to be widespread. On average, Latin Americans believe that two-thirds of all public employees are corrupt, and only 30 percent of respondents see "much" or "some" recent progress in reducing corruption.[12] The sense that corruption is pervasive and unyielding is a major cause of the general lack of faith in the system. A third dimension on which Latin Americans assess their economic system concerns the privatization of state enterprises. Only in the last five years of economic growth has the image of privatization started to improve, and even now only a minority holds a favorable view of the process.[13]

Overall, views of the market economy remain mixed. Only 50 percent of Latin Americans on average say that the economic system works well, and in 2007 only 26 percent say that they are satisfied with the market economy; 47 percent nevertheless believe that it is the only way a country can develop.[14] The latter figure is especially striking considering that 50 percent of people in the region report difficulties in making ends meet every month.[15] Worse still, 86 percent have no bank account and thus no access to formal credit. In other words, the majority of people in the region have very limited access to the market economy, and this practical difficulty—more than ideology—shapes their attitudes toward the market economy. When people mention access to a fair income as a component of democracy, they have in mind the inequality that excludes more than half the population from the economic system, which they see as being used by the powerful for their own interests.

After five straight years of economic growth, people are beginning to have more positive views of the economy. Concern with unemployment has declined, and it is no longer regarded as by far the region's most important problem. In 2007, 21 percent called the economy "good"—rising from a historical average of 8 percent between 1996 and 2004—while those who rated the economy as "bad" or "very bad" decreased from 59 percent in 2003 to 28 percent in 2007. At the same time, those who rated it as "regular" rose from 33 percent to 50 percent during the same period. For the first time in memory, for at least half the population the region is richer. It has taken a quarter-century to bring poverty down to the levels of the 1980s, a fairly modest achievement in economic performance. If people are clinging to democracy, it is because they believe that democracy can take the region beyond this point.

Latin America has reached a new level of experience and expectation, and what was tolerable ten years ago is no longer tolerable today. Higher levels of education yield higher levels of criticism aimed at the unfairness of the system. The Chilean case is emblematic in this respect. Social uproar has exploded in Chile after seventeen years of democratic rule—and after poverty has been reduced by more than half. Chile, with its robust economy and stable institutions, has evolved and grown wealthier. But the overwhelming perception of inequality before the law and of an unfair system remains. In other words, in spite of economic success, no significant social transformation has taken place, because too few are benefiting from this success.

There is also another element in the socioeconomic mix—a new lower-middle class that has emerged as Latin America has reduced poverty back to the levels of the 1980s. Very little attention is being given to the more subtle structural poverty of this new class, which no longer starves but is far from secure. Empowered politically but with low incomes, this new class may represent a greater threat to governability than the truly poor. They have Internet access, mobile phones, and flat-screen televisions, but no reading glasses, no dental health, no possibility of access to psychological or psychiatric attention, and no access to higher education. The most frustrated democrats are those who have attained secondary education, because they realize that they are on a dead-end street in terms of opportunity.

In this context, mounting political demands and increased political conflict are inevitable. Yet they could prove to be tools for democratic consolidation, for they force open difficult issues and push societies to address bottlenecks. Conflict exposes the contradictions behind what I have called "the smiling mask."[16] While the instability of democracy may be messy, it is a preferable alternative to revolution when the demand for social transformation is not being satisfied.

The Trust Factor

Trust in institutions has been a dominant variable in attempts to explain the evolution and consolidation of democracy in Latin America. The picture that emerges is discouraging, generating a kind of self-fulfilling prophecy of defeat, as levels of trust have remained stubbornly low over the course of the decade. One should be cautious, however, about inferring too much about the process of consolidation from this single attitudinal dimension.

While people in developed nations express high levels of interpersonal trust, meaning trust in unknown third parties, people in developing countries do not. Over the decade from 1996 to 2006, the level of this type of trust has not changed; only 20 percent trusted others in 1996, and only 21 percent in 2006. General social trust is simply not part of Latin American culture.

What we instead find in Latin America is "network trust," whereby people create bonds within a limited scope of interaction among a close community.[17] This type of trust is defined by the capacity to have direct personal contact or experience with others—family members, friends, colleagues, neighbors, or even someone more removed, such as a telephone operator. The level of trust is related to the quality of the interaction or experience—the closer the interaction, the greater the trust. It is this most primitive type of trust, based on experience, skin color, and eye contact, that holds these societies together.

Conversely, for political or societal institutions in Latin America, trust is scarce. Since 1995, no political or governmental institution has enjoyed the confidence of even 40 percent of the population, and the only major private institution that has done so is the church, which enjoys the trust of 72 percent of Latin Americans on average (see Table 4). Still, there is evidence at the country level of changes in trust in institutions during the past decade.

In Colombia, for example, trust in the police increased from 40 to 51 percent, and trust in the military rose from 44 to 59 percent. In Costa Rica, trust in the police increased from 26 percent to 41 percent in the same period. Other countries have experienced a significant decrease in trust in the military—most dramatically in Ecuador, where trust in the military plummeted from 76 percent in 1996 to 35 percent in 2006. More broadly across Latin America, trust rose in 2006 above the historical average for the decade with respect to several institutions: the military (to 44 percent), the presidency (to 47 percent), and the judiciary (to 36 percent).

The same cannot be said for political parties and parliament, which have

TABLE 4—TRUST IN INSTITUTIONS (IN PERCENTAGES)

DEMOCRATIC INSTITUTIONS		PRIVATE INSTITUTIONS	
Armed Forces	39	Church	72
President	37	Radio	49
Police and County Council	33	Television	44
Judiciary and Government	30	Large Companies	37
Public Administration	29	Private Companies and Banks	36
Congress	27	Entrepreneurial Associations	33
Political Parties	19	Trade Unions	26
		Stock Exchange	23

Figures represent averages for the 176,447 interviews conducted in eighteen countries by the Latinobaró-metro, 1995–2006.

remained stuck at fairly constant levels of distrust. Since 1996, trust in political parties has never risen above 28 percent in the region; falling to a low of 11 percent in 1998, it averaged 19 percent during the course of the decade. There remains a crisis of representation in Latin America, but it can be seen as part of a process of elite renewal that has begun but is far from complete. Getting rid of the old elites is easier than creating new ones. Most of the instability to come will derive from the search for new political leaders, and trust in democratic institutions will be shaped by the capacity of the ruling elites to produce the expected transformation of societies as a whole. To repeat, the disenchantment on the left with leftist governments reflects evaluations of this factor—for in the end, what matters is not being in office, but having the power to effect real change.

The hunger for change and the willingness to reward it are evident in the impact of the election of an indigenous person as president of Bolivia. Morales's victory boosted trust in most of Bolivia's democratic institutions (albeit from very low levels): in Congress, from 21 percent in 2005 to 32 percent in 2006; in political parties, from 10 percent to 17 percent; in the judiciary, from 25 percent to 37 percent; and in the armed forces from 33 percent to 44 percent. This is perhaps the most dramatic indication that trust in institutions is a consequence of people's experience with the performance of those institutions and the impact of the institutions on their lives. Trust is not a value-related element of democracy, but one way in which citizens evaluate their political system.

In addition, statistical analysis shows that democratic institutions are bound together, so that trust tends not to change in one institution unless it changes in others as well.[18] In other words, it is the performance of the system as a whole that produces a given level of trust. Reforming the justice system alone, for example, will not increase trust in democratic institutions if the other institutions themselves have undergone no change. On the other hand, a major shift, such as Bolivia's election of an Indian to the presidency, produces higher trust in all institutions.

Trust in democratic institutions, and in others generally, is correlated with democracy's capacity to generate inclusion. Poverty, since it forces people to stay within a limited area, explains in part why trust has developed in networks. In the absence of social mobility, people must seek objects of trust at close range. And the story of Latin America remains one of extremely limited social mobility: 86 percent of those born in the last generation to parents with only primary education themselves attain only primary education. In four generations, this bleak statistic has improved only modestly (from 96 percent). An individual's future is determined from birth, and people expect democracy to change this. But in order to increase levels of trust in democratic institutions in Latin America, more extensive changes are needed. Immigration, which is introducing an interesting element of social mobility and opportunity through open borders, may bring forth such a transformation. By fostering social mobility through immigration, economic integration could serve as a powerful tool for democratization.

As Latin America approaches the two-hundredth anniversary of its first independence, the Latinbarómetro data suggest that the region will achieve a second independence—one with full, functioning democracy. Universal suffrage has brought the possibility of changing "the priest" and keeping "the mule," as the old Mexican saying goes.[19] Finding the right successor for the priest—namely, political leadership that can deliver the expected social and economic improvements—is the first and most important task. Political conflict and instability may be necessary to achieve these societal transformations, and thus ultimately to secure democracy among increasingly critical and expectant populations. As our data have shown, the problem in the countries of Latin America is not so much how undemocratic the people are, but how undemocratic democratic rule can be.

NOTES

1. The Latinobarómetro was launched in 1995 and its findings were first reported in the *Journal of Democracy* in 1997; see Marta Lagos, "Public Opinion in New Democracies: Latin America's Smiling Mask," *Journal of Democracy* 8 (July 1997): 125–38.

2. All results are calculated on the basis of ten years of data from 176,447 interviews in eighteen countries. Data mentioned without full reporting have been published in the Latinobarómetro reports from 1995 to 2006, available at *www.latinobarometro.org*. Averages in comparative public-opinion analyses are not weighted by the population size of countries. For a detailed depiction of these two items, see Figures 1 and 2 at *www.journalofdemocracy.org/articles/gratis/LagosGraphics-19-1.pdf*.

3. The analysis here is confined to the single measure of support for democracy, an indicator with three alternatives: 1) "Democracy is preferable to any other form of government"; 2) "Sometimes an authoritarian government can be preferable"; or 3) "Indifference to the type of regime." However, the findings are similar if another measure of democratic support is employed—for example, an index composed of a selected number of variables.

4. People were identified as being "left," "center," or "right" based on their response

to the following question: "On a scale from 0 to 10, with 0 being the extreme left and 10 the extreme right, where do you place yourself? Left: 0–3; center: 4–6; and right: 7–10."

5. The survey was taken in October 2006, after ten elections had taken place; only the Venezuelan election took place afterward.

6. Carlos Huneeus and Luis Maldonado, "Demócratas y nostálgicos del antiguo régimen. Los apoyos a la democracia en Chile," *Revista Española de Investigaciones Sociológicas* (Madrid) 103 (July–September 2003): 9–49.

7. In 2007, however, there was an increase in support for an authoritarian regime as a consequence of significant reforms on the government's agenda, which have created a polarized political climate.

8. MORI survey on political leadership, 22 July 2007.

9. The open-ended question is "What does 'democracy' mean to you?" The closed question is "People often differ in their views on the characteristics that are important for a democracy. If you have to choose only one of the characteristics on this list, which one would you choose as most essential to a democracy? Civil liberties that ensure the right to criticize openly; a competitive party system; an economic system that ensures a fair income; a justice system that treats everybody equally; respect for minorities; government of the majority; or parliament members who represent their voters."

10. Russell J. Dalton, Doh C. Shin, and Willy Jou, "Understanding Democracy: Data From Unlikely Places," *Journal of Democracy* 18 (October 2007): 142–56.

11. For a good example of such an approach, see Seymour Martin Lipset and William Schneider, *The Confidence Gap: Business, Labor, and Government in the Public Mind,* rev. ed. (Baltimore: Johns Hopkins University Press, 1987).

12. Only in Uruguay (41) and Chile (48) was the average percentage of public employees perceived to be corrupt below 50 percent, and not in a single Latin American country did a majority of the public perceive progress in the last two years in fighting corruption. Both figures are from the 2005 Latinobarómetro report.

13. Those with a favorable view of privatization increased from 22 percent in 2003 to 35 percent in 2007.

14. This figure of 47 percent was down from 63 percent in 2006.

15. This was the percentage in 2005 who said that their total family income was "not sufficient" to cover their needs, and that "we have major problems." The figure was down from 62 percent in 2003 but nevertheless higher than the range of 46 to 53 percent during the period 1996 to 2001. See the Table "Subjective Income, 1996-2005," at *www.journalofdemocracy.org/articles/gratis/LagosGraphics-19-1.pdf.*.

16. See Lagos, "Latin America's Smiling Mask."

17. Latinobarómetro report, 2003.

18. In other words, democratic institutions depend on each other for their respective levels of trust. See the Table "Factor Analysis: Trust in Institutions" at *www.journalofdemocracy.org/articles/gratis/LagosGraphics-19-1.pdf.*

19. After independence, Mexican peasants referred to the change of power from one oligarchy (Spaniards) to another (whites), by saying "It is just another priest on a different mule."

6

AUTHORITARIAN NOSTALGIA IN ASIA

Yu-tzung Chang, Yun-han Chu, and Chong-Min Park

Yu-tzung Chang *is associate professor of political science at National Taiwan University. He is co-principal investigator and program manager of the Asian Barometer.* **Yun-han Chu** *is Distinguished Research Fellow at the Institute of Political Science at Academia Sinica and director of the Asian Barometer.* **Chong-Min Park** *is professor of public administration at Korea University in Seoul and directs the Asian Barometer Survey in South Korea. This essay originally appeared in the July 2007 issue of the* Journal of Democracy.

From Bangkok to Manila, Taipei, Seoul, and Ulaanbaatar, East Asia's "third-wave" democracies are in distress. The most dramatic sign of trouble has been the September 2006 military coup in Thailand, where the opposition had earlier boycotted a parliamentary election. (Thailand was also the scene of the region's last full-scale democratic breakdown, a 1991 coup.) In Taiwan and the Philippines, the losers of the most recent presidential elections have challenged the results. In South Korea, the incumbent president has found himself crippled by flagging popular support and deserted by his own party's National Assembly deputies. Mongolia is mired in party stalemate. Even the region's oldest democracy, Japan, has been beset by endless corruption scandals and consistent failures to come to grips with the challenges of deflation, stagnation, and the need for structural economic reform. Under these stressful circumstances, can democracy still endure and flourish in East Asia?

Although many forces can affect a democracy's survival chances, no democratic regime can stand long without legitimacy in the eyes of its own people. Scholars have long known that beliefs and perceptions regarding legitimacy have much to do with whether a regime—particularly one founded upon popular consent—will endure or break down.[1] What elites think matters, but for democracy to become stable and effective, the bulk of the citizenry must develop a deep and resilient commitment to it. A necessary condition for the consolidation of democracy is met when an overwhelming proportion of citizens believe that "the democratic regime is the most right and appropriate for their society, better than any other realistic alternative they can imagine."[2]

Data from the first and second Asian Barometer Surveys (ABS)[3] can help us systematically to assess the extent of normative commitment to democracy that citizens feel in Japan, South Korea, Taiwan, Mongolia, the Philippines, and Thailand. The assessment involves seeking answers to the following interrelated questions: Has the growth of democratic legitimacy in East Asia stagnated or even eroded? How detached are East Asians from authoritarian alternatives? What do East Asians think of how democracy works in their countries? Is there a link between how citizens rate democracy's performance and how committed to democracy they feel? Is popular support for democracy deeply rooted in a liberal-democratic political culture? Let us begin by briefly explaining the strategies that we have chosen for measuring democratic legitimacy.

Measuring Democratic Legitimacy

Public opinion plays a crucial role in determining legitimacy. International donors, think tanks, and experts can publish all the ratings they like, but a democracy will be consolidated only when most of those who live within its borders believe that democracy actually is better for their society and that democracy of an acceptable quality is being supplied. In a nutshell, the citizens are the final judges of the legitimacy as well as the characteristics of their democracy. Surveys such as the Asian Barometer open a window on whether citizens think that their political institutions are delivering acceptable degrees of democracy and good governance. In particular, such surveys make possible an empirical assessment of the extent of normative commitment to democracy among the public at large and thus tell us much about how far a given political system has really traveled toward democratic consolidation.[4]

Those who seek to gauge popular support for democracy have long asked respondents to choose among three statements: "Democracy is always preferable to any other kind of government," "Under some circumstances, an authoritarian government can be preferable to a democratic one," and "For people like me, it does not matter whether we have a democratic or a nondemocratic regime." But the single-item measurements thus reached always lack conceptual breadth and depth, and are less reliable than measurements drawn from multiple indicators.[5]

Like any other complex concept, normative commitment to democracy consists of many attitudinal dimensions. Richard Rose, Doh Chull Shin, and their colleagues have respectively highlighted four other important aspects of democratic legitimacy.[6] First is the *desire for democracy,* the level of democracy that citizens want for their political regime.[7]

Second is the *suitability of democracy,* the degree to which citizens feel that democracy is appropriate for their country.[8] Third is the *efficacy of democracy,* which involves the effectiveness of the democratic regime in addressing the country's major problems.[9] Fourth is the *priority* that citizens place on democracy as compared to other societal goals.[10] The ABS contains specific items designed to measure these four additional dimensions, thus generating a five-item battery that can be used to gauge popular support for democracy.

As important as such support is, robust legitimacy entails more. It also requires that citizens profess "authoritarian detachment"—in other words, that they reject nondemocratic alternatives. Referring to Winston Churchill's famous 1947 quip that democracy "is the worst form of government except all those other forms that have been tried from time to time," Rose and his colleagues argue that democracy often survives not because most people believe in its intrinsic legitimacy, but rather because there are simply no preferable alternatives.[11] This suggests that aversion to authoritarianism weights as heavily as attachment to democracy in sustaining a democratic regime. Hence, our surveys asked respondents a set of three questions exploring whether or not they would favor the return to any of the three conceivable authoritarian alternatives: strongman rule, single-party rule, and military rule.

One of the ABS's important methodological innovations is its use of items meant to probe further into the substance and depth of popular commitment to democracy. These items intentionally omit the word "democracy" itself since use of the "d-word" could invite answers that might seem socially desirable, but which may not be deeply felt. In our time, after all, even the least democratic rulers and regimes habitually speak of "democracy"—it is a word whose very prestige has led to its excessive and at times less-than-honest use. Fortunately for us, however, there is no need to invoke the "d-word" in order to probe respondents' value orientations toward such fundamental organizing principles of liberal democracy as liberty, the rule of law, the separation of powers, and the duty of government to answer to the governed.

The batteries for measuring popular attachment to democracy, detachment from authoritarianism, and liberal-democratic value orientation have been consistently applied in two rounds of surveys between 2001 and 2006, yielding for the first time a database that is longitudinal across time rather than a "snapshot" of opinion at a given moment.

Teetering Support for Democracy

When we began our analysis we did not expect to find a strong and resilient popular base for democratic legitimacy in East Asia's new democracies, let alone any enhancement of it over time. We knew that many East Asian democracies display socioeconomic features that in principle should be friendly to the growth of democratic legitimacy (sizeable middle classes, well-educated people, and many ties to the global economy). Yet at the same time we feared that the region's overall geopolitical configuration, political history, and predominant cultural legacies would act as strong drags on the development of robust democratic political cultures.

Let us discuss these three factors in more detail. First, over the last three decades East Asia has in a significant way defied the global democratic trend known as the third wave. Most of the region's people remain under one form or other of authoritarian or at best semidemocratic rule. In 2006, only six of the region's eighteen sovereign states received a Freedom House (FH) rating of Free. Five of the six Free countries, moreover, had become democratic only during the recent era of the third wave. (The five were Mongolia, the Philippines, South Korea, Taiwan, and Thailand—the last of which has now received an FH ranking of Not Free in the wake of its 2006 military coup.) Furthermore, with the shift of the region's center of economic gravity from Japan to China, East Asia has become one of the few places in the world where regime characteristics pose no barrier to trade and investment and perhaps the only region where newly democratized countries have become economically integrated with and dependent on nondemocratic countries.

Second, few of the region's former authoritarian regimes have been thoroughly discredited. Indeed, all too many people are wont to credit them with having fostered social stability, stunning economic growth, and an apparently greater resistance to "money politics" or other corrupt dealings. Because many an East Asian authoritarian order permitted limited pluralism—allowing some forms of electoral contestation as well as the existence of an opposition—citizens in the region's new democracies have not known the dramatic increases in rights and freedoms that their counterparts in many other third-wave democracies have witnessed. Moreover, many of East Asia's new democracies have found their performance hampered by grave governance challenges flowing from political strife, bureaucratic paralysis, recurring scandals, sluggish economic growth, and foggy economic outlooks. At the same time, the authoritarian or semiauthoritarian regimes of Singapore, Malaysia, China, and Vietnam have seemingly shown themselves able to handle economic globalization as well as other complex problems. The achievements (real or putative) of the region's less-than-democratic regimes both past and present have saddled its young democracies with unreasonably high public expectations.

Finally, there is the argument—proffered by such influential Western scholars as Lucian Pye and Samuel P. Huntington—that dominant East Asian cultural traditions pose an obstacle to the acquisition of democratic values.[12] Echoing this view for their own purposes, certain figures in the region have embraced the idea of "Asian values" that privilege group

TABLE 1—SUPPORT FOR DEMOCRACY (IN PERCENTAGES)

COUNTRY	SURVEY YEAR	PREFERABILITY: DEMOCRACY IS ALWAYS PREFERABLE TO ANY OTHER KIND OF GOVERNMENT[1]	DESIRABILITY: TO WHAT EXTENT WOULD YOU WANT OUR COUNTRY TO BE DEMOCRATIC NOW?[2]	SUITABILITY: DEMOCRACY IS SUITABLE FOR OUR COUNTRY[2]	EFFICACY: DEMOCRACY IS CAPABLE OF SOLVING THE PROBLEMS OF OUR SOCIETY[3]	PRIORITY: DEMOCRACY IS EQUALLY OR MORE IMPORTANT THAN ECONOMIC DEVELOPMENT	MEAN SCORE (0–5)	N
Taiwan	2001	40.4	72.2	59.0	46.8	23.5	2.42	1415
	2006	47.5	83.1	67.1	54.3	24.2	2.76	1587
South Korea	2003	49.4	95.4	84.2	71.7	30.1	3.31	1500
	2006	42.7	94.1	79.2	55.2	32.3	3.04	1212
Philippines	2002	63.6	88.1	80.2	60.7	21.8	3.14	12.3
	2005	50.6	70.8	56.6	55.9	26.4	2.60	1200
Thailand	2001	82.6	93.0	88.1	89.6	51.3	4.04	1544
	2006	72.7	84.6	82.4	66.2	47.9	3.54	1546
Mongolia	2002	57.1	91.6	86.3	78.4	48.6	3.62	1144
	2006	38.9	94.7	84.7	76.7	32.2	3.27	1211
Average[4]	2001–2003	58.9	88.1	79.5	69.8	35.2	3.31	6806
	2005–2006	51.4	85.3	74.1	61.5	32.9	3.05	6756
Japan	2003	67.2	87.1	76.3	61.4	44.0	3.36	1419

1. Trichotomous variable recoded into dichotomous variables
2. Six or above on a 10-point scale
3. Dichotomous variables
4. Values in the Average row refer to those of emerging democracies and exclude Japan.
Source: Asian Barometer Survey, 2001–2006.

over individual interests, authority over liberty, and duties over rights. Such values, it is said, draw a sharp line between East Asia and the West and make the former less prone to embrace liberal democracy.

The ABS confirms that East Asian citizens feel ambivalent about democracy, and that the region's new democracies have seen their popular legitimacy stay flat or even drop slightly. On the one hand, a great majority of ordinary citizens finds the ideal of democracy appealing. Between 2001 and 2003, fully 88 percent of those surveyed across all five new democracies (Mongolia, the Philippines, South Korea, Taiwan, and Thailand) deemed democracy to be "desirable for our country now," while 80 percent considered democracy "suitable for our country," and 70 percent believed that "democracy is capable of solving the problems of our society" (see Table 1). On the other hand, fewer than three out of five respondents (59 percent) considered democracy "preferable to all other kinds of government," while barely more than a third (35 percent) said that it was "equally or more important than development." Even in Japan, the region's oldest democracy, only two-thirds of respondents said that "democracy is always preferable."

More disturbingly, when we surveyed people in the five new democracies again in 2005–2006, every indicator of average support for democracy showed a decline. The preference for democracy and the perceived efficacy of democracy each dropped by about 8 percentage points. Some countries declined sharply on other measures, too. Between the two surveys, a quarter of Thais and a sixth of South Koreans lost confidence in democracy's efficacy, and the belief among Mongolians that "democracy is always preferable" fell 18 points, to only 39 percent. Outside East Asia, such a low level of support was found only in some struggling Latin American democracies.[13] In 2005, only 56 percent of Filipinos still said they believed that "democracy is suitable" (a 23-point drop in four years). Only in Taiwan did support for democracy strengthen during this period (albeit from a rather low base).

To measure the overall level of attachment to democracy, we constructed a 6-point (0-to-5) index of the number of prodemocratic responses to the five questions discussed above (see the second column from the right in Table 1). On this index, South Korean and Japanese citizens show lukewarm support for democracy, with mean scores only at about the region's average. Thailand in 2001 registered the highest level of overall support (4.0), reflecting the euphoria and optimism most Thais felt at the beginning of a new administration under since-deposed premier Thaksin Shinawatra, whose party had just captured an unprecedented single-party majority in parliament. Taiwan registered the lowest mean score (2.4). This came in 2001, just a year after the first-ever alternation in power (produced by the 2000 elections) and at a time when the island was suffering the worst economic recession it had known since the 1972–73 oil crisis.

Most East Asian democracies are still wrestling with a fragile and fluid foundation of popular support. Crises of governance have taken a toll on popular commitment to democracy, pushing down the region's average score from 3.3 around 2002 to 3.0 around 2006. Now, East Asians on average accept only three out of five possible reasons to embrace democracy. And, as elsewhere, East Asians' attachment to democracy appears context-dependent. The more abstract the context, the stronger is the normative commitment; the more concrete the context, the weaker the commitment. Nearly everyone embraces democracy as an abstract idea, but significantly fewer endorse it as their preferred form of government under all circumstances, and fewer still say that if forced to choose between the two, they would prefer democracy even to economic development.

Authoritarianism's Lingering Support

The absence of full-blown positive sentiment toward democracy in these East Asian countries would be less worrisome to the degree that authoritarian alternatives also lack support. Here as well, however, the evidence is less than reassuring. In the three less-developed countries among our group (Mongolia, the Philippines, and Thailand), pockets of support for authoritarianism are growing rather than diminishing.

If we look at popular rejection of each individual authoritarian alternative—strongman rule, single-party rule, and military rule—antipathy for authoritarianism appears quite high. In the first-wave surveys, more than two-thirds in every country except Mongolia opposed replacing democracy with strongman rule. Rejection of single-party rule was less emphatic but still exceeded two-thirds in all countries except Thailand (where it stood at 61 percent). Military rule was rejected even more vigorously, at levels exceeding 80 percent in every country except the Philippines (63 percent). Yet the aggregate picture raises some cause for concern. Only in Korea, Japan, and Taiwan did a majority reject all three alternatives. In Mongolia, the Philippines, and Thailand, only 39 to 46 percent of respondents rejected all three authoritarian options.

More alarmingly, the gap between the two sets of countries widened significantly in the second survey. Rejection of all three authoritarian options rose from 56 to 69 percent in Taiwan and from 71 to 77 percent in South Korea, but it dropped from 44 to 28 percent in Mongolia and declined slightly to 39 percent in the Philippines. In both of the latter countries, the yearning for a "strong leader" to decide everything grew substantially. Worrisome signs also popped up in Thailand on the eve of the 2006 military coup. While the aggregate measure of authoritarian detachment improved (from 46 to 55 percent), the percentage of Thais who disapproved of military rule dropped 9 points, and the percentage of those who objected to strongman rule dropped 8 points.

TABLE 2—DETACHMENT FROM AUTHORITARIANISM (IN PERCENTAGES)

COUNTRY	SURVEY YEAR	DISAGREE WITH THE FOLLOWING:			
		STRONG LEADER[1]	NO OPPOSITION PARTY[2]	MILITARY RULE[3]	REJECT ALL THREE
Taiwan	2001	68.3	70.3	81.6	55.7
	2006	76.1	82.9	88.2	69.1
South Korea	2003	84.4	86.7	89.8	71.3
	2006	82.7	87.8	90.5	76.8
Philippines	2002	69.4	69.6	62.7	39.6
	2005	58.5	64.6	73.0	38.5
Thailand	2001	76.6	61.3	81.2	46.1
	2006	68.8	73.1	71.3	54.7
Mongolia	2002	59.2	72.4	85.8	44.4
	2006	34.5	70.9	82.8	28.4
Average[4]	2001–2003	72.4	72.1	80.7	52.2
	2005–2006	65.0	76.1	81.1	54.5
Japan	2003	79.1	66.7	94.4	57.4

1. "We should get rid of parliament and elections and have a strong leader decide things."
2. "No opposition party should be allowed to compete for power."
3. "The military should come in to govern the country."
4. Values in the Average row refer to those of emerging democracies and exclude Japan.
Source: Asian Barometer Survey, 2001–2006.

Comparing Tables 1 and 2 reveals another important contrast between the two sets of countries. On measures of support for democracy, Thailand and Mongolia appear stronger than Taiwan and South Korea, but the former two (and the Philippines) lag well behind on authoritarian detachment. This suggests that Thailand, Mongolia, and the Philippines each have a large number of equivocal and confused citizens whose inconsistent political orientations burden their democracies with a fragile foundation of legitimacy. In Taiwan and South Korea, authoritarianism has gradually lost its appeal, but democracy has not yet lived up to their citizens' high expectations.

Evidence from Eastern Europe, Africa, and Latin America suggests that popular support for democracy is directly affected by citizens' assessments of how well democracy works.[14] Some early studies of East European transitions identified perceptions of change in economic circumstances as the most important factor influencing support for democracy.[15] Later studies qualified this view by finding that citizens' perceptions that "good governance" (rule of law, corruption control, and the like) was in place had a still larger impact on democratic support.[16] In analyzing data from Africa, Robert Mattes and Michael Bratton also found that people judged democracy through direct experience with their own governments' political and (to a lesser extent) economic performance.[17]

Our surveys used three succinct indicators to gauge how citizens assessed the working of democracy. The first was overall satisfaction "with the way democracy works in our country." The second measures perceptions of the extent of corruption in the national government, and the third taps people's assessments of general economic conditions over the last few years (often seen as a telling indirect measure of regime effectiveness). From these responses we can glean possible reasons for the waning of popular support for democracy and the revival of authoritarian nostalgia in several of our cases.

In each of the five new democracies, negative assessments of democratic performance increased markedly on at least one of the three items. Dissatisfaction with the way democracy works declined slightly in Taiwan (to 39 percent) but increased in each of the other four countries, still to a very low level (15 percent) in Thailand, but to 44 percent in South Korea and to 59 percent in the Philippines.[18] This explains why in 2005 the Philippines registered the lowest mean score (2.6) on the five-item battery measuring support for democracy and the second-lowest overall level of authoritarian detachment in the region, while these two indices of democratic legitimacy have improved somewhat between 2002 and 2006 in Taiwan. This macro-level observation is backed up by individual-level statistical analysis, which shows a significant correlation between the level of dissatisfaction and the mean score of the support-for-democracy battery.[19]

Moreover, in all East Asian democracies (including Japan), citizens were appalled by stories of rampant corruption at the level of the national government. Across the region, no other factor seems to have done as much to hurt public confidence in democratic institutions.[20] During the first wave of surveys, more than 45 percent of respondents in Japan, South Korea, and Taiwan—and more than 60 percent in Mongolia and the Philippines—perceived that "almost everyone" or "most officials" were "involved in corruption and bribe-taking in the national government." Such cynical assessments have persisted in South Korea and the Philippines and have intensified in Taiwan (to 58 percent) and Mongolia (to 69 percent). Resentment of corruption has evidently helped to feed the dramatic rise in Mongolians' yearning for strongman rule.

Most of East Asia's democratic regimes cannot rely on economic performance because the region's growth momentum has not fully recovered to (and may never again reach) the levels seen before the 1997 financial crash. Still, significant differences exist among countries because citizens assess their respective national economic conditions differently. In countries where rapid economic growth was the rule for decades, recent performance might "feel" much worse than statistics indicate. Therefore, we are not surprised to find that slightly more than four-fifths of Japanese in 2003, three-quarters of South Koreans in 2006, and just over three-fifths of Taiwanese (in both surveys) felt that the national economic condition had gotten worse in the last few years. The combination of this disparaging assessment of the economy with the perception of rampant corruption helps explain why so many citizens in Taiwan and South Korea (and to some extent in Japan as well) still doubt that democracy is effective, or that it is always preferable. Where people have experienced (within memory) a variant of soft authoritarianism that delivered social stability, economic development, and at least the appearance of resistance to money politics, democracy now seems to be having a hard time winning hearts.

The Uneven Spread of Liberal-Democratic Values

To what extent is popular support for democracy in East Asia deeply rooted in a liberal-democratic political culture? This is a crucial question for gauging the region's democratic future, as it tests how robust is the observed popular commitment to democracy. If citizens' embrace of democracy is not anchored in liberal values affirming freedom and the rule of law, the foundation of regime legitimacy will remain shallow and fragile. This also provides a vantage point for examining the debate over "Asian exceptionalism."[21] If a liberal-democratic culture can take root in East Asian soil, especially in societies with a strong Confucian legacy, the core assumption of the "Asian values" thesis is turned on its head.

Due to limited space, we present here only the results of three items selected from a more elaborate battery. The three items were worded to repudiate the notions of political liberty, separation of powers, and the rule of law—which are presumed by some established scholars to contradict traditional Asian concepts of good governance.[22]

In Table 3, we report the percentage of respondents who disagreed with each of the three statements and thus revealed their propensity for liberal-democratic values. We also calculate a 4-point index (0 to 3) based on the number of liberal responses and report the findings in the righthand column of the table.

As we see in Table 3, across East Asia the acquisition of liberal-democratic values has been slow and uneven. The average number of liberal views hovered around the midpoint of 1.5. But here again, the richer countries in our group offer a sharp contrast to their less-developed neighbors. In Japan, South Korea, and Taiwan, a great majority of citizens embrace political liberty, separation of powers, and rule of law. Their mean scores were way above the region's average. In Taiwan, 60 percent of respondents in 2001 and 71 percent in 2006 disagreed that "the government should decide whether certain ideas should be allowed to be discussed in society." In South Korea, the rejection rate was about 60 percent in both surveys, and in Japan it was 55 percent. In South Korea, more than 69 percent of respondents have consistently rejected the notion that "when judges decide important cases, they should accept the view of the executive branch."

TABLE 3—POPULAR BELIEF IN LIBERAL-DEMOCRATIC VALUES
(IN PERCENTAGES)

COUNTRY	SURVEY YEAR	DISAGREE WITH THE FOLLOWING:			MEAN (0–3)
		REGULATED DISCUSSION[1]	POLITICAL JUDICIARY[2]	DISREGARD THE LAW[3]	
Taiwan	2001	60.2	53.7	58.3	1.72
	2006	71.1	57.0	67.9	1.96
South Korea	2003	60.1	69.0	76.7	2.06
	2006	58.5	71.5	74.3	2.04
Philippines	2002	39.7	38.7	70.2	1.49
	2005	40.8	32.3	59.3	1.32
Thailand	2001	46.9	40.1	49.2	1.36
	2006	43.9	27.7	33.6	1.05
Mongolia	2002	22.3	71.0	59.6	1.53
	2006	13.5	42.9	43.4	1.00
Average[4]	2001–2003	47.2	54.2	62.6	1.64
	2005–2006	46.9	46.0	55.3	1.48
Japan	2003	55.6	62.2	72.0	1.90

1. "The government should decide whether certain ideas should be allowed to be discussed in society."
2. "When judges decide important cases, they should accept the view of the executive branch."
3. "When the country is facing a difficult situation, it is okay for the government to disregard the law in order to deal with the situation."
4. Values in the Average row refer to those of emerging democracies and exclude Japan.
Source: Asian Barometer Survey, 2001–2006.

Less overwhelming but still strong majorities have done so in Taiwan and Japan as well. Almost three-quarters in Japan and Korea disagreed that "it is okay for the government to disregard the law in order to deal with [a difficult] situation." In Taiwan, the proportion rose from 58 percent in 2001 to 68 percent in 2006. Thus, a liberal-democratic culture seems to be emerging in these three socioeconomically advanced democracies.

By contrast, Filipinos, Mongolians, and Thais gave much more illiberal responses, and the gap between them and Taiwan, South Korea, and Japan is widening. In all three of the former countries, only a minority defended freedom of expression. In Mongolia, support for this freedom (expressed via disagreement with the first item in Table 3) declined to a miniscule 13 percent in 2006. The proportions supporting judicial independence shrank from 40 to 28 percent in Thailand, from 38 to 32 percent among Filipinos, and from 71 to 43 percent among Mongolians. There is a similar pattern of diminishing support for the rule of law, dropping for example from 49 to 33 percent in Thailand. Clearly, liberal-democratic values have not yet taken hold in Mongolia, the Philippines, and Thailand—on the contrary, the political culture in each country seems to have taken an authoritarian turn. Moreover, this deterioration reinforces the three concurrent trends observed earlier: dwindling popular support for democracy, declining popular resistance to authoritarian alternatives, and growing dissatisfaction with the working of democracy. From the viewpoint of regime legitimacy, these young democracies appear vulnerable to any well-orchestrated hostile intervention by a strategically positioned antidemocratic elite.

Table 3 also helps us decipher the meaning behind some of the baffling statistics we observed earlier. In Thailand, support for democracy as a concept far outstripped the regional average, but this support was not backed by belief in liberal-democratic values and hence has proven quite shallow—as the relative quiescence of the country since the 2006 coup suggests. In fact, Thailand's mean score on liberal-democratic values dropped to 1.05 on the 0-to-3 scale, just above Mongolia and way below the region's average.

Lastly, the figures in Table 3 provide little support for the "Asian-values" thesis. A liberal-democratic culture is emerging in Japan, South Korea, and Taiwan—the very countries which, among all East Asian democracies, are the most thoroughly imbued with Confucian principles and ideals. Their Confucian legacy might not have been conducive to the acquisition of liberal-democratic values, but it appears to have done nothing to hinder the process either.[23]

How does democracy's standing in East Asia appear in global perspective? The short answer is: about average. Democracy is in trouble in East Asia, but at the same time it is in no worse shape there than it is in other developing regions of the planet. East Asia is not alone in showing symptoms of democratic recession, ambivalence toward democracy's legitimacy, and faltering confidence in democracy's effectiveness as a system of governance. Compared to levels of popular support for democracy, strength of authoritarian detachment, and satisfaction with the performance of democracy observed in other regions, our six East Asian democracies appear on a par with similarly situated societies elsewhere in the world.[24]

The lesson we draw is not that East Asian cultures preclude liberal democracy from taking root, but that this form of government must win citizens' support through better performance. People's disenchantment with the gap between democratic promises and democratic realities is growing in all of East Asia's emerging democracies. Many citizens feel that progress toward democratic goals such as the rule of law, accountability, and responsiveness has been too sluggish and too scanty. There is also a broad feeling that the performance of democratic regimes has not lived up to expectations, especially as regards social equity, economic growth, and law and order. As a result, public confidence in democracy's superiority has waned. This does not mean that democratic consolidation in East Asia is a lost cause, but that it will require steps to make democratic regimes more effective, honest, and responsive.

Nonetheless, meeting citizens' expectations for strong economic growth combined with social equity is more difficult in an era when globalization can aggravate economic inequality and instability while hampering the capacity of states to manage and cushion the resulting stresses. Globalization also accelerates the hollowing-out of national politics. It shifts the locus of governing power away from a nation's capital to international organizations (such as the World Bank), multinational firms, foreign institutional investors, and private transnational actors. It pains most citizens to realize that, in a globalized world, their elected governments all too often can do little to shield them and their families from the challenges thrown up by a dynamic world economy.

These are challenges that third-wave democracies face everywhere, but East Asian democracies confront them in a delicate, if not more difficult, regional context. Many East Asian democracies are still struggling against a haze of nostalgia for authoritarianism, as citizens compare life under democracy with either the growth-oriented authoritarianism of the recent past or with their prosperous nondemocratic neighbors of the present. Either way, these region-specific benchmarks tend to set the performance bar for democratic regimes at an unreasonable height.

The economic and geopolitical rise of China over the last decade has also made the regional environment more hospitable for nondemocracies. The dramatic decline of Japan's economic vitality and regional influence during this period has further eclipsed the sway of the United States (and the community of industrialized democracies as a whole) over the political future of the region. The Japanese themselves, meanwhile, feel lukewarm enough about their own system that they are likely to sound an uncertain trumpet when it comes to calling the rest of the region to the liberal-democratic standard. China is showing her socialist neighbors a viable path for growing out of a planned economy, and is proving (so far, at least) that sequenced transition from communism to a form of authoritarian developmentalism is possible. If China fails to embark on a path of democratization, government by consent may still hold its own in the region, but the prospect of new democratic breakthroughs will recede.

NOTES

We wish to thank all our colleagues who carried out the Asian Barometer Survey in their respective countries, especially Robert Albritton, Thawilwadee Bureekul, Damba Ganbat, Linda Guerrero, Ken'ichi Ikeda, and Doh Chull Shin. We gratefully acknowledge generous financial support from Taiwan's National Science Council and Ministry of Education, National Taiwan University, the Academia Sinica, the Henry Luce Foundation, the World Bank, and the Korean Research Foundation Grant funded by the Korean Government (MOEHRD) (KRF-2005-042-B00016).

1. Juan J. Linz and Alfred C. Stepan, *The Breakdown of Democratic Regimes* (Baltimore: John Hopkins University Press, 1978).

2. See Larry Diamond, *Developing Democracy: Toward Consolidation* (Baltimore: Johns Hopkins University Press, 1999), 65.

3. The Asian Barometer Survey (ABS) represents the region's first collaborative initiative to develop a regional network of democracy studies based on surveying ordinary citizens. Between June 2001 and February 2003, the ABS surveyed eight East Asian countries and territories: Japan, South Korea, Mongolia, Taiwan, the Philippines, Thailand, Hong Kong, and China. The ABS launched its second-round survey in October 2005, enlarging its geographical scope to cover five more countries in the region. By March 2007, the fieldwork in South Korea, Mongolia, Taiwan, the Philippines, Thailand, and Indonesia had been completed, and the surveys in China, Hong Kong, Japan, Indonesia, Vietnam, Cambodia, Malaysia, and Singapore were still underway. The ABS survey in Thailand was conducted in April and May of 2006, just four months before the military coup. All ABS data were collected through face-to-face interviews of randomly selected eligible voters in each participating country. For further details, visit *www.asianbarometer.org*.

4. Yun-han Chu, Larry Diamond, and Doh Chull Shin, "Halting Progress in Korea and Taiwan," *Journal of Democracy* 12 (January 2001): 122–36; Doh Chull Shin, "Democratization: Perspectives from Global Citizenries," in Russell Dalton and Hans-Dieter Klingemann, eds., *The Oxford Handbook of Political Behavior* (Oxford: Oxford University Press, 2007), 259–82.

5. Robert Adcock and David Collier, "Measurement Validity: A Shared Standard for Qualitative and Quantitative Research," *American Political Science Review* 95 (September 2001): 538.

6. William Mishler and Richard Rose, "What Are the Political Consequences of Trust? A Test of Cultural and Institutional Theories in Russia," *Comparative Political Studies* 38 (November 2005): 1050–78; Doh Chull Shin and Jason Wells, "Challenge and Change in East Asia: Is Democracy the Only Game in Town?" *Journal of Democracy* 16 (April 2005): 88–101.

7. The ABS asks: "Here is a scale: 1 means complete dictatorship and 10 means complete democracy. To what extent would you want our country to be democratic now?"

8. The exact wording of the item reads: "Here is a similar scale of 1 to 10 measuring the extent to which people think democracy is suitable for our country. If '1' means that democracy is completely unsuitable for [name of country] today and '10' means that it is completely suitable, where would you place our country today?"

9. Respondents were asked: "Which of the following statements comes closer to your own view? 'Democracy cannot solve our society's problems,' or 'Democracy is capable of solving the problems of our society.'"

10. The ABS asks the respondents: "If you had to choose between democracy and economic development, which would you say is more important?"

11. Richard Rose, William Mishler, and Christian Haerpfer, *Democracy and Its Alternatives: Understanding Post-Communist Societies* (Baltimore: Johns Hopkins University Press, 1998), 31.

12. Lucian W. Pye, *Asian Power and Politics* (Cambridge, Mass.: Belknap, 1985); Samuel P. Huntington, *The Clash of Civilizations and the Remaking of World Order* (New York: Simon and Schuster, 1996).

13. Latinobarómetro, *Latinobarómetro Report 2005* (Santiago de Chile: Corporación, 2005).

14. See, for example, Michael Bratton and Eric C.C. Chang, "State Building and De-

mocratization in Sub-Saharan Africa: Forwards, Backwards, or Together?" *Comparative Political Studies* 39 (November 2006): 1059–83; Geoffrey Evans and Stephen Whitefield, "The Politics and Economics of Democratic Commitment: Support for Democracy in Transition Societies," *British Journal of Political Science* 25 (October 1995): 485–514.

15. Adam Przeworski, *Democracy and the Market: Political and Economic Reforms in Eastern Europe and Latin America* (Cambridge: Cambridge University Press, 1991), 184; Herbert Kitschelt, "The Formation of Party Systems in East Central Europe," *Politics and Society* 20 (March 1992): 7–50.

16. Stephen Whitefield and Geoffrey Evans, "Political Culture versus Rational Choice: Explaining Responses to Transition in the Czech Republic and Slovakia," *British Journal of Political Science* 29 (January 1999): 129–54; Pamela Waldron-Moore, "Eastern Europe at the Crossroads of Democratic Transition: Evaluating Support for Democratic Institutions, Satisfaction with Democratic Government, and Consolidation of Democratic Regimes," *Comparative Political Studies* 32 (February 1999): 32–62.

17. Robert Mattes and Michael Bratton, "Learning about Democracy in Africa: Awareness, Performance, and Experience," *American Journal of Political Science* 51 (January 2007): 192–217.

18. Space does not permit presentation of the table with our results on these performance dimensions. That may be found at *www.journalofdemocracy.org*.

19. When all the cases for the five new democracies were pooled together, the correlation coefficients came to -0.22 for the first-wave ABS and -0.19 for the second-wave ABS.

20. Eric C.C. Chang and Yun-han Chu, "Corruption and Trust: Exceptionalism in Asian Democracies?" *Journal of Politics* 68 (May 2006): 259–71.

21. Francis Fukuyama, "The Illusion of Asian Exceptionalism," in Larry Diamond and Marc F. Plattner, eds., *Democracy in East Asia* (Baltimore: Johns Hopkins University Press, 1998).

22. Most notable are Pye, *Asian Power and Politics,* as well as Daniel A. Bell et al., eds., *Towards Illiberal Democracy in Pacific Asia* (New York: St. Martin's, 1995).

23. Chong-Min Park and Doh Chull Shin, "Do Asian Values Deter Popular Support for Democracy in South Korea?" *Asian Survey* 46 (May–June 2006): 341–61.

24. For instance, on whether "democracy is always preferable," the mean support across East Asia's five new democratic regimes was 59 percent in 2001–2003 and 51 percent in 2005–2006. This is very close to the 53 percent average in Latin America in 2005 and in Eastern Europe recently. Richard Rose, *Insiders and Outsiders: New Europe Barometer 2004* (Glasgow: Centre for the Study of Public Policy No. 404, 2005), 68.

7

THE FRAGILITY OF SUPPORT FOR DEMOCRACY IN SOUTH ASIA

Peter R. deSouza, Suhas Palshikar, and Yogendra Yadav

Peter R. deSouza *is director of the Indian Institute of Advanced Studies in Shimla, India.* ***Suhas Palshikar*** *is professor of political science at the University of Pune in India.* ***Yogendra Yadav*** *is codirector of Lokniti–Programme for Comparative Democracy and senior fellow at the Centre for the Study of Developing Societies in Delhi, India. This material appeared in a slightly different form as a chapter in* The State of Democracy in South Asia, *published by the Centre for the Study of Developing Societies in December 2006. This essay was originally published in the January 2008 issue of the* Journal of Democracy.

The citizens of South Asia share the contemporary global aspiration for democracy. As the idea of democracy travels to different parts of the world and to various social groups and communities, ordinary citizens come to attach positive connotations to the word "democracy" as understood in the various languages of this region. They buy into the idea of democracy as well as what is today the most commonly accepted institutional form of democracy, namely, rule by elected representatives. More than an abstract preference or a simple acquiescence, most South Asians believe that democracy is suitable for their country and prefer democracy over authoritarianism. While support for the institutional form of democracy is determined by access to education, media exposure, and the experience of living under democratic conditions, support for the idea of democracy cuts across social barriers.

If the end of the twentieth century was marked by the triumph of democracy all over the world, the beginning of the twenty-first century has been characterized by an anxiety about the extent, depth, and implications of this triumph. As democracy becomes the "only game in town" in more and more countries in the various regions of the world, the idea of democracy has also acquired a currency that it may not have had at any other point in human history. Yet this global march of democracy does not by itself mean popular support for it. Do citizens simply acquiesce in the new form of government just as they had acquiesced in the earlier forms of government? Do they only accept the idea of democracy on an abstract plane, or are they willing to endorse the institutional form of democracy over its alternatives? In short, do the citizens really support democracy? This question is especially worth asking in South Asia, for the answer is neither well known nor self-evident.

South Asia does not fully fit into the story of the global triumph of democracy. The countries in this region have not experienced a linear progression toward democracy; more often than not, theirs has been a story of forward movements followed by setbacks and regression. The region's story is far from a narrative of unalloyed democratic triumph, especially if we include such nearby countries as Afghanistan, Myanmar (Burma), Bhutan, and the Maldives. The larger neighborhood, be it China or West and Central Asia, is hardly conducive to democratic sentiments. Furthermore, those who believe that certain preconditions must obtain if democratic culture is to take root often list given levels of economic development and prosperity among these prior necessities. South Asia is one of the world regions where this condition is clearly not met, for it continues to be home to the largest number of poor people on earth.

Finally, the world since 9/11 has seen the rise of a hypothesis proposing a disconnect between Islam and democracy. South Asia is home to more than a quarter of the global Muslim population; Muslims are either the majority or a significant minority in all five countries of this region. Thus if the citizens in this region support democracy, it would have implications far beyond South Asia. But despite the significance of this question—Do the people of South Asia really support democracy?—it had long been impossible to offer any credible answer, as South Asia remained outside the purview of the "barometers" of public opinion and attitudes about democracy. *The State of Democracy in South Asia* study carried out the first-ever simultaneous survey of attitudes toward democracy in the five countries of South Asia—Bangladesh, India, Nepal, Pakistan, and Sri Lanka—based on a large and representative sample of adult citizens.[1] The survey provides enough evidence to suggest widespread support for democracy throughout the region.

When asked to spell out what the word "democracy" meant to them, nearly everyone who responded offered positive descriptions. Negative "top-of-the-mind" associations were fewer than one out of ten in each of the five countries. This confirms a similar finding of the World Values Survey conducted in 2001 in three countries of the region. In that survey, as many as 98 percent of the respondents in Bangladesh and 93 percent in India indicated their approval of the "democratic system." Pakistan, however, was second to last, just ahead of Russia in that global survey, with a mere 68 percent approving of democracy.[2]

Support for democracy, however, goes beyond a liking for the word "democracy" and extends to expressing approval of the institutional form of democratic government. People in the region overwhelmingly favor the rule of "leaders elected by the people," with only a handful of respondents disagreeing with the idea of representative democracy. In Pakistan and Nepal, the two countries that did not have representative democracy at the time of the survey, about a quarter of the respondents offered no response to this question.

People not only approve of democratic arrangements, but they find them suitable for their own contexts. Seven out of eight respondents in South Asia—a higher proportion than one finds in East Asia—held that democracy was "suitable" or "very suitable" for their own country. Doubt or uncertainty regarding the suitability of democracy surfaced in the form of "no response": nearly a third of the persons interviewed in the region—many more in Pakistan and Bangladesh—did not offer any response to this question.

Finally, the citizens of South Asia do not simply *like* democracy, they *prefer* it to authoritarian rule. With the exception of Pakistan, about two-thirds of those who responded preferred democracy over any other form of government. Only one out of ten responses overtly supported the idea that "sometimes dictatorship is better than democracy." But there is a significant number of people who are either indifferent or ignorant about this crucial choice. About half the respondents in Pakistan and a quarter in other countries said that the distinction between a democratic and a nondemocratic form of government made no difference to them. Roughly a third of those interviewed either did not understand this question or could give no response.

A comparison of the findings from South Asia with the responses to this question from the rest of the world suggests that unless we see "no response" as a sign of ambiguity, support for democracy in the region is not very different from what it is anywhere else. For every one South Asian response that endorses dictatorship, there are six South Asian responses that prefer democracy; this compares favorably with the ratio obtained for the same question in East Asia, Latin America, and the postcommunist countries of Europe.

What do we make of this support for the idea of democracy? When people say that they desire or prefer democracy, are they saying anything significant? Or are they just paying lip service to a universal norm, to what is seen as the only legitimate model for governing a country? The evidence presented thus far permits a limited conclusion: "Democracy" has become an object of desire—something that is viewed positively, is considered suitable, and is generally preferred over its opposite. This is not a trivial finding coming from a region where conditions are considered unfriendly to the growth of democracy. Moreover, when the study took place in 2005, the region had two of the few surviving military dictatorships and executive monarchies of our time. When the people living under nondemocratic regimes are paying even lip service to the idea of democracy, they are making a significant statement. But does this support for the idea of democracy translate into an endorsement of the institutional form of representative democracy and the negation of its alternatives? What do people mean by the "democracy" that they say they support?

The "Funnel of Democracy": Support Is Equivocal

One way to measure the depth of support for democracy is to ask whether those who affirm the representative form of democratic government reject its various real-life alternatives. This is what the "funnel of democracy" seeks to capture. As we move from unambiguously anti-democratic alternatives to the more subtle forms of nondemocratic alternatives, we find a sharp drop in the proportion of those who continue to negate alternatives to democracy. The shape of the resultant funnel captures the depth of support for democratic government: the wider the base of the funnel, the more robust the support for the institutional form of democratic government.

The funnel of support for democracy in the region as a whole has a conical shape—a very wide mouth but a fairly narrow base (see Figure 1).[3] The proportion of supporters of the representative form of democratic government drops sharply with successive stages. Thus, unlike in many longstanding democracies, in South Asia an affirmation of democratic government does not lead to the negation of authoritarian options. At the same time, the situation in South Asia does not resemble that of Latin America or postcommunist Europe, where more citizens reject authoritarianism than support a democratic form of government. In all South Asian countries, the proportion of those who support democracy is much higher than the proportion of those who negate its alternatives. The pattern varies across countries, from a wineglass-shaped funnel in the case of Pakistan to a relatively broad-based funnel in the case of India, because different stages have varying effects in different countries.

At stage one—the affirmation of rule by elected representatives—support for democratic government is very broad in all five countries. But the pattern begins to diverge by stage two. At this stage, those who entertain the idea of dictatorship or feel indifferent about the choice between democracy and dictatorship are excluded. More than half the responses from Pakistan drop out here, as compared to one-quarter to one-third for the other countries.

The fragility of support for democracy begins to show as we move through stages three and four, the rejection of the two obviously non-democratic forms of government: military rule and monarchy, respectively. Six out of every ten respondents in Pakistan and Bangladesh, the two countries with a record of army rule, endorsed the idea that

FIGURE 1—THE FUNNEL OF DEMOCRACY IN SOUTH ASIA

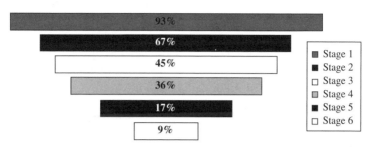

Stage 1: Includes all those who support government by elected leaders
Stage 2: Excludes those who prefer dictatorship sometimes or are indifferent between democracy and dictatorship
Stage 3: Excludes those who want army rule
Stage 4: Excludes those who want rule by king
Stage 5: Excludes those who want a strong leader without any democratic restraint
Stage 6: Excludes those who want the rule of experts rather than politicians

Note: Percentages calculated from merged data set with equal weights for each country (Bangladesh, India, Nepal, Pakistan, and Sri Lanka).

the country should be governed by the army. This is one of the highest levels of support for army rule recorded in any part of the world. Even in the other three countries, where opponents of government by the military outnumber its supporters, the level of endorsement for army rule cannot be dismissed as trivial.

It is true that in countries with no experience of army rule, respondents do not understand what they are endorsing. Their response is best interpreted as support for the army as an institution—for its discipline and professionalism, which present such a stark contrast to the messy realities of civilian politics, and for its role as a symbol of national pride—rather than as a demand for the replacement of democratic representatives by the army. This is not peculiar to South Asia. What is perhaps special is the willingness to accept a political role for the army in countries such as Bangladesh, where the people have a history of struggling against and successfully dislodging army rule. Some of this may be attributed to poor education and a lack of awareness about army rule. In all the region's countries, it is the least-educated citizens who are the most likely to endorse army rule.

Compared to support for army rule, support for monarchy is a minor factor in all South Asian countries except Nepal, which at the time of the survey was a land ruled for all practical purposes by an executive monarch. A majority of the respondents in Nepal endorsed the idea of "rule by the king." They did not, however, understand that to mean an all-powerful executive monarchy: Those citizens who understood these fine distinctions preferred constitutional monarchy to an active rule of the kind that the king was to inaugurate after February 2005. Since the popular uprising and restoration of the parliament in 2006, public opinion has registered a dramatic shift in favor of a republican form of government. While it remains to be seen if democratic Nepal opts for the republican form of government, it nevertheless seems unlikely that monarchy will remain an important factor in South Asia. The only other monarch in the region, the king of Bhutan, has already announced several steps leading to a transition toward constitutional monarchy.

The first four stages involving overt support for democracy and rejection of its obvious alternatives lead to a considerable narrowing of the funnel in each country except India and Sri Lanka. Close to half the responses in these two longstanding democracies manage to pass the first four filters. But they do not pass the remaining stages very well. Throughout the region, there is a two-thirds approval of the rule of a "strong leader who does not have to bother about elections." Only in India do those who disapprove of such a rule outnumber those who approve of it. The introduction of this fifth stage leads to a significant attrition of support for democratic government in all of these countries, especially in Nepal and Sri Lanka. This should come as no surprise in a region that has a long tradition of strong leaders such as Indira Gandhi, Zulfikar Ali Bhutto, and Sheikh Mujib-ur Rahman, who owed their power to democratic popularity but once safely entrenched, tended to bypass institutional norms of liberal democracy.

The same is true in even greater measure of support for decision making by "experts rather than politicians": Four out of every five respondents agreed with this suggestion. This sixth and final check reduces the support for democratic government to a single digit in all countries except India. To be sure, the last two conditions are stiff for any democracy in the world. Yearning for a strong leader and preferring experts over politicians are universal themes in contemporary public opinion. Besides, the support for strong leaders or experts need not always reflect a nondemocratic orientation; it very often stems from a desire for effective rule and seeks fulfillment within a democratic frame.

Democrats Outnumber Nondemocrats

Another way of measuring the depth of support for democratic government is to calculate the proportion of "democrats" in the citizenry and to examine the nature of the relationship between the democrats and "nondemocrats." In this sense, the depth of democracy is measured by how favorable the ratio of democrats to nondemocrats is within a society. This way of measuring support for democracy has the advantage of bringing greater precision and rigor to a comparison across countries, but at the cost of focusing narrowly on just one kind of support for democracy as an institutional form of government.

The picture of support for democracy in South Asia that this analysis yields is mixed—positive on balance but not free of reasons for worry. A

TABLE—LEVEL OF SUPPORT FOR DEMOCRACY BY COUNTRY
(IN PERCENTAGES)

COUNTRY	STRONG DEMOCRAT	WEAK DEMOCRAT	NONDEMOCRAT	SUPPORT FOR DEMOCRACY RATIO
Bangladesh	19	62	19	1.03
India	41	43	15	2.71
Nepal	22	54	24	0.92
Pakistan	10	49	41	0.24
Sri Lanka	36	50	14	2.52
South Asia	26	52	22	1.17

Note: The figure for South Asia is from a merged data set with equal weights for each country. The ratio of support for democracy is the proportion of strong supporters divided by the proportion of skeptics. "Don't know" (including those who could not understand the questions) have been treated as a missing value.

little more than a quarter of the respondents can be described as "strong democrats," for they are consistent in supporting democracy and in opposing obviously nondemocratic forms of government. A strong democrat here is someone who supports rule by elected representatives *and* always prefers it to any other form of government *and* is opposed to rule by the army or the king. The proportion of strong democrats is higher in India and Sri Lanka than the regional average, but substantially lower in Pakistan.

On the other end of the spectrum, slightly fewer than a quarter of respondents fall in the category of nondemocrats, those who prefer a nondemocratic alternative to democracy. Thus a nondemocrat here is someone who prefers dictatorship (or is indifferent to the choice between democracy and dictatorship) *and* who supports either army rule or rule by the king. Here again, the picture is relatively better in India and Sri Lanka, which have lower proportions of nondemocrats. The proportion of nondemocrats in Pakistan is twice as high as in the rest of the region (see Table).

If we look at regional averages, the proportion of strong democrats is marginally higher than that of nondemocrats. This is reflected in the Support for Democracy Ratio (SDR) of 1.17 in the region. This ratio is the proportion of strong democrats to nondemocrats; an SDR of 1.0 would indicate a perfect balance between the two extreme categories. A higher SDR indicates deeper support for democracy. It is therefore not surprising that the two countries with the longest and least interrupted experience of democracy are the countries with the highest support for democracy. The proportion of strong supporters of democracy in India and Sri Lanka is two-and-a-half times that of the nondemocrats and thus suggests a robust dominance of democratic sentiment. In Bangladesh and Nepal, there appears to be a precarious balance of democratic and nondemocratic forces, with an SDR of around 1.0. The situation in Pakistan does not appear encouraging for democracy. Although the strong and weak democrats together outnumber nondemocrats, the balance of the two extreme categories is rather unfavorable, with an SDR of just 0.24. This means that in Pakistan, there are four nondemocrats for every strong democrat.

This reading, however, needs to be qualified. First, what appear to be the characteristics of a country need not reflect anything essential about the culture and society of that country. As our analysis shows, this reflects above all the experience of democracy in Pakistan. Second, as noted above, this measure is limited to the support for representative democracy as a form of government; support for the idea of democracy has a wider base in Pakistan. Third, we do not know how stable are the attitudes of support for democratic government, or how well our measure captures the dimension of stability. It is likely that our measure reflects the popular mood of cynicism and exasperation born from the existence of army rule on the one hand and the uninspiring experience with party politics and Islamist forces on the other. We do know, for instance, that in Nepal, support for democracy leapt upward after the democratic surge of May 2006. It could well be that another round of movement for democracy in Pakistan may lead to dramatic changes in popular support for democracy.

The burden of interpretation thus hangs on the majority of the respondents in South Asia, more in Bangladesh and fewer in India, who fall into the residual category of "weak democrats." They are democrats because they support at least one of the key attributes of a democratic government, but should be labeled "weak" since they are not quite consistent in negating nondemocratic forms of government. Nearly half these weak democrats affirm support for democracy but do not clearly negate one of the nondemocratic options. Another third of respondents are ambivalent, for they either support both democracy and its alternatives or support neither. This leaves a small fraction of weak democrats who lean toward being nondemocrats, supporting nondemocratic options without quite negating the democratic option. Thus it is reasonable to infer that democrats, including both strong and weak, outnumber nondemocrats in all the countries. This is as true in Pakistan as it is in the region's other countries. Yet this conclusion remains tentative, for weak democrats can swing in either direction.

Education, Exposure, and Experience

Analyses of support for democracy across different countries in the region may give the impression that some countries or their dominant religions are more democratic than others. This needs to be checked carefully by a detailed breakdown of support for democracy as that support relates to different social variables within and across these countries. A quick analysis shows that support for democracy within each of these countries varies sharply among different social groups. Those who are socially privileged tend to support democracy much more than do those at the lower end of the social order. This is true of various aspects of social privilege: Elites, or those in higher occupations, are much more supportive of democracy than the mass public; men support democracy substantially more than women do, particularly in Bangladesh, Nepal, and Pakistan; urban dwellers support democracy more than do villagers in Bangladesh, Sri Lanka, and Pakistan, although this is not true in Nepal and India; in each of the countries, those who are well-off tend to support democracy at higher rates than do those with lower incomes.

This first impression needs to be fine-tuned, for much of what appears to be the effect of income, gender, and urbanity reflects the unequal degrees of access to education enjoyed by different social groups. In determining the level of support for democracy, formal education turns out to be the strongest factor: The higher a respondent's level of educational attainment, the greater that respondent's support for democracy is likely to be. In this respect, completing school with a matriculation degree or its equivalent is a crucial step that leads to a leap in support for democracy. In South Asia, someone with a graduate degree is seven times more likely to support democracy than is a nonliterate person. This relationship holds with varying degrees of intensity across all five countries of the region. The relationship is strongest in Nepal, which has the region's lowest literacy rate, and is weakest in Sri Lanka, which has the highest level of literacy. This suggests that once education ceases to be a scarce commodity, its effect begins to diminish. The effect of education is reinforced by exposure to the media: the higher the exposure, the greater the support for a democratic government.

Once the effects of formal education and media exposure are taken into account, other factors become less important than initially thought. For example, there is no difference in support for a democratic government among urban and rural residents; if anything, educated villagers tend to support democracy more than do equally educated urbanites. Additionally, among respondents with equal education there is only a weak relationship between being well-off and supporting democracy, and the relationship disappears if we look only at those who have completed schooling (see Figure 2 on p. 98). Finally, gender matters much less than it seemed at first. Men and women with equal levels of education and exposure to the media tend to support democratic government in equal measure.

While formal education explains a good deal of the differences in the levels of support for democracy, it does not quite explain the differences between countries. It does not explain, for instance, why a nonliterate person from India is twice as likely to support democracy as is a college graduate from Pakistan. For this we need to turn to another kind of learning, the learning that takes place through living in a democracy (see Figure 3 on p. 99). The overall ratio of support for democracy in these five

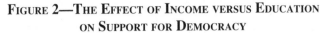

FIGURE 2—THE EFFECT OF INCOME VERSUS EDUCATION
ON SUPPORT FOR DEMOCRACY

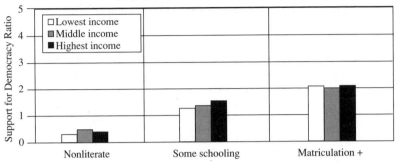

countries roughly follows the extent of their experience with democratic regimes: India and Sri Lanka are at the top, followed by Bangladesh and then Nepal and Pakistan. (Although Nepal has less democratic experience than Pakistan, its experience is more recent and therefore more influential for the current population.) This intuitive sense is confirmed by a careful analysis of the relationship between the proportion of one's adult life, since age fifteen, spent under a democratic regime and one's support for democracy. For those who have never or only very briefly experienced democracy, the SDR is 0.27—there are four nondemocrats to each democrat in this group. The ratio steadily goes up with an increase in the proportion of adult life spent under democracy and turns favorable (more democrats than nondemocrats) at about the 75 percent mark. For those who have never lived under a nondemocratic system, the SDR is 2.39; there are more than two democrats for each nondemocrat in this group. Thus what appears to be a difference in support for democracy among the countries is better seen as a difference in exposure to democracy.

A combination of these three factors—formal education, media exposure, and the informal political education that democracy provides—accounts for many of the differences in support for democracy in South Asia. The lowest support for democracy (SDR of 0.1; one democrat to ten nondemocrats) comes from nonliterate people who have never or only rarely experienced democracy. The level of support with the same degree of exposure to democracy is four times greater among those who have completed matriculation, and eleven times greater for those who have always lived under democracy but are nonliterate. The highest level of support for democracy (an SDR of 3.81, nearly four democrats to each nondemocrat) is recorded among those who have completed secondary school and have always lived in a democracy (see Figure 3).

The religious diversity that characterizes South Asia makes the region a promising laboratory in which to test the notion that believers in Islam are reluctant supporters of democracy. The fact that democracy has a checkered record in the two Muslim-majority countries of the region

FIGURE 3—COMBINED EFFECT OF EDUCATION AND
EXPERIENCE OF DEMOCRACY

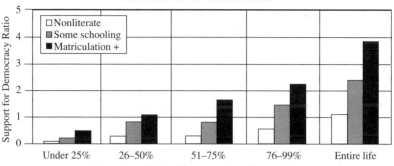

Proportion of adult life spent under a democratic regime

might lend strength to this suspicion. But a careful breakdown of the support for democracy among major religious and ethnic communities in each country shows otherwise. Followers of Islam are a significant presence in all five countries, but their level of support for democracy varies by country. If Muslims living in Pakistan record the lowest level of support for democracy, Muslims in Sri Lanka register the highest. Likewise, Hindus living in India, Nepal, and Pakistan register strikingly different levels of support for democracy. As a rule, different religious communities are closer to their compatriots in their attitude toward democracy than they are to their coreligionists in other countries.

What matters more than religion is the minority status of the community. In countries where the majority-minority question has acquired public salience, the minorities tend to invest themselves more heavily in democracy than the majority community does. Thus the Tamils and Muslims in Sri Lanka, Hindus and ethnic minorities in Bangladesh, and non-Punjabis in Pakistan express greater faith in democracy. This pattern, however, does not hold in India, where the majority-minority lines are drawn differently at different levels, leading to a crisscrossing and fuzziness of boundaries; nor does it hold in Nepal, where this is not yet a public-political issue. If we go by self-identification, the relationship is clear: Those who think that they belong to a minority tend to be more supportive of democracy.

If we see support for democracy not as a function of some immutable cultural trait but as a product of different kinds of learning, we can say that the current uneven distribution of support for democracy in the different countries of South Asia can, and is likely to, change in the future. As formal education, exposure to the media, and democratic experience become more widespread, we are likely to witness an upswing in the levels of support for democracy as a form of government.

How do we reconcile the widespread support for the idea of democracy with the somewhat shallow and uneven support for democracy as an institutional form? Clearly there is no seamless translation of the idea of democracy into an agreed institutional form, nor is there a consensus on what is incompatible with democracy. One possible approach would be to treat general support for the idea of democracy as a surface phenomenon that cannot be taken at face value unless verified by support for the institutional form of democracy and the negation of nondemocratic alternatives. According to this approach, effective support for democracy in South Asia is fairly limited. One can hope that it will grow with the spread of education, a greater penetration of the mass media, and more experience with modern democracy.

There is, however, an alternative and richer method of interpreting this difference that merits careful consideration. In this approach, support for the idea of democracy and the institutional form of democracy are two distinct but not incompatible dimensions of expressing an aspiration for democracy. Thus support for the idea of democracy need not always be verified by the negation of apparently nondemocratic forms of government; a simultaneous affirmation of democracy and its alternatives need not be seen as a sign of incoherence or contradiction. Ordinary citizens may have many models of democracy in their minds that they are unable to articulate in coherent and general terms, especially if they have not had the benefit of formal education or exposure to the media, which reinforce each other.

Thus an overwhelming support for strong leaders and experts or limited support for religious leaders can be interpreted in different ways.[4] It can be seen as a sign that support for democracy is vulnerable. It can also be viewed as an expression of unease with the received model of democracy and a desire to combine the existing model with other virtues: discipline (as exemplified by the army), order (as personified by a strong leader), wisdom (as embodied by experts) and values (as represented by religious leaders). People may see modern politics as much too competitive, faction-ridden, and devoid of values; hence the attraction that may be exerted by any alternative which promises to enforce order and reduce social divisions. While the people of South Asia do not wish to give up on popular rule, they appear willing to relax some of the legal-institutional requirements associated with a modern liberal democracy. Rather than choosing a nondemocratic government over a democratic one, they seem to be demanding a redefinition of what it means to be democratic.

An analysis of how the two dimensions—conceptual and practical—relate to each other shows that they are mutually reinforcing. In other words, stronger support for the idea of democracy in general terms is associated with a higher score on the index of support for democracy as an institutional form. The index of support for a democratic government directly and positively correlates with a belief in the suitability of democracy in one's own country. Those who believe that democracy is suitable or very suitable for their country are much more likely to be democrats than those who find democracy unsuitable for their country. A similar, though less strong, relationship exists between being satisfied with the working of democracy and the index of support for a democratic government. The relationship is understandably weaker in Nepal and Pakistan, where respondents found it difficult to relate to the question about "satisfaction with the way democracy works in our country." The more active one is in politics, the more likely one is to support democracy; and the higher the degree of one's participation—from being a one-time voter to a regular voter to a participant in nonelectoral political activity and finally to being a member of political organizations—the higher is likely to be one's support for democratic governance.

Support for the idea of democracy and support for the institutional form of democratic governance therefore fit together in a meaningful pattern that holds positive implications for democracy's future in the region. Those who are more active participants and who feel more satisfied with the working of the political system are likely to be more supportive of a democratic government. In addition, the division between strong democrats and nondemocrats does not follow the social fault lines of these societies. Although democracy has yet to become the only game in town in the region, the factors that drive support for democracy are such that one can expect a strengthening of democratic sentiment where it is currently weak.

NOTES

1. For details of the study, see *www.democracy-asia.org*.

2. European and World Values Surveys Four-Wave Integrated Data File, 1981–2004, v.20060423, 2006, European Values Study Foundation and World Values Survey Association; available at *www.worldvaluessurvey.org*.

3. A complete set of supporting graphics can be found at *www.journalofdemocracy. org/articles/gratis/YadavGraphics-19-1.pdf*.

4. Nearly 40 percent of respondents agreed with the suggestion that "religious leaders rather than politicians" should make the major decisions in the country. The pattern across the five countries, however, is mixed: majority support in Bangladesh and Pakistan, ambivalence in Nepal, and clear rejection in Sri Lanka and India. This suggests that popular perceptions are shaped by the extent to which the state has adopted an official religion and has allowed religious leaders some space in the secular domain. The Sunni *ulama* play a significant political role in Pakistan, although they may not directly contest elections. The rise of the politics of Hindutva ("Hindu-ness") in India and of Islamist parties in Bangladesh has heralded religious leaders' entrance into electoral politics. Likewise, the political clout that Sri Lanka's Buddhist monks wield is a clear indicator of the presence of religious leaders in the political process. Not surprisingly, religious leaders who enjoy political popularity do not formally demand the rejection of electoral democracy; instead, they use the mechanisms of electoral democracy to expand the role of religion in the political arena. Therefore, the distinction between politician and religious leader may not always be clear. Moreover, widespread support for religious leaders indicates a vulnerability to subdemocratic or parademocratic forms of politics.

8

FORMAL VERSUS INFORMAL INSTITUTIONS IN AFRICA

Michael Bratton

Michael Bratton is University Distinguished Professor of Political Science and African Studies at Michigan State University. He is also founder and director of the Afrobarometer, a collaborative international survey-research project that measures public opinion regarding democracy, markets, and civil society in eighteen African countries. This essay originally appeared in the July 2007 issue of the Journal of Democracy.

Few political scientists would dispute that political institutions help to shape the attitudes and behavior of citizens. Indeed, one of the leading paradigms in the study of political life today is known as the "new institutionalism."[1] This body of theory assumes that ordinary people—when they think and act politically—take their cues from the structure of rules, procedures, and customs prevailing in the polity in which they live. As such, political institutions provide a revealing aperture through which to view—and to explain—regularities in public opinion and mass participation.

But a lively debate persists about the relative importance of formal and informal institutions. What is the operative framework for studying the politics of new democracies? Is it a sovereign constitution, along with the rule-governed agencies and legal procedures with which a constitution is associated? Or is real-world politics driven by more contextual dynamics, in which "actual existing" social and power relations—not words on paper—determine who gets what, when, and how? Put differently, do citizens respond primarily to the inscribed regulations of formal institutions or to the unwritten codes embedded in everyday social practice?

According to Douglass C. North's classic formulation, political institutions can be "any form of constraint that human beings devise to shape human interaction," and can work through "both formal constraints—such as rules that human beings devise—and informal constraints—such as conventions and codes of behavior."[2]

Most practitioners of the new institutionalism disregard North's qualification and focus only on formal institutions, thereby underrating the impact of the informal realm. This bias may be reasonable for established democracies, where the rule of law guides political actors and a widespread ethic of "constitutionalism" reinforces written constitutions. But these conditions rarely hold in emergent democracies, where legal limits on state power are usually novel and untested.[3] Even if the rule of law is not completely absent in such societies, it is often weakly developed or sometimes ignored with impunity, usually in deference to personal or communal ties. Under these conditions, the influence of formal institutions may be sharply attenuated as political actors align themselves with more familiar relationships and routines.

Such considerations bear on the study of how ordinary Africans arrive at assessments of democracy. When they judge the new political regime, are they thinking of its formal institutions, such as elections, multiple parties, and control of executive power by independent legislatures and courts? Or do African publics still view politics in their countries mainly through the lens of such informal institutions as clientelism, corruption, and trust in (or fear of) "Big Men"? If, as expected, public opinion is mediated by both formal and informal institutions, which are the more salient? And assuming that informal institutions remain important, do they on balance help or harm democracy?

As exemplified by North's broad usage, the term "institution" is one of the loosest in the social-science lexicon. It has been used variously to refer to the rules of the political game, to organizations that link individuals to the political system, or even to "stable, valued and recurring patterns of (political) behavior."[4] In this article, I mean by *formal institutions* the organized routines of political democracy, such as regular elections for top officeholders and legal constraints on the political executive. By *informal institutions* I mean the patterns of patron-client relations by which power is also exercised. Sadly, neither of these two types of political institutions, nor their interactions, are well understood as they exist in and touch on Africa.

One group of Africa scholars—whom we may characterize as "formalists"—contends that the nature of official state institutions decisively shapes citizens' stances toward democracy. Relevant institutions include the constitution (whether it is unitary or federal, presidential or parliamentary); the electoral system (whether it is majoritarian, plurality-based, or proportional); and the party system (whether it is fragmented or one party dominates it). Donald Horowitz, for example, has argued that a federal constitution helps to ease political conflict in deeply divided societies.[5] Andrew Reynolds recommends proportional representation as an electoral formula to protect minority rights.[6] And Daniel N. Posner discovers that the competitiveness of the party system affects whether ethnic groups mobilize along language or tribal lines.[7]

Other scholars—whom we might dub "informalists"—remind us that official state institutions are usually weak in Africa, where unwritten rules hold far more sway. Indeed, Goran Hyden asserts that "Africa is the best starting point for exploring the role of informal institutions" and that these derive from a social logic he calls "the economy of affection."[8] As examples of informal institutions, he includes charisma (an authority relationship based on personal trust); clientelism (the expression of political loyalty to providers of patronage); pooling (horizontal exchanges within small groups); and collective self-defense (for example, the development of shared norms of sovereignty and noninterference).

Within this rich social matrix, three informal institutions seem especially pertinent to struggles for democracy in Africa: clientelism, corruption, and "Big Man" presidentialism. René Lemarchand has argued that, by distributing material rewards to clients, political patrons help to integrate a diversity of cultural groups into a national political community.[9] By contrast, Sahr Kpundeh argues that corruption—defined as the misuse of public office for private gain—"adversely impedes development . . . and participatory governance."[10]

And Nicolas van de Walle draws attention to presidentialism, especially in its informal guises:

> Regardless of constitutional arrangements . . . power is intensely personalized around the figure of the president . . . He is literally above the law, controls in many cases a large proportion of state finance without accountability, and delegates remarkably little of his authority on important matters . . . Only the apex of the executive really matters.[11]

Corruption, clientelism, and "Big Man" presidentialism—all dimensions of neopatrimonial rule—tend to go together as a package. They are "stable, valued and recurring patterns of behavior" to which all political actors are acutely attuned. Indeed, these practices are so ingrained in African political life as to constitute veritable political institutions.

Before turning to empirical analysis, a few final points of conceptual clarification are in order. First, I distinguish formal and informal institutions for analytical purposes only; in reality, these structures thoroughly interpenetrate one another. Indeed, hybrid regimes such as the neopatrimonial variety so common in Africa arise precisely when informal practices of presidential dominance, official corruption, and patron-client ties seep into the formal operations of the state. Second, the assumption that both types of institutions affect the development of democracy is only a first step. The more critical question is which matters *more:* formality or informality? Guillermo O'Donnell argues that in Latin America "the actual rules being followed" often trump mere "parchment" institutions.[12] As a working hypothesis, one would expect this balance to prevail in African countries as well.

Finally, in an important insight, Gretchen Helmke and Steven Levitsky show that informal institutions are a double-edged sword with regard to democracy.[13] Illicit procedures (such as corruption) usually undermine the fair and equal treatment of citizens. Yet in situations where formal institutions remain weak, personal connections (ties of personal loyalty to an incumbent president, for example) can help to secure legitimacy for a fragile democratic regime.

Data and Measurement

Data from the Afrobarometer (AB), a comparative series of public attitude surveys on democracy, governance, markets, and civil society, will help us to analyze the manner and extent of political institutions' effects on popular attitudes toward democracy in Africa.[14] Because the AB uses a standard questionnaire with identical or functionally equivalent items, it affords unique opportunities to compare results across countries and over time. Still, caution should be used in extrapolating findings to the continent as a whole: Survey work can go forward only in Africa's more open and stable societies, so the most authoritarian and conflict-ridden countries have to be left out. The trends reported here are based on three rounds of AB surveys. Round 1 took place in a dozen countries between 1999 and 2001 ("circa 2000"); Round 2 covered sixteen countries from 2002 to 2003 ("circa 2002"); and Round 3 was carried out in eighteen countries in 2005 and 2006 ("circa 2005").[15]

Let us look first at the "demand side" of public opinion. Do Africans *want* democracy and, if so, has popular support been rising or falling? Moreover, as the collective memory of democratic transition fades, are Africans more or less nostalgic for previous systems of authoritarian rule? The analysis then moves to the "supply side" by asking whether Africans think that they are *getting* the political regimes they desire. Now that they have experienced democracy in practice, are Africans satisfied with the quality of rule delivered by their leaders? And, over time, how much democracy do they think their respective countries have achieved?

The analysis finally turns to possible institutional explanations for democratic attitudes. Unlike in conventional macro-level studies, here political institutions are measured from a micro-level perspective. For example, do Africans prefer multiparty elections to other sets of rules for choosing leaders? Do they think that elections are adequate mechanisms for ejecting nonperforming politicians? Do they think the president ought to obey the constitution? Do they conclude that he actually does so?

Regardless of methodology, informal institutions are harder to observe than formal ones. Survey-based indicators are admittedly approximate and fail to capture the full dimensions of complex informal phenomena. But the following indicators represent a sustained effort to capture empirically some key, but slippery, concepts.

Clientelism is measured by an average construct of two related survey questions that ask respondents to "choose either A or B": first, either "A) As citizens, we should be more active in questioning our leaders," or "B) In our country these days, there is not enough respect for authority"; and second, either "A) Since leaders represent everyone, they should not favor their own family or group," or "B) Once in office, leaders are obliged to help their home community." I classify as clients those individuals expressing loyalty toward hometown patrons (in both cases option B).

The indicator of *corruption* is more straightforward: "How many national assembly representatives/local government councilors do you think are involved in corruption?" Regardless of actual levels of graft, those saying "most" or "all" perceive widespread official corruption.

In closing, *presidentialism*—ties of personal loyalty to a presidential "Big Man"—is probed with a question asking: "How much do you trust the President?" Those saying "a lot" or "completely" are taken to be complicit in the informal aspects of presidentialism because, even if the ruler oversteps his constitutional role, these individuals are likely to give him the benefit of the doubt.

Trends in Attitudes Toward Democracy

In 2005, a decade and a half after regime transitions began in earnest in Africa, a clear majority (62 percent) of citizens interviewed prefer democracy to any other kind of government. But is the term "democracy" broadly understood? Almost three-quarters (73 percent) of the more than 25,000 respondents to AB Round 3 could attach a meaning to the "d-word." And, among this better-informed group, 75 percent prefer a democratic regime.

People have the most confidence in democracy in Ghana, Kenya, and Senegal, all countries in which recent elections have brought about an alternation of ruling groups. But support for democracy is a minority sentiment in Madagascar, where leadership alternation was violently resisted by the last loser; and Tanzania, where many residents of the island of Zanzibar were unhappy with the outcome of the previous election. Low levels of support for democracy, however, should not be mistaken for support for a nondemocratic alternative, as large numbers say they "don't know" enough about regime alternatives (Tanzania) or have no regime preference (Madagascar).

To probe the depth of expressed democratic commitments, the survey asks people whether they harbor nostalgia for any of the autocratic forms of government previously common in Africa. Fully 73 percent of all Africans polled, for example, now reject military rule. Compared to the 62 percent who support democracy, this result suggests that feelings of hostility toward authoritarianism are more common than feelings of support for democracy. More people can specify the type of regime that they *do not* want than the kind of regime that they *do* desire. They may be attached to the general *idea* of democracy, but have limited knowledge of or commitment to its specific component *institutions*.

There is little relation between popular rejection of military rule and a country's experience. In those countries where no military coup has ever succeeded (Zambia, Kenya, and Zimbabwe), as well as in those where successful coups have led to long periods of praetorians in power (Ghana and Lesotho), more than four out of five people reject this regime. It is troubling to discover, however, that a majority of Namibians—a population with memories of strong-arm rule from apartheid-era South Africa but no other history of military intervention in politics—say that they would be unconcerned if "the army came in to govern the country."

Similarly, there is little connection between a legacy of single-party rule and its rejection today. With few exceptions, Africans everywhere now seem to prefer a plural polity: On average, 71 percent reject one-party rule. Citizens of Zimbabwe and Zambia have experienced de facto or de jure one-party monopolies, while people in Nigeria and Botswana have never experienced either. Yet at least four out of five respondents in all these countries reject one-party rule. Tanzanians remain more sympathetic to single-party rule than all other Africans, perhaps because the ruling Chama Cha Mapinduzi has always held power in Tanzania, bridging the one-party and multiparty eras. And the liberation-movement heritage in Mozambique, Namibia, and Uganda—and even in South Africa—leads significant minorities still to find appeal in the idea of a vanguard party.

Democracy's trajectory in Africa is reflected in trends in the levels of popular demand for various types of political regimes. Are prodemocratic attitudes rising or falling? In the twelve countries for which we have three observations, mass support for democracy has fallen slightly over the past six years, from 69 to 61 percent (see Table 1).[16]

The proportion of people who reject military rule has also dipped (from 82 to 73 percent). Because people continue to reject one-party and one-man rule—the latter at very high levels—the greatest threat to popular support for democracy appears to come from people who are beginning to feel nostalgia for military rule.

But these changes are evident only at the margins. As of our most recent observation in 2005, clear majorities were still dismissing military rule and backing democracy. Moreover, a half or more of all respondents have always rejected *all three* authoritarian alternatives. Finally, to the extent that people learn to be politically consistent—that is, by *simultaneously* rejecting all forms of autocracy *and* embracing democracy—*demand for democracy* is basically holding steady.

Lest we mistakenly take Africa-wide averages to be more representative than they really are, let us examine the cases of extreme change within countries. Popular support for democracy is down most sharply in Tanzania, perhaps because people are becoming confused about whether

TABLE 1—TRENDS IN ATTITUDES TO DEMOCRACY, 12 AFRICAN COUNTRIES, 2000–2005 (IN PERCENTAGES)

	CIRCA 2000	CIRCA 2002	CIRCA 2005
DEMAND			
Support democracy	69	62	61
Reject military rule	82	78	73
Reject one-party rule	69	66	70
Reject one-man rule	80	78	78
Reject all three authoritarian alternatives	59	50	52
Express demand for democracy*	44	37	46
Display political patience	46	56	56
SUPPLY			
Satisfied with democracy	58	52	46
Perceive extensive democracy	50	49	48
Perceive supply of democracy†	54	51	47
Expect democratic future	—	—	54

* reject all three authoritarian alternatives and also support democracy
† average of satisfaction with, and extent of, democracy

a one-party–dominant system is truly a democracy. But popular support is up by 10 percentage points in Lesotho, mainly because of the introduction between 1999 and 2002 of a more proportional electoral system. Because this institutional reform was the only major change between elections, herein lies *prima facie* case evidence that formal institutions are beginning to matter in building democratic attachments.[17]

Finally, the most promising sign for democracy's prospects concerns popular political patience. The survey question asked: "Choose either A or B: A) Our present system of elected government should be given more time to deal with inherited problems; or B) If our present system cannot produce results soon, we should try another form of government." The proportion selecting A—the patient option—actually rose and then stabilized (at 56 percent), suggesting that, even as some democratic commitments weaken with time, Africans are nonetheless willing to accept democracy, "warts and all."

Turning to the supply of democracy, many citizens are beginning to perceive that democracy has distinct shortcomings—"warts" if you will—that include defamatory political discourse, a poor record of service delivery, and new opportunities for corruption. These concerns are reflected in the sharply declining proportion of Africans interviewed who say that they are "satisfied with the way democracy works in [my country]." Down an average 13 percentage points (from 58 percent circa 2000 to 45 percent circa 2005), the direction of this trend applies to eight of the twelve countries for which the three observations are available.

Satisfaction with democracy has risen only in Ghana, Lesotho, Namibia, and South Africa. The continental average is pulled sharply downward by Nigeria, where satisfaction with democracy has collapsed by 58 percentage points in just six years—a steep decline that parallels popular approval of President Olusegun Obasanjo's job performance. Standing in sharp contrast to Nigeria is its smaller West African neighbor Ghana, where democracy's approval rating is up 16 percentage points. This again draws attention to formal political institutions such as Ghana's impressive and steadily improving national Electoral Commission, which has clearly helped democracy to consolidate in that country.

In 2005, for the first time, mass satisfaction with democracy dipped below 50 percent.[18] This means that in nine of the eighteen countries surveyed, fewer than half of all citizens were satisfied. In Madagascar, Malawi, Nigeria, and Zambia, those who approved of democracy's performance amounted to barely a quarter of the population. Judging by this yardstick, these were the Afrobarometer countries in which democracy was at greatest risk. And just 14 percent of Zimbabweans were satisfied with democracy's condition—a sign of just how far, under Robert Mugabe, that country has fallen from the ranks of Africa's open societies.

Several hopeful signs offset this bad news. First, as an alternate measure of democracy's health, the survey asked: "In your opinion, how much of a democracy is [your country] today?" This indicator—which we call the "extent of democracy"—has remained stable over the three rounds of surveys, with about half those interviewed continuing to say that they live in a reasonably high-quality democracy. An apparent slight decline is not statistically significant.

Second, our respondents expressed hope about the future stability of democracy. When asked for the first time in 2005, "In your opinion, how likely is it that [your country] will remain a democracy?" some 54 percent replied that they thought democracy was more likely than not to endure. Taken together with the positive finding about popular patience, these results suggest that Africans have not yet given up on democracy. Indeed, they seem to have emerged from the elated honeymoon of regime transition with the sober view that democracy is imperfect, but still better than the alternatives and thus worth keeping.

To conclude the description of recent trends, I want to make a passing comment about the reliability of the Afrobarometer data. If public opinion constitutes an accurate portrayal of real levels of and trends regarding democracy, then aggregate survey results should correlate with standard measures based on expert opinion. As a test, I compare AB assessments of the "extent of democracy" with the familiar Freedom House (FH) index. Figure 1 confirms that the different research methods tend to validate each other: The AB and FH country-level results correlate very closely (Pearson's r greater than 0.8); accordingly, most observations hug the same regression line. The few exceptions are minor: Zimbabweans tend

FIGURE 1—FREEDOM HOUSE SCORES BY
PERCEIVED EXTENT OF DEMOCRACY, 2005

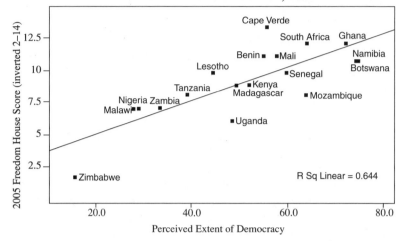

to see a little more democracy than do scholars, while the experts are slightly more sanguine about democracy in Cape Verde than that country's citizens. For the most part, however, ordinary Africans and specialists arrive at almost identical assessments.

Explaining Democratic Attitudes

If survey research says basically the same thing as expert opinion, why bother with the time and expense that surveys require? The reason is that survey data give us a fuller, more fine-grained picture. They permit us to peer below the country level to portray results by different social, economic, regional, and cultural groups. Survey data can also reveal *how* individuals arrive at their opinions, including via routes that run through formal as well as informal institutions.

For example: *Who* among the electorate *wants* democracy? When sociodemographic influences are regressed on *demand for democracy,* the results are revealing. Being a woman or living in a rural area suppresses demand. And aging raises it. Predictably, education is the most important social factor shaping demand for democracy, with an impact three times larger than age or habitat. Perhaps surprisingly, however, Muslims are *more* likely to demand democracy than adherents of other religions, though this result may reflect the inclusion in the Afrobarometer of Mali and Senegal, where democratic procedures readily coexist with moderate forms of Islam.

Take an even more interesting question: *On what basis* do Africans conclude that they are *getting* democracy? What institutional points of reference, if any, do they use? With the popularly perceived *extent of democracy* as the object to be explained, we can postulate that people will base this opinion on their assessments of the quality of political institutions, both formal and informal. Previous analysis has shown that the two most powerful attitudinal predictors of the extent of democracy concern a formal political institution (whether citizens see the last election as "free and fair") and an informal personal tie (whether citizens trust the incumbent national president).[19]

Do the qualities of these institutions continue to predict the supply of democracy circa 2005? And which is the more important: the formal or the informal institution? Model 1 in Table 2 shows the powerful impacts of *both* formal elections *and* informal trust. In a regression analysis, the qualities of these two institutions together predict a third of the variance in popular estimates of the extent of democracy (see adjusted R square). This compares favorably with the 8 percent of variance that is explained by a respondent's education, which is usually held to be a strong predictor of democratic attitudes.[20]

Indeed, the quality of national elections seems to be the principal standard by which ordinary Africans judge their country's degree of democracy. But people also look for excellence in leadership. They must trust the incumbent president before they will judge that democracy is taking root.

Strikingly, the formal institution seems to matter more than the informal one. Here we have additional, cross-national evidence that the rules of democracy (that is, high-quality elections) are formative for popular regime assessments. This finding casts doubt on Staffan Lindberg's assertion that *any* kind of election, regardless of quality, will strengthen the regime.[21] But since this finding also contradicts conventional wisdom about the weakness of institutions in Africa, it must be explored and tested further. To that end, we note that when the impact of the same two predictors is tracked over time, we find citizens' judgment that elections have been "free and fair" accounting for a larger proportion of the explained variance in "extent of democracy" in 2005 (64 percent) than was the case in 2002 (59 percent). Because the explanatory power of the official institution increased significantly from 2002 to 2005, we can tentatively infer that formal rules are gradually displacing informal ones in the public mind.

As a set of formal institutions, however, democracy consists of more than elections alone. Do Africans also endorse the full array of democracy's component institutions? Here we consider four formal institutions, including elections.

First, the Africans we interviewed overwhelmingly prefer to "choose leaders through regular, open and honest *elections*" rather than "adopt other methods." Over time, this preference has held steady among four out of five respondents, and is especially strong in Ghana and Benin. In my opinion, popular support for open elections is now an institutionalized norm of African politics.

FIGURE 2—FORMAL INSTITUTIONS: POPULAR DEMAND VERSUS
PERCEIVED SUPPLY, 18 AFRICAN COUNTRIES, 2005 (IN PERCENTAGES)

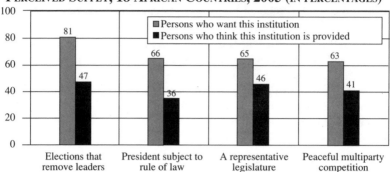

Second, competitive elections imply support for another formal institution of democracy: *multiple political parties*. People say that they prefer
"many political parties . . . to make sure [they] have real choices in who
governs them" versus finding multiparty competition "unnecessary . . .
[because] parties create division and confusion." Abandoning earlier reservations, publics approved of multiple parties at a rate that shot up by an
average of 12 percentage points over the three short years from 2002 to
2005, with even greater increases appearing in Lesotho and Zimbabwe.

Third, Africans want their executive presidents held accountable,
at least to *parliament*. A gradually rising proportion of citizens—two-
thirds by 2005—require that "the members of parliament (rather than the
president) make laws." This sentiment is most widespread in Senegal and
Mozambique.

Finally, the only formal democratic institution that may be losing support is the rule of law. The proportion that wants the president to "obey the
laws and the courts, even if he thinks they are wrong," has recently fallen
from three-quarters to two-thirds of all respondents. But this anomalous
result may simply be an artifact of a change in the wording of a question
that earlier had made explicit reference to constitutional term limits on
presidents.

On balance, therefore, growing numbers of Africans seem to support
several key political institutions that constitute the formal foundation of
a democratic regime. But is this progress on the demand side (the institutions that people *want*) matched by equal satisfaction on the supply side
(the institutions that people *get*)?

Figure 2 suggests that Africans are not getting the institutions they
want. While 81 percent call for open elections, just 47 percent think
that elections actually "enable voters to remove leaders from office."
Whereas 66 percent wish to subject the president to the rule of law, a
mere 36 percent believe that, in practice, the president "never ignores
the constitution." While a similar two-thirds demand a representative

TABLE 2—EXPLAINING THE PERCEIVED EXTENT OF DEMOCRACY:
FORMAL AND INFORMAL INSTITUTIONS

	MODEL 1	MODEL 2
Constant	1.314*	2.615*
FORMAL INSTITUTIONS		
Free and fair elections	.427*	
Elections that remove leaders		.033†
Peaceful multiparty competition		.045*
A representative legislature		.121*
President subject to rule of law		.097*
INFORMAL INSTITUTIONS		
Clientelism		.033*
Corruption		-.121*
Trust in the president	.242*	.255*
Adjusted R square	.330	.187

Unless otherwise indicated in row heading, cell entries are standardized regression coefficients (beta).
* p<.001, † p<.01

legislature, fewer than half think they have actually elected a parliament that "reflect(s) the views of voters." Finally, while a clear majority (63 percent) yearns for peaceful multiparty competition, a large minority (41 percent) still fears that, in reality, "competition between political parties leads to violent conflict."

Because the performance of all formal institutions systematically falls short of popular expectations, we postulate that people will seek to make up for perceived institutional deficiencies by counting on the informal ties characteristic of clientelism, corruption, and presidentialism—each of which represents a dimension of neopatrimonial rule. Some 28 percent of Africans interviewed exhibited clientelist tendencies when they agreed that they should "respect [the] authority" of leaders who "help their home communities." Twenty-six percent of respondents thought "all" or "most" MPs and local councilors to be "involved in corruption." And, as before, the 64 percent of adults who say that they trust the incumbent president "somewhat" or "a lot" give us a sense of the personal ties that underlie presidentialism.

To weigh the relative importance of specific institutions in shaping the perceived extent of democracy, I enter all four formal institutions and all three informal institutions into a more comprehensive regression analysis (see Model 2 in Table 2). Based on the size and the signs of the regression coefficients, we arrive at several interesting conclusions.

First, once a full range of institutions is considered, an informal linkage stands out. People are most likely to judge the extent of democracy in terms of their trust in the incumbent president. The evidence therefore suggests that African politics has not yet moved fully from the realm of personalities and factions to the realm of policies and formal institutions.

Second, other informal institutions perform as expected: Clientelism (in the form of loyalty to hometown patrons) has a positive effect on the perceived extent of democracy; but the perception that elected leaders are corrupt has an effect that is strongly negative. Our data therefore confirm theoretical claims that informal institutions can have either positive or negative effects as regards democracy. In this light, clientelism and corruption are best viewed as two sides of the same coin of distributive politics: Citizens defer to authority when they benefit materially, but question and condemn their leaders when benefits accrue to others, especially political elites.[22]

Third, all formal institutions are statistically significant, reaffirming that—if effectively applied—written rules can help to form popular attachments to democracy. Among the four formal institutions that we have considered, however, a representative legislature seems to have the most effect on ordinary people's judgments of democratic progress. We conclude, therefore, that Africans demand *more* than clean elections. They also require that their leaders spend the time between elections being responsive to popular needs and accepting accountability for their performance in office.

The Institutionalization of Democracy in Africa

Is democracy becoming institutionalized in Africa? It is, if only in part. A decade and a half after the first African regime transitions and despite growing popular disillusionment with democracy in practice, the general *idea* of "rule by the people" remains an attractive prospect for solid majorities of citizens. But popular attachment to the specific *institutions* of a democratic regime—and how willing citizens feel to apply formal criteria of institutional development to the evaluation of regime performance—is a much more varied and tentative matter.

Survey research suggests that regular, open elections are now an institutionalized feature of African politics. Ordinary people use the quality of elections—are they "free and fair"?—as the main gauge of democracy's development in their countries. Moreover, the reform of electoral institutions—for example, the introduction of a proportional electoral system in Lesotho and the creation of an effective electoral commission in Ghana—can have additional positive effects.

Yet even as elections take root, people still question the competitiveness of formal institutions. Many harbor doubts that elections can bring about alternations of incumbent presidents and ruling parties, while others are realizing that an "electoral" democracy alone does not ensure the presence of a responsive and accountable leadership between elections.

Public support for such other formal institutions of democracy as multiple parties, independent courts, and assertive legislatures lags behind support for elections. In addition, the supply of all formal institutions fails to meet popular demands. People continue to think that presidents ignore constitutions, that legislatures fail to represent popular desires, and that multiparty competition all too easily spills over into political violence. As such, Africans estimate that the key elements in a well-functioning democracy—notably institutions that check the executive—are performing below par.

Because formal rules mandating public accountability are persistently weak, people turn to other standards for judging the extent of democratic growth. Informal values and patterns of behavior continue to shape Africans' orientations toward their respective polities. When asked to appraise the quality of democracy in their own countries, citizens still fall back on personal ties of trust—especially trust in the "Big Man" president who continues to personify the government and the regime. As long as loyal clients are rewarded by the distribution of material benefits, informal ties can help to generate legitimacy for a democratic regime. But if political elites monopolize available resources, then citizens tend to see corruption, an informal institution that is clearly corrosive to democracy.

NOTES

1. James March and Johan Olsen, "The New Institutionalism: Organizational Factors in Political Life," *American Political Science Review* 78 (September 1984): 734–49. See also their "Elaborating the 'New Institutionalism,'" in R.A.W. Rhodes, Sarah Binder, and Bert Rockman, eds., *The Oxford Handbook of Political Institutions* (Oxford: Oxford University Press, 2006).

2. Douglass C. North, *Institutions, Institutional Change and Economic Performance* (New York: Cambridge University Press, 1990), 4.

3. H.W.O. Okoth-Ogendo, "Constitutions Without Constitutionalism: Reflections on an African Political Paradox," in Issa Shivji, ed., *The State and Constitutionalism: An African Debate on Democracy* (Harare: SAPES Trust, 1991), 3–25.

4. Samuel P. Huntington, *Political Order in Changing Societies* (New Haven: Yale University Press, 1968), 12.

5. Donald L. Horowitz, *A Democratic South Africa? Constitutional Engineering in a Divided Society* (Berkeley: University of California Press, 1991).

6. Andrew Reynolds, *Electoral Systems and Democratization in Southern Africa* (Oxford: Oxford University Press, 1999).

7. Daniel N. Posner, *Institutions and Ethnic Politics in Africa* (New York: Cambridge University Press, 2005). See also his article with Daniel J. Young, "The Institutionalization of Political Power in Africa," *Journal of Democracy* 18 (July 2007): 126–40.

8. Goran Hyden, *African Politics in Comparative Perspective* (New York: Cambridge University Press, 2006), 7 and 78.

9. René Lemarchand, "Political Clientelism and Ethnicity in Tropical Africa: Competing Solidarities in Nation-Building," *American Political Science Review* 66 (February 1972): 91–112.

10. Sahr J. Kpundeh, "Corruption and Corruption Control," in E. Gyimah-Boadi, ed., *Democratic Reform in Africa: The Quality of Progress* (Boulder, Colo.: Lynne Rienner, 2004), 121.

11. Nicolas van de Walle, "Presidentialism and Clientelism in Africa's Emerging Party Systems," *Journal of Modern African Studies* 41 (June 2003): 310.

12. Guillermo O'Donnell, "Another Institutionalization: Latin America and Elsewhere," Kellogg Institute Working Paper No. 222, University of Notre Dame, 1996.

13. Gretchen Helmke and Steven Levitsky, *Informal Institutions and Democracy: Lessons from Latin America* (Baltimore: Johns Hopkins University Press, 2006).

14. Afrobarometer surveys are based on randomly selected national probability samples ranging in size from 1,200 to 2,400 respondents per country and representing a cross-section of citizens in each country aged 18 years or older. Samples are selected from the best available census frames and yield a margin of sampling error of no more than plus or minus three percentage points at a 95 percent confidence level. All interviews are conducted face-to-face by trained fieldworkers in the language of the respondent's choice. Response rates average above 80 percent.

15. Benin, Botswana, Cape Verde, Ghana, Kenya, Lesotho, Madagascar, Malawi, Mali, Mozambique, Namibia, Nigeria, Senegal, South Africa, Tanzania, Uganda, Zambia, and Zimbabwe. Zimbabwe is included since, at the time of the first survey in 1999, it was still a relatively open society. Uganda is also covered because, even in the country's conflict-wracked northern zones, survey research has proven possible.

16. The figure of 61 percent diverges from the previously reported average of 62 percent because it refers to only 12 countries. AB does not yet have three observations for all 18 countries.

17. For in-depth analysis, see Wonbin Cho and Michael Bratton, "Electoral Institutions, Partisan Status, and Political Support in Lesotho," *Electoral Studies* 25 (December 2006): 731–50.

18. Although only 46 percent expressed high levels of satisfaction ("fairly" plus "very" satisfied), even fewer (36 percent) expressed low levels ("not very" and "not at all").

19. Calculated from AB Round 1 data. See also Michael Bratton, Robert Mattes, and E. Gyimah-Boadi, *Public Opinion, Democracy and Market Reform in Africa* (New York: Cambridge University Press, 2005), 278.

20. Because educated people have developed their critical faculties, education is negative for the perceived extent of democracy, whereas the institutional indicators are positive.

21. Staffan Lindberg, *Democracy and Elections in Africa* (Baltimore: Johns Hopkins University Press, 2006).

22. I am indebted to E. Gyimah-Boadi for helping me think through this puzzle. Other useful comments from Wonbin Cho, Adrienne LeBas, and Daniel Posner were received gratefully.

9

THE "ALTERNATION EFFECT" IN AFRICA

Michael Bratton

Michael Bratton is University Distinguished Professor of Political Science and African Studies at Michigan State University. He is also founder and director of the Afrobarometer, a collaborative international survey-research project that measures public opinion regarding democracy, markets, and civil society in eighteen African countries. This essay originally appeared in the October 2004 issue of the Journal of Democracy.

More than a decade has passed since the third wave of global democratization broke on Africa's shores. This African wave came to world attention in February 1990, when the South African apartheid government decided to lift the ban on the African National Congress and release Nelson Mandela from three decades of imprisonment. Only four years later, vast crowds cheered Mandela's presidential inauguration as the new nation's multicolored flag replaced the hated banner of the apartheid state. And in 1999, young Nigerians danced in the streets to celebrate the downfall of a brutal military dictatorship and to welcome a new civilian regime.

Mass public celebrations have often greeted the ouster of longstanding authoritarians and the birth of democracy at the polls. But how long does such enthusiasm last? Are Africans' preferences for democratic government enduring or ephemeral?[1] This essay reports that, consistent with trends in other world regions, mass democratic commitments in Africa are far from fixed. Instead, popular support for democracy tends to drift downward over time. Reassuringly, however, it seems that Africans' commitment to democracy can be refreshed by alternations in power by way of elections.

In short, there are signs of an incipient pattern in the evolution of public opinion in Africa's new democracies. Mass political optimism invariably marks the immediate aftermath of founding elections, and the public mood is especially buoyant in countries where the preceding regime has been deeply repressive—as in South Africa and Nigeria. Indeed, landmark democratic transitions often generate rashly unrealistic expectations about the benefits that democracy will bring. But on the "morning after," initial popular exuberance dissipates. If political life reverts to familiar patterns, people begin to question the desirability and quality of the new order, and they tend to sober up sharply if elected elites betray their popular mandate by indulging in corrupt or manipulative behavior. In cases where a rotten team of incumbents survives subsequent elections, it does not take long until the general public becomes disillusioned with democracy.

Can alternations in power restore popular faith in democracy? More than any other political event, a peaceful vote and subsequent transfer of power from one group to another should serve in the public mind to validate "rule by the people." But in reality, does electoral alternation help to relegitimize democracy?

Surveys of public opinion in Africa offer an opportunity to test whether the election of new ruling parties can in fact reinvigorate stalling attitudes toward democracy. This essay draws upon data from the Afrobarometer—a comparative series of public attitude surveys on democracy, market reform, and civil society.[2] The first round of surveys took place between July 1999 and October 2001, and covered more than 21,000 adult citizens in 12 countries. The second round reached more than 23,000 persons in 15 countries between June 2002 and October 2003. In each round, trained fieldworkers conducted face-to-face interviews in a local language of the respondent's choice. For the sake of consistency, however, the key term of "democracy" was expressed in a national language, whether English, French, Portuguese, or Swahili. By this standard, an average of more than three-quarters of the respondents in the surveys' randomly selected national samples was able to attach a meaning to the term.

In order to arrive at reliable conclusions about trends in public opinion, analysts generally prefer to have at least three observations, separated by intervals of several years. Otherwise, momentary shifts in volatile attitudes—or mere measurement errors—may be misinterpreted as lasting changes in the public mood. Because so far only two observations are available for most countries in the Afrobarometer, we take several precautions to diminish the chances of arriving at faulty conclusions: We note if interview questions change between surveys, we break down Afrobarometer "averages" by country, and we draw attention only to differences of 10 percentage points or more. For any given Afrobarometer survey the margin of sampling error is plus or minus 3 points, which doubles to 6 points when two surveys are compared. Therefore, we use an even larger margin—at least 10 percentage points—before speculating about changes in public opinion.

This essay reports a few preliminary differences in popular attitudes toward democracy between Afrobarometer Rounds 1 and 2. As with similar analyses,[3] two familiar clusters of attitudes are examined: On the demand side, we review popular support for democracy and rejection of

FIGURE 1—SUPPORT FOR DEMOCRACY
BY COUNTRY, OVER TIME

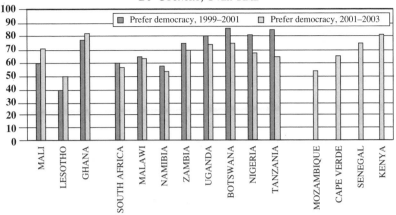

authoritarian rule; on the supply side, the analysis concerns mass satisfaction with democracy and estimates of democracy's extent. Moreover, on a continent where little is known about public opinion, we find it worth announcing early warnings about attitude stability or change, even if these are tentative. Until more data is collected over a longer period, however, we resist proclaiming firm conclusions about general trends.

Democracy Yes, Authoritarianism No?

To gauge support for democracy, survey respondents were asked a standard question: "Which of these statements is closest to your own opinion? a) Democracy is preferable to any other form of government; b) In some circumstances a nondemocratic government can be preferable; c) For someone like me, it doesn't matter what kind of government we have." In the 12 countries covered by Afrobarometer Round 1, an average of 69 percent expressed a preference for democracy.[4] In Round 2, that figure slipped to 63 percent for the 11 countries covered in both rounds and to 64 percent for all 15 countries.

This slight decline of 5 or 6 percentage points falls within the margin of sampling error for survey comparisons, and does not meet our 10-point standard for inferring a real change in public opinion. Thus, while we can surmise that popular support for democracy is more likely to have fallen than risen, the survey results do not show proof of serious erosion in democracy's support base in the surveyed countries between 1999 and 2003. The surveys also suggest that attrition was mostly due to individuals shifting from expressing support for democracy to saying "don't know."[5] From that finding, we infer that the emerging African democracies have not matched popular expectations, causing some people to doubt the desirability of the new order.[6]

The picture sharpens when the data are broken down by country. The three clusters of countries that appear in Figure 1 each represent different findings. In the first group, which includes Mali, Lesotho, and Ghana, popular support for democracy is increasing—by as much as 10 percentage points in Mali and Lesotho. Support for democracy in Lesotho rose from a low 40 percent in 2000 to a somewhat more robust 50 percent in 2003. In the intervening period, the country adopted a more representative electoral system and, in May 2002, conducted peaceful legislative elections. It is likely that growing support for democracy among people in Lesotho can be attributed to their satisfaction with the electoral reforms that ended one-party control of the legislature and opened its doors to minority parties. But gains in democratic support in Lesotho are offset by an equally large increase in the segment of the population that regards nondemocratic government as acceptable under certain circumstances. In Ghana, we find a much more consistent attachment to democracy: Four out of five Ghanaians declare it their preferred form of government while concomitantly dismissing all forms of authoritarianism.

In the second group of countries in Figure 1, support for democracy seems to be fading. In three of these eight cases, the drop is 10 percentage points or more. In Nigeria, support went down 14 points between 2000 and 2003, while the share of respondents who said they might be willing to accept military or other nondemocratic rule more than doubled from 9 to 19 percent. In this country, democracy's loss was clearly autocracy's gain. Despite this negative trend, two-thirds of the surveyed Nigerians still supported democracy in 2003—a level close to the cross-national average.

In the third cluster, which includes Mozambique, Cape Verde, Kenya, and Senegal, we cannot comment on change because we have data only from one observation. A 2001 pilot survey in Mozambique, however, found 58 percent support for democracy. In 2002, when a full Afrobarometer survey was first completed, that number had slipped to 54 percent. Counting Mozambique, three times as many African countries—9 out of 12—experienced declines in support for democracy as underwent increases.

As Africans learn about democracy, do they still harbor nostalgia for strong government? We probed reactions to several nondemocratic alternatives that Africans have experienced in recent years: military rule, one-man rule, and one-party rule. Three questions were posed: "There are many ways to govern a country. Would you approve or disapprove of the following? a) The army comes in to govern the country; b) Elections and parliament are abolished so that the president can decide everything; c) Only one political party is allowed to stand for election and hold office."[7]

As with prodemocratic opinion, anti-authoritarian sentiments dropped slightly between the two Afrobarometer survey rounds. But none of these changes was ever greater than the margin of sampling error for survey

FIGURE 2—NUMBER OF AUTHORITARIAN ALTERNATIVES REJECTED
ROUND 1 (1999–2001) VERSUS ROUND 2 (2002–2003)

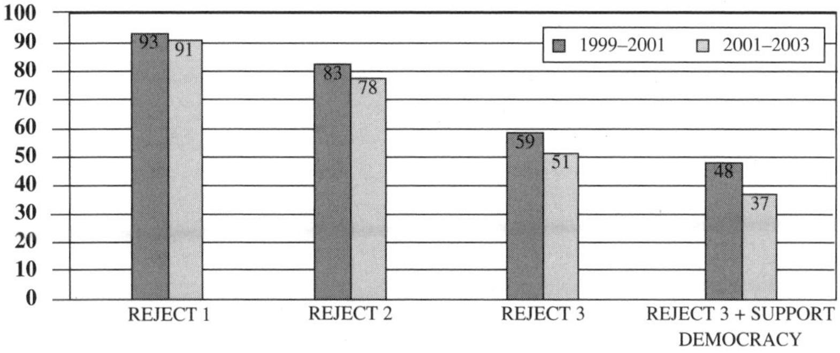

comparisons: On average, the number of people rejecting military rule fell 5 points (from 82 to 77 percent) and the number rejecting presidential dictatorship, 4 points (from 80 to 76 percent). The average proportion rejecting one-party government was generally lower, and dropped a barely perceptible 2 points (from 69 to 67 percent). Against the backdrop of these numbers, it is noteworthy that at least two-thirds of all Africans surveyed continued to reject each authoritarian alternative.

We find that the results of Round 2 confirm our Round 1 findings: Africans have grown thoroughly weary of military rule and presidential dictatorship; more of them reject military and personal autocracies than support democracy; yet many remain willing to accept one-party rule. Nostalgia for a single-party state is most prevalent where national-liberation movements have long dominated politics, as in Mozambique, where only 42 percent—a minority of the electorate—rejects the one-party state (other examples are Namibia and Uganda).

Attention must be drawn to an important decline in the compound attitude that we call "demand for democracy." It taps the depth of popular democratic commitment by testing whether individuals who say they support democracy also reject all three (military, one-party, or presidential) forms of authoritarian rule. The logic of this construct is that individuals who pay lip service to democracy must also demonstrate sincerity by discarding any residual longings for strong government. As Figure 2 shows, it is also easy for Africans to reject at least one form of autocracy, as do on average 91 percent. But anti-authoritarian sentiments are actually extremely shallow, as evidenced by the rapid decay in the number of people who reject *multiple* forms of autocracy. Just 51 percent, barely half of all survey respondents, reject all three.

Even more shocking is that fewer than half the respondents demand democracy *and* reject authoritarianism. In Round 1, just 48 percent manifested this deep commitment, mainly because of the continuing popular appeal of the one-party model. By the end of 2003, the proportion of the population that was both prodemocratic *and* fully anti-authoritarian had

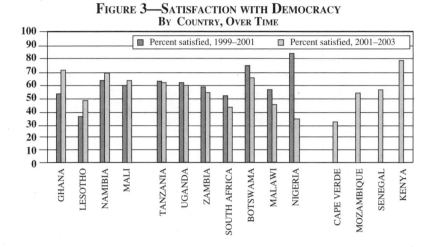

FIGURE 3—SATISFACTION WITH DEMOCRACY
BY COUNTRY, OVER TIME

slumped sharply to a mere 37 percent overall. In other words, we estimate that just over one-third of survey respondents are deeply committed to democracy. Shallow democratic commitments, it seems, can indeed erode with unsettling speed.

Evaluating the Delivery of Democracy

Turning from the demand side to the supply side, we inquired about the delivery of democracy in the surveyed countries. The first question is standard: "Overall, how satisfied are you with the way democracy works in your country?"[8] The decrease in democratic attitudes reappears, this time among those on the "satisfied" side of the scale: Whether measured across the original 11 countries or the expanded sample of 15 countries, satisfaction with democracy stood at 54 percent by 2003, down from 58 percent earlier. This apparent change arose mainly from the recent disappointment of those who were once "very satisfied" and an increase in those who are "not very satisfied." Popular satisfaction with democracy is therefore becoming more moderate, as people's initial optimistic hopes are confronted with the harsh realities of post-transitional governance. The "fairly satisfied" group remains unchanged at 37 percent in Round 1 and 2; in this case, Round 2 data serve to confirm the Afrobarometer's original findings.

As Figure 3 demonstrates, Ghana and Nigeria represent the extremes. Between 1999 and 2002 in Ghana, satisfaction with democracy rose 18 points—one of the largest attitude shifts detected so far (though the figure may be inflated by the exclusion of "don't know" responses).[9] The change is most likely real, and due to the peaceful alternation of ruling parties that occurred in the December 2000 elections, widely regarded as free and fair. Ghanaians have since given the new government high marks for economic management and reconfirmed their patience with its economic-reform program, which indicates that they are relatively content with the performance of the ruling party in particular and the political regime in general.

The trend in Nigeria leads in the opposite direction. Satisfaction with democracy plummeted from 84 percent in January 2000, soon after the restoration of civilian rule, to 35 percent in October 2003, in the wake of President Olusegun Obasanjo's reelection. (An August 2001 intermediate survey showed a middling level of satisfaction—57 percent.) Nigerians probably wanted this former army general to serve as an interim leader during the country's transition from military to civilian rule, but he ignored popular preferences and eventually chose to run for a second term. In this case, the Afrobarometer's findings confirm a straight downward trend in the population's satisfaction with democracy. So it appears that, even as average satisfaction with democracy holds steady across the continent, there is considerable volatility within certain countries.

How much democracy do Africans think they are getting? In the Afrobarometer surveys, the perceived extent of democracy is tapped by a distinctive question: "In your opinion, how much of a democracy is your country today? Is it a full democracy, a democracy with minor problems, a democracy with major problems, or not a democracy at all?" As a quick yardstick of regime consolidation—at least as viewed from a popular perspective—we have yet to find a better single indicator.

As Figure 4 shows, the perceived extent of democracy rose slightly between the two surveys. In Round 1, 50 percent rated their country a viable democracy (either "full democracy" or "minor problems"); in Round 2, some 54 percent felt that way. Although this shift represents the first slight increase we have detected in attitudes toward democracy, we recognize that a 4-point difference could readily be due to sampling error across surveys. Moreover, among the 11 countries sampled in both surveys, we find *no* change in the perceived extent of democracy. The incremental gain is rather a result of political exuberance in the four new countries included in Round 2—in 2003, an optimistic 76 percent of Kenyans rated their new democratic regime a viable democracy. The safest general assumption, therefore, is that the perceived extent of democracy among Africans has remained constant in the period covered by the Afrobarometer.

As was the case regarding satisfaction with democracy, however, it appears that people have begun to tone down favorable judgments. As they learn about the performance of elected governments, they become more skeptical about democracy's consolidation. A clear plurality of respondents (37 percent) regards their country, perhaps realistically, as "a democracy with minor problems." The 10-point upsurge in this category is nearly proportionate to the decrease in the "full democracy" category, which leads us to assume that Africans are recognizing, in the aftermath of transition euphoria, that real democracies are often imperfect.

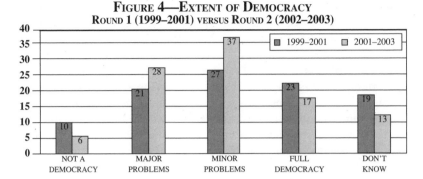

FIGURE 4—EXTENT OF DEMOCRACY
ROUND 1 (1999–2001) VERSUS ROUND 2 (2002–2003)

While it may seem that the perceived extent of democracy has hardly changed at the cross-national level, stark contrasts appear at the country level. In five countries—Ghana, Lesotho, Mali, Tanzania, and Uganda—people tend to believe that the extent of democracy is slowly increasing with time. In six other countries—Botswana, Malawi, Namibia, Nigeria, South Africa, and Zambia—people see emerging deficits in the delivery of democracy. Volatility is greater on this specific attitude than any of the others, with temporal changes in 10 of 11 countries (all except Namibia) exceeding 10 percentage points.

On the upside, Mali displays a sharp rise, with the proportion of respondents seeing an almost or completely "full" democracy increasing by 18 points (from 45 to 63 percent). While Malians are learning about democracy—as indicated by the declining number of "don't knows"—it also seems that the May 2002 electoral alternation further induced people to regard any problems with democracy as "minor" rather than "major." At the other extreme, Malawi registered the largest decline in the perceived extent of democracy: a 24-point drop between 1999 and 2003. During this period, former president Bakili Muluzi sought an unconstitutional third term, accusations of official corruption multiplied, and the country suffered a crippling food crisis. The perceived extent of democracy also slumped in Zambia, where the number of people rating the country a "full democracy" dropped 15 percentage points, and the number of people seeing "major problems" went up 22 percentage points. In the period between surveys, Zambians experienced elections (in December 2000) in which no presidential candidate or political party won a majority and where accusations of electoral fraud abounded.

The Alternation Effect

When discussing the role of elections in the fate of new democracies, one has to consider Samuel P. Huntington's "two-turnover test."[10] The logic behind the test is that democracies can be regarded as consolidated only if governments can routinely be removed by electoral means, and the only reliable indicator that they can be removed is that they *have* been removed. Huntington argues that after two cycles of peaceful leadership replacement, most political actors have both won and lost without revolting, which indicates that they have accepted the rules of the electoral game. While he goes too far in reducing democratic consolidation to electoral alternation—after all, institutions other than elections are required for democracy's long-term stability—it may be that a turnover in power has the salutary effect of restoring public faith in democracy. If so, elections are more than mere formalities, and their regular conduct is central to democratization. In addition to infusing government with new blood, elections may contribute to the maturation of nascent democratic cultures.

To illustrate this idea, we conducted a brief test. For each country surveyed in both Afrobarometer rounds, we calculated the number of months elapsed from that country's last electoral alternation of ruling parties, counting backward from December 2003. The resulting variable ranged from 19 months (to the May 2002 elections in Mali and Lesotho) to 169 months (to Namibia's founding election of November 1989). In Tanzania and Uganda, countries that have never changed ruling parties by way of elections, we calculated the months elapsed since their founding competitive elections. In Malawi, Namibia, South Africa, and Zambia, the first present-era multiparty contest led to a leadership turnover. While these countries have not seen any subsequent alternation of ruling parties, Malawi and Zambia at least experienced a change of presidents due to constitutional term limits, and Nelson Mandela decided to leave office before a second term. (We excluded Botswana and Zimbabwe from the test since the transition to multiparty democracy occurred in these countries long before the third wave reached Africa.)[11]

In estimating the effects of electoral alternation on mass attitudes to democracy, the independent variable was the passage of time since the last electoral alternation, and the dependent variables were the amount of change in each attitude discussed in this article. As expected, we found that the passage of time was negatively related to *every* positive trend in democratic attitudes—on both the demand and supply sides.[12] In other words, the farther back in the past an electoral alternation (or, failing that, a transition to competitive elections) had occurred, the more disillusioned people were with democracy. By contrast, the more recent these defining political events, the more optimistic citizens tended to be.

This argument is particularly well demonstrated by changing attitudes toward the extent of democracy. Figure 5 shows a very strong relationship between the proximity of an electoral alternation and shifts in the amount of democracy people perceive in their country. At one extreme, Ghana, Lesotho, and Mali all underwent a turnover of ruling parties via multiparty elections in the course of the last three years. Accordingly, the average citizen in these countries perceives substantial increases in

FIGURE 5—CHANGE IN EXTENT OF DEMOCRACY
THE EFFECT OF ELECTORAL ALERNATION

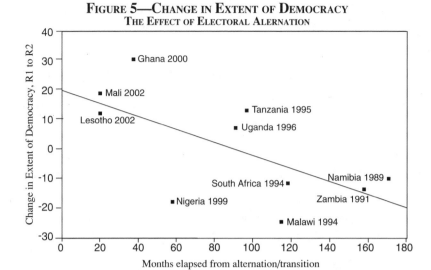

the extent of democracy. In every case, the margin of change exceeds 10 percentage points—and was as high as 30 points in Ghana. At the other extreme, a decade or more has elapsed since an alternation of ruling parties at the polls in Malawi, Namibia, Zambia, and even South Africa. As expected, citizens of these countries perceive that the extent of democracy is in decline. Again, the margin of change always exceeds 10 percentage points—and reaches 24 points in Malawi.

Our argument that electoral alternation benefits democratic culture also appears to hold in countries for which we have only one round of data. Elections in Senegal and Kenya led to a switch of ruling parties in April 2001 and December 2002, respectively, and their populations now perceive more democracy than the cross-national average. Moreover, consistent with the closer temporal proximity of Kenya's election, the perceived extent of democracy was at the time of the survey higher there than in Senegal (76 versus 58 percent).

These results suggest an electoral cycle in the evolution of public opinion, especially with regard to perceptions of the supply of democracy. At first, transitions to multiparty democracy generate optimism, even in the absence of alternation. Thereafter, initial commitments to democracy gradually deteriorate, often in response to disappointing government performance. But democratic legitimacy can be renewed, either by improved policy performance or by the replacement of an underperforming government at the polls.

These findings are encouraging, but there is also a negative side. To begin with, a change in ruling parties remains a rare occurrence in African political life. Since the flood of founding elections in the early 1990s, only six of the 32 presidential elections held in the 15 countries covered by Afrobarometer Round 2 have resulted in alternations in power.[13] Much as before, dominant parties tend to cruise to reelection; they sometimes even succeed in installing handpicked presidential successors without ever losing power.

Moreover, the positive dividend of electoral alternation does not fully offset the possibility that public opinion regarding democracy may be trending downward. The occasional ruling-party turnover has not prevented prodemocratic attitudes from settling at levels somewhat lower than those which followed Africa's landmark transitions. Assuming that there was no sampling error, popular support for democracy in Africa declined between 1999 and 2003 at about the same rate as such support did in Latin America between 1996 and 2002.[14] And judging by the Latin American experience, it could drop even lower in the future.[15] Neither continent matches the gains of Eastern Europe, where support for the postcommunist democratic regimes actually rose between 1991 and 1995, before returning to original levels by 1998.[16]

Moreover, democratic preferences are not evenly distributed *within* the surveyed countries. For example, supporters of the party that won the last election tend to be the most overoptimistic, and are strongly inclined to perceive a greater supply of democracy than those who voted for the party that lost the election.[17] Yet the "winners" are less likely than the "losers" to express deep commitment to democracy by explicitly demanding a democratic government.[18] On one hand, losers seem to cling to the hope that democracy will eventually end their political exclusion; on the other hand, winners are especially shallow democrats, whose attachment to democracy lasts only as long as they remain in power.

At the level of the individual, the downward trend in democratic commitment implies that as ordinary people learn about democracy, they are less likely to harbor unattainable expectations about what a new set of leaders can achieve. Africans seem to be realizing that while democracy provides a voice in decision making, it does not automatically deliver social renewal and economic recovery. At the country level, fading democratic support runs counter to conventional hopes that democracy becomes consolidated as more and more citizens take it as their own. The survey participants' relatively shallow and short-lived commitment to democracy does not bode well for the development of an African culture of democracy. In this context, elections that lead to change in ruling parties offer one of democracy's best present hopes in Africa.

NOTES

1. "Key Findings on Public Opinion in Africa," Afrobarometer Briefing Paper 1 (April 2002), available at *www.afrobarometer.org*.

2. The Afrobarometer project is a joint enterprise of the Institute for Democracy in South Africa (Idasa), the Center for Democratic Development (CDD-Ghana), and Michigan

State University (MSU). Hence I use a collective "we" in describing methods and reporting results.

3. Michael Bratton, Robert Mattes, and E. Gyimah-Boadi, *Public Opinion, Democracy, and Market Reform in Africa* (New York: Cambridge University Press, 2004).

4. Averages are calculated on pooled data, weighted to standardize each national sample to N=1200. That is, each country carries equal weight in aggregate means, regardless of sample size or overall population.

5. That is, more people were unable to choose between the available response options and could not proffer any answer.

6. The increase in "don't know" responses also derives from persons in Ghana and Botswana who did not recognize the word "democracy" in English. Comparisons may be affected by this change of question wording between Rounds 1 and 2.

7. Response categories form a five-point scale from "disapprove strongly" through "disapprove," "neither," and "approve," to "approve strongly." In the text and figures, summary figures for rejection of authoritarian rule combine "disapprove" and "disapprove strongly."

8. Response categories form a four-point scale from "not at all satisfied" through "not very satisfied" and "fairly satisfied" to "very satisfied." In the text and figures, summary figures for satisfaction combine "fairly" and "very."

9. See endnote 5.

10. Samuel P. Huntington, *The Third Wave: Democratization in the Late Twentieth Century* (Norman: University of Oklahoma Press, 1991), 266–67.

11. These outlying cases tend to cancel each other out: While Botswana undermines the argument that democratic attitudes decline in the absence of alternation, the case of Zimbabwe embodies it.

12. Always significant, the correlation coefficients (Pearson's r) ranged from -.081 for change in satisfaction with democracy to -.665 for change in the perceived extent of democracy.

13. In Lesotho and South Africa, we counted parliamentary elections.

14. Down 5 points, from 61 to 56 percent. See "Alarm Call for Latin America's Democrats," *Economist,* 28 July 2000; and "Democracy Clings On in a Cold Economic Climate," *Economist,* 26 August 2002.

15. Down to 43 percent in 2003. See United Nations Development Programme report, "Democracy in Latin America: Towards a Citizens' Democracy" (2004).

16. Up from 58 percent to 65 percent, then back to 57 percent. Richard Rose and Christian Haerpfer, *Trends in Democracies and Markets: New Democracies Barometer, 1991–98,* (Glasgow: University of Strathclyde Studies in Public Policy No. 308, 1998).

17. For a two-item construct of perceived supply of democracy (an average of satisfaction and extent), Pearson's r=.204, p<.001.

18. For the four-item construct of demand for democracy (an average of support democracy plus reject three alternatives), Pearson's r=-.043, p<.001.

10

THE ARAB ASPIRATION
FOR DEMOCRACY

Amaney Jamal and Mark Tessler

Amaney Jamal *is assistant professor of politics at Princeton University.*
Mark Tessler *is Samuel J. Eldersveld Collegiate Professor and director of
the International Institute at the University of Michigan. This essay originally appeared in the January 2008 issue of the* Journal of Democracy.

Over the course of the last quarter-century, democratic currents have
swept across much of the developing and postcommunist worlds. The
Arab world, however, has remained largely untouched by this global
democratic trend. The first *Arab Human Development Report,* published
by the United Nations Development Programme in 2002, lamented that
political systems "have not been opened up to all citizens" and that
"political participation is less advanced in the Arab world than in other
developing regions."[1] The 2003 report reiterated this assessment, stating
that the Arab world's freedom deficit "remains critically pertinent and
may have become even graver" since the 2002 report was issued.[2] A series
of articles in the January 2004 issue of *Comparative Politics* described
the "resilient and enduring authoritarianism" in the Arab world, and later
that same year Thomas Carothers and Marina Ottaway concluded that in
most Arab countries "real progress toward democracy is minimal."[3] Nor
has the situation changed very much in the last few years, as the 2005
Arab Human Development Report confirms.

Despite—or perhaps because of—the persistence of authoritarianism
across the Arab world, popular support for democracy there is widespread. The evidence for this may be gleaned from twenty different
surveys carried out in nine different Arab countries between 2000 and
2006.[4] Indeed, cross-regional data from the World Values Survey indicate that support for democracy in the Arab world is as high as or higher
than in any other world region.[5] While this might appear anomalous in
a region where ordinary citizens have had little experience with democracy, the absence of democracy may be the very factor that leads so

TABLE 1—SUPPORT FOR DEMOCRACY

	ALL COUNTRIES	JORDAN	PALESTINE	ALGERIA	MOROCCO	KUWAIT
Despite drawbacks, democracy is the best system of government	86% N=5,740	86% N=1,143	83% N=1,270	83% N=1,300	92% N=1,277	88% N=750
Having a democratic system of government in our country would be good	90% N=5,740	93% N=1,143	88% N=1,270	81% N=1,300	96% N=1,277	93% N=750

Note: See question wording at *www.journalofdemocracy.org/articles/gratis/TesslerGraphics-19-1.pdf*.

many citizens to desire a democratic alternative to the political systems by which they are currently governed.

The most recent of these surveys were carried out in 2006 as part of the Arab Barometer survey project.[6] Data were collected through face-to-face interviews with representative national samples in Morocco, Algeria, Palestine, Jordan, and Kuwait. The Arab Barometer survey instrument was jointly developed by the present authors and team leaders from the five countries in which the surveys have thus far been carried out.[7] The interview schedule also included items used in the regional Barometers in Africa, Asia, and Latin America, with which the Arab Barometer is cooperating as part of the Global Barometer project.

As suggested above, data from the Arab Barometer, as yet unreported elsewhere, once again reveal high levels of support for democracy. More specifically, 86 percent of those interviewed believe that democracy is the best form of government, and 90 percent agree that democracy would be a good or very good system of governance for the country in which they live. These findings are shown in Table 1, which also provides percentages for the individual participating countries. It shows that, despite some cross-national variation, there is overwhelming support for democracy in every country.

The Arab Barometer also provides data that shed light on political participation and can help us to probe how respondents understand democracy and think about democratization. Many but not all citizens are politically engaged. For example, 52 percent of the Arab citizens surveyed report that they have voted in elections, and 56 percent report that they regularly follow the news. Interestingly, despite their preference for democratic governance, 83 percent believe that political reforms should be implemented gradually. Some also state that democracy has a number of important drawbacks, even if they nonetheless consider it to be the best political system. For example, 31 percent state that democracy is bad for the economy and 33 percent state that it is bad at maintaining order. These findings are shown in Table 2 (p. 132), which also presents percentages for the individual countries.

There is considerable variation in the way that citizens in the Arab world think about democracy. On the one hand, a solid majority expresses support not only for democracy as an abstract concept but also for many of the institutions and processes associated with democratic governance. For example, 62 percent of those interviewed believe that competition and disagreement among political groups is a good thing for their country, and 64 percent believe the government should make laws according to the wishes of the people. On the other hand, when asked to identify the most important factors that define a democracy, about half the respondents emphasized economic considerations rather than political rights and freedoms.

In Algeria, Jordan, and Palestine (the question was not asked in Kuwait and Morocco), only about half the respondents stated that the most important aspect of democracy is the opportunity "to change the government through elections" or the "freedom to criticize the government." The other half attached greatest importance to democracy's (presumed) ability to "provide basic necessities like food, clothing, and shelter for everyone" or to "decrease the income gap between rich and poor."[8]

Such findings suggest that economic issues are central to the way that many Arab citizens think about governance and, accordingly, that many men and women probably have an instrumental conception of democracy. When asked to identify the most important problem facing their country, fully 51 percent of the entire five-country sample described that problem in economic terms, citing such considerations as poverty, unemployment, and inflation. Only 5 percent stated that authoritarianism is the most important problem. Slightly higher percentages mentioned the U.S. occupation of Iraq (8 percent) and the Arab-Israeli conflict (7 percent) as the most important problem.

Coupled with the finding that most Arabs want political reform to be implemented gradually, this suggests that majorities in the Arab world attach higher priority to solving economic problems than to securing the political rights and freedoms associated with democracy. One way to read this is that Arab-world majorities support democracy, at least in part, because it promises to make governments more accountable and more attentive to the concerns of ordinary citizens, particularly their economic concerns. In other words, for at least some respondents, it is not so much that democracy is the "right" political system in a conceptual sense, but rather that democracy is a "useful" form of government that has the potential to address many of a country's most pressing needs.

This conclusion is reinforced by other findings from the Arab Barometer surveys. Respondents were much more likely to be critical of their government for poor economic performance than for a lack of freedom. Indeed, slender majorities view their governments favorably on political

TABLE 2—POLITICAL ENGAGEMENT AND EVALUATIONS
OF DEMOCRACY

	ALL COUNTRIES	JORDAN	PALESTINE	ALGERIA	MOROCCO	KUWAIT
Voted in the last election	52%	59%	71%	45%	50%	23%
Follows news about politics often or very often	56%	49%	78%	45%	49%	23%
Political reform should be introduced gradually	83%	77%	91%	79%	81%	88%
In a democracy, the economy runs badly	31%	38%	41%	38%	10%	28%
Democracies are bad at maintaining order	33%	36%	42%	43%	12%	33%
Competition and disagreement are not a bad thing for our country	62%	60%	50%	61%	67%	79%
The government should make laws according to the wishes of the people	61%	58%	59%	59%	81%	62%
Percentage of people giving a political feature of democracy as the most important*	48%	39%	58%	50%	—	—

* Percentage of people choosing "opportunity to change government" or "freedom to criticize government" rather than "reduce income gap between rich and poor" or "provide basic necessities like food."

grounds. For example, 54 percent believe that they have the power to influence government decisions; 50 percent believe that the courts are fair; 53 percent believe that they can criticize the government without fear; and 57 percent believe that they can join organizations without fear. By contrast, only 33 and 31 percent, respectively, believe that their government is doing a good job of fighting unemployment and narrowing the gap between rich and poor.

Democracy and Islam

Across all sectors of the Arab world, as in other Muslim-majority countries, there is a vibrant and nuanced discourse on the compatibility of Islam and democracy. Although some Muslim clerics and religious thinkers contend that democracy is not possible in a political system guided by Islam, others disagree. Equally important, it appears that neither Arab intellectuals nor ordinary citizens accept the view that Islam and democracy are incompatible. Rather, from mosque sermons to newspaper columns, from campus debates to coffee-shop discussions, large numbers of Arabs and other Muslims contend that the tenets of Islam are inherently democratic.[9]

In Western discourses, by contrast, it has often been asserted that Islam is opposed to democratic rule, and assertions along these lines are frequently advanced to explain the persistence of authoritarianism in the Arab world. The argument that Islam stifles democracy includes several interrelated assertions. First, some contend, as does Samuel P. Huntington in *The Clash of Civilizations,* that Islam and democracy are inherently incompatible because Islam recognizes no division between "church" and "state" and emphasizes the community over the individual.[10] Individualism, Huntington maintains, is a necessary component of a liberal-democratic order. Second, some scholars assert that Islamic law and doctrine are fundamentally illiberal and hence create an environment within which democracy cannot flourish. Francis Fukuyama, among others, makes this argument.[11] Finally, some claim that Islam fosters antidemocratic attitudes and values among its adherents. On the one hand, according to this argument, the religion does not advocate a commitment to political freedom. On the other, Islam is said to promote fatalism, the unquestioning acceptance of "Allah's way," and thus to nurture acceptance of the status quo rather than the contestation needed for a vibrant democracy.[12] As a result, according to this collection of arguments, the religious orientations and attachments of Muslim citizens create a normative climate that is hostile to democracy.

Arab Barometer data permit an examination, admittedly limited to the individual level of analysis, of these competing views of the relationship between democracy and Islam. To the extent that religious orientations and attachments do discourage democracy, support for democracy should be lower among more religious men and women. This is not the case, however. In fact, more religious Muslims are as likely as less religious Muslims to believe that democracy, despite its drawbacks, is the best political system. The Barometer has identified the frequency of Koran reading as a valid and reliable measure of religiosity. Respondents are categorized according to whether they read the Koran every day, several times a week, sometimes, or rarely or never. Strikingly, at least 85 percent of the respondents in each category state that democracy is the best political system. Thus, since public support for democracy is necessary for a successful and consolidated democratic transition, and since available evidence indicates that religiosity does not diminish this support for democracy among Muslim publics, it seems clear that the persistence of authoritarianism in the Arab world cannot be

TABLE 3—VARIATION IN THE SUPPORT FOR DEMOCRACY
BY ATTITUDES TOWARD A POLITICAL ROLE FOR ISLAM

| | PERCENTAGE SAYING THAT DESPITE DRAWBACKS, DEMOCRACY IS THE BEST SYSTEM OF GOVERNMENT | |
	Strongly Agree/Agree that Men of Religion Should Influence Government Decisions	Strongly Disagree/ Disagree that Men of Religion Should Influence Government Decisions
All Countries	54%	46%
Jordan	52%	48%
Palestine	55%	45%
Algeria	58%	42%
Morocco	63%	37%
Kuwait	39%	61%

explained by the religious orientations and attachments of ordinary men and women.

A different question bearing on the relationship between democracy and Islam concerns the role of Islam in political affairs. Many Arab citizens express support for the influence of Islam in government and politics. This is not the view of all citizens, however. In contrast to support for democracy, which is expressed by the overwhelming majority of the respondents in the Arab Barometer and other recent surveys, men and women in every country where surveys have been conducted are divided on the question of whether Islam should play an important political role. For example, whereas 56 percent of the respondents in the Arab Barometer surveys agree with the statement that men of religion should have influence over government decisions,[13] 44 percent disagree, indicating that they believe Islam should *not* play an important political role.

Further, the division of opinion observed among all respondents is present to the same degree among those who express support for democracy. Among respondents who believe democracy to be the best political system, despite any possible drawbacks, 54 percent believe that men of religion should have influence over government decisions while 46 percent disagree. This is shown in Table 3, which juxtaposes these items measuring support for democracy and support for a political role for Islam. Although there is modest variation from country to country, Table 3 shows that respondents who support democracy are divided more or less equally between those who favor secular democracy and those who favor a political system that is both democratic and gives an important role to Islam. Consistent with findings reported earlier, it shows that among the relatively few respondents who do not support democracy, there is also a division of opinion regarding a political role for Islam.

How do Muslim Arabs who express support for democracy but also want their religion to have a meaningful role in political life understand what might be called "Islamic democracy"? Aspects of this question pertaining to Islam itself—to views about the particular ways that democratic political life might incorporate an Islamic dimension—are beyond the scope of this essay.

More pertinent to the present study is the question of whether those who support Islamic democracy possess democratic values, both in absolute terms and relative to those who support secular democracy. Table 4 (p. 136) presents data with which to address this question. The Table compares respondents who favor secular democracy and those who favor Islamic democracy with respect to three normative orientations that relevant scholarship has identified as necessary (along with support for democracy) to the long-term success of a democratic transition. These values are: 1) respect for political diversity and dissent, measured by the importance that respondents attribute to the presence of political leaders who are open to different political opinions; 2) social tolerance, measured by respondents' stating that they would harbor no objection to having neighbors of a different race; and 3) gender equality, measured by a question asking whether men and women should have equal job opportunities and wages. While these are only some of the values that are important for democracy, responses to questions about them will offer insights about the presence or absence of democratic values among Muslim Arab men and women in general and, in particular, about similarities or differences in the values of citizens with dissimilar preferences regarding the place of Islam in democratic political life.

Several conclusions may be drawn from Table 4. First, most men and women in every country express democratic values. Almost all respondents consider it important that political leaders be open to diverse ideas. Social tolerance, as reflected in openness to having neighbors of a different race, is also very high. Indeed, overall, there is only one instance in which less than two-thirds of those surveyed answered in a manner inconsistent with democracy. This instance occurs among those Algerian respondents who say that they favor Islamic democracy. Of these, only 57 percent say that they favor equal job opportunities and wages for men and women (compared to 71 percent among secular democrats).

Second, there are very few significant differences between respondents who favor secular democracy and those who favor Islamic democracy. The former are more likely to endorse a norm that is consistent with democracy in most instances, but differences are almost always very small. In only two of the fourteen country-specific comparisons shown in Table 4 is the difference between those who favor secular democracy and those who favor Islamic democracy greater than 10 percent (12 percent in one instance and 14 percent in the other). In almost all

TABLE 4—DEMOCRATIC VALUES AND SUPPORT OF A POLITICAL ROLE FOR ISLAM AMONG RESPONDENTS WHO SUPPORT DEMOCRACY

THOSE WHO SUPPORT DEMOCRACY		PERCENTAGE AGREEING WITH STATEMENT ABOUT DEMOCRATIC VALUES		
		It is important to have political leaders who are open to different political opinions	Do not mind having neighbors of a different race	Men and women should have equal job opportunities and wages
All Countries	Secular Democracy	95	86	76
	Islamic Democracy	95	82	70
Jordan	Secular Democracy	94	79	66
	Islamic Democracy	92	67	66
Palestine	Secular Democracy	96	NA	79
	Islamic Democracy	97	NA	72
Algeria	Secular Democracy	95	83	71
	Islamic Democracy	96	80	57
Morocco	Secular Democracy	93	94	78
	Islamic Democracy	95	89	77
Kuwait	Secular Democracy	96	88	85
	Islamic Democracy	98	92	84

the remaining comparisons, the difference is actually 5 percent or less. Thus, the overall conclusion suggested by Table 4 is that democratic values are present to a significant degree among Muslim Arab citizens, most of whom support democracy, and that this is the case whether or not an individual believes that his or her country should be governed by a political system that is Islamic as well as democratic. These observations reinforce previous assessments related to Arab Muslims' views regarding the compatibility of democracy and Islam.

A final question pertaining to the relationship between democracy and Islam concerns the reasons that some respondents favor secular democracy while others prefer a political system that is democratic and also incorporates an Islamic dimension. Of particular concern is whether a preference for democracy that has an Islamic dimension reflects the influence of religious orientations, political judgments and evaluations, both, or neither. One hypothesis is that piety and religious attachments may lead Muslim Arabs to favor Islamic democracy. Another is that discontent with governments and regimes that are essentially secular may predispose citizens to favor a system that incorporates an Islamic dimension. It is also possible that a preference for Islamic democracy reflects concern with preserving a measure of continuity—that is, with keeping a measure of tradition in place even as a shift to something new (democracy) is taking place.

We tested these propositions via a regression analysis that assesses the impact on political-system preference of personal religiosity and political evaluations. Frequency of Koran reading is again used as a measure of personal religiosity. Political evaluations include an item that asks about trust in the head of the government, another that asks whether ordinary citizens have the ability to influence the policies and activities of the government, and a third that asks whether democracies are not good at maintaining order. Binary logistic regression is used since only those who favor democracy (whether with or without an Islamic dimension) are included in the analysis.[14] Age, educational level, and economic well-being served as control variables.

The regression analysis shows that personal religiosity is not significantly related to political-system preference in any of the five countries in which Arab Barometer surveys were conducted. This is consistent with earlier findings; not only does religiosity not lead men and women to be less supportive of democracy, it does not lead them to be more supportive of a political system that incorporates an Islamic dimension.

Political evaluations, by contrast, are significantly related to political-system preference in every country. There is some cross-national variation in the particular evaluations that are most salient, and the direction of the relationship is not the same in every instance. A preference for a democratic system that incorporates an Islamic dimension is disproportionately likely among: 1) Jordanian respondents who have little trust in the head of government, believe that ordinary citizens have the ability to influence the activities and policies of the government, and believe that democracies are not good at maintaining order; 2) Palestinians who have these same sentiments; 3) Algerians who believe that democracies are not good at maintaining order; 4) Moroccans who believe that democracies *are* good at maintaining order; and 5) Kuwaitis who have little trust in the head of government, believe that ordinary citizens have little ability to influence the activities and policies of the government, and believe that democracies are not good at maintaining order.

These differences invite inquiry into the ways in which particular national circumstances determine how political judgments shape citizens' attitudes about the desired connection between democracy and Islam. Even in the absence of such inquiry, however, findings from the Arab Barometer make clear that explanatory power is to be found in political judgments rather than religious orientations.

The Desire for a Strong Leader

Despite the support for democracy that overwhelming majorities of respondents express in the Arab Barometer surveys, there are some respondents who state that it would be good or very good for their country to have a strong nondemocratic leader who does not bother with parliament and elections. This opinion is expressed by 17 percent of the respondents in the five surveys taken together, although it is somewhat higher in some countries and somewhat lower in others, ranging from 26 percent in Jordan to 10 percent in Algeria. Further, this undemocratic attitude is expressed only slightly less frequently among individuals who express support for democracy—being about 15 percent overall and ranging from 25 percent in Jordan to 8 percent in Algeria and Kuwait. These findings are shown in Table 5.

Since these percentages are fairly low, they are consistent with the finding that most ordinary citizens in the Arab world believe that democracy, whatever its drawbacks, is the best political system—and the one by which they believe their own country should be governed. On the other hand, the inverse correlation between support for democracy and approval of a strong leader who does not have to bother with parliament and elections is not as strong as might be expected. In other words, as noted above, there are some men and women who support democracy and also state that an undemocratic leader would be good for their country.

How should this apparent contradiction be understood? While it is possible that at least some of these individuals simply do not understand what democracy involves, it is probable that in many cases the juxtaposition of these contradictory attitudes reflects concern that a democratic transition could be destabilizing or disproportionately harmful to some citizens even if it helps the country overall, and that it should therefore be implemented in a "guided" fashion by a strong leader who is able to ensure that political change will be carried out in an orderly fashion. This is consistent with the finding, reported earlier, that almost all respondents want political reforms to be implemented gradually. It may also be significant that support for an undemocratic leader is expressed most frequently, both among all respondents and among those who support democracy, in Jordan and Morocco, two poor countries in which a monarch who is not responsible to the electorate is the guarantor of political order and political continuity.

We have also carried out a regression analysis (similar to that pre-

TABLE 5—SUPPORT FOR DEMOCRACY AND ATTITUDES ABOUT STRONG
LEADERS WHO DO NOT HAVE TO BOTHER
WITH PARLIAMENT AND ELECTIONS

THOSE WHO SAY THAT HAVING A STRONG LEADER WHO DOES NOT HAVE TO BOTHER WITH PARLIAMENT AND ELECTIONS IN OUR COUNTRY WOULD BE GOOD	DESPITE DRAWBACKS, DEMOCRACY IS THE BEST SYSTEM OF GOVERNMENT	
	Strongly Agree/ Agree	Strongly Disagree/ Disagree
All Countries	15%	25%
Jordan	25%	37%
Palestine	14%	14%
Algeria	8%	18%
Morocco	16%	37%
Kuwait	8%	30%

sented with respect to the connection between attitudes toward democracy and political Islam) to shed light on the connection between support for a democratic political system and support for an undemocratic leader. Again, binary logistic regression has been used since the analysis includes only those who support democracy and do not approve of undemocratic leadership and those who support democracy and do approve of undemocratic leadership.[15] Also, once again, the same measures of personal religiosity and political evaluations are employed, as are the control variables of age, educational level, and economic well-being.

The results are consistent both with the conclusions about religiosity reported above and with the hypothesis offered to explain why some individuals who favor democracy might also express approval of an undemocratic leader. On the one hand, in *none* of the five countries for which data are available is this combination of supposedly contradictory attitudes more common among those individuals who are more religious.

On the other hand, political assessments have explanatory power in four of the five countries, Kuwait being the exception. In Algeria, Jordan, and Palestine, individuals who believe that democracies are not good at maintaining order are more likely than others to couple support for democracy with support for strong leadership. In Morocco, those who believe that democracies are not good at maintaining order are less likely than others to combine a preference for strong leadership with support for democracy. In Morocco and Jordan (both of which are monarchies) individuals who believe that citizens have the ability to influence government activities and policies are disproportionately likely to favor democracy, but also express support for a strong leader who does not have to bother with parliament and elections. Thus, as the Arab Barometer data have shown with respect to all the questions investigated, the political-system preferences and views about governance held by ordinary men and women are not shaped to a significant degree by religious orientations or attachments. By contrast, these preferences and views do appear to be influenced in important ways by people's judgments and perceptions relating to political considerations.

Support for Democracy, But of What Kind?

Data from the Arab Barometer survey make clear that there is broad support for democracy in the Arab world. In a way that is perhaps fed by the very persistence of authoritarianism in Arab polities, the vast majority of Arab men and women believe that democracy is the best political system and that it would be a good way for their country to be governed. This is not the whole story, however. People understand democracy in different ways. Often, they value it mainly as an instrument. They want to see it implemented gradually, and they disagree among themselves about whether or not it should include an important role for Islam. Thus, an understanding of political-system preferences and popular views about governance requires attention to multiple dimensions of support for democracy.

The Arab Barometer data also illuminate debates about the compatibility of Islam and democracy. More specifically, findings from these surveys suggest that Islam does not foster antidemocratic attitudes. On the one hand, personal religiosity does not diminish support for democracy. Nor even does it foster a preference for a political system that is Islamic as well as democratic. On the other hand, those who do favor Islamic democracy are not significantly less likely than those who favor secularism to embrace democratic norms and values. But while Islamic orientations appear to play no significant role in shaping citizens' attitudes toward democracy, the Arab Barometer data offer strong evidence that judgments pertaining to political circumstances and performance do make a difference.

It is unclear whether popular support for democracy can and will actually transform into pressure for political reform and democratic openings in the Arab world. Earlier surveys also found a widespread preference for democratic governance, which is a sign that undemocratic regimes and popular desires for democracy can coexist for considerable periods of time. Findings from the Arab Barometer suggest the possibility that this may be partly the result of a desire for stability that parallels the desire for democratic governance. This is reflected in the widespread emphasis on gradualism, as well as the support of some Arabs for a strong leader who does not have to bother with parliament and elections—a support fostered, in part, by a belief that democracies are poor at maintaining order. Concerns about stability almost certainly reflect the geostrategic situation in the region, particularly the destabilizing developments that have shaped politics in Iraq, Palestine, Lebanon, and

Algeria in recent years. In some countries, concerns about stability may also be encouraged by political leaders who justify their opposition to reform by insisting that democratization will bring divisiveness and disorder. All of this may reduce the pressure from below for a democratic transition and serve the interests of regimes committed to preserving the authoritarian status quo.

But while findings from the Arab Barometer say little about whether there are likely to be transitions to democracy in the Arab world in the years ahead, they do offer evidence that citizens' attitudes and values, including those relating to Islam, are not the reason that authoritarianism has persisted. Indeed, the Arab Barometer indicates that if and when progress toward democracy does occur, most Arab-world citizens will welcome it even as they debate the precise character and content of the democratic political systems that they believe should be established. As a result, those who wish to advance the cause of democracy in the Arab world should focus their investigations not on the alleged antidemocratic impulses of ordinary women and men, but rather on the structures and manipulations, and perhaps also the supporting external alliances, of a political leadership class that is dedicated to preserving its power and privilege.

NOTES

1. *Arab Human Development Report* (New York: UN Development Programme, 2002); ch. 7, *www.undp.org/rbas/ahdr/bychapter.html.*

2. *Arab Human Development Report* (New York: UN Development Programme, 2003); Introduction, *www.undp.org/rbas/ahdr/english2003.html.*

3. Marina Ottaway and Thomas Carothers, "Middle East Democracy," *Foreign Policy,* November–December 2004, 22–28. See also Marcia Posusney and Michelle Angrist, eds., *Authoritarianism in the Middle East* (Boulder, Colo.: Lynne Rienner, 2005).

4. See, for example, Mark Tessler and Eleanor Gao, "Gauging Arab Support for Democracy," *Journal of Democracy* 16 (July 2005): 83–97; Mark Tessler, "Do Islamic Orientations Influence Attitudes Toward Democracy in the Arab World? Evidence from Egypt, Jordan, Morocco, and Algeria," *International Journal of Comparative Sociology* 2 (Spring 2003): 229–49; Mark Tessler, Mansoor Moaddel, and Ronald Inglehart, "Getting to Arab Democracy: What Do Iraqis Want?" *Journal of Democracy* 17 (January 2006): 38–50.

5. Ronald Inglehart et al., eds., *Human Beliefs and Values: A Cross-cultural Sourcebook Based on the 1999–2002 Values Surveys* (Mexico City: Siglo XXI, 2004).

6. The Arab Barometer team consists of partners in five Arab countries: Fares Braizat of the Center for Strategic Studies, Jordan; Khalil Shikaki of the Center for Policy and Survey Research, Palestine; Ghanim al-Najjar of Kuwait University, Kuwait; Mohammed Abderebbi of Hassan II University–Mohammadia, Morocco; and Abdallah Bedaida of the University of Algiers, Algeria. The first wave of the Arab Barometer project was funded by the Middle East Partnership Initiative (MEPI) of the U.S. Department of State.

7. Additional surveys in the first wave of the Arab Barometer are scheduled to be carried out in Yemen and Lebanon in early 2008.

8. The characteristics attributed to democracy were assessed by the following item: "People often differ in their views on the characteristics that are essential to democracy. If you have to choose only one thing, what would you choose as the most important characteristic, and what would be the second most important?" The response code listed the four attributes discussed in the text and also gave respondents the option of specifying another characteristic. Almost 99 percent of the respondents selected one of the four listed characteristics.

9. For excellent discussions of the compatibility of Islam and democracy, see Khaled Abou Fadl, *Islam and the Challenge of Democracy* (Princeton: Princeton University Press, 2004); John Esposito and John Voll, *Islam and Democracy* (New York: Oxford University Press, 1996); José Casanova, "Civil Society and Religion: Retrospective Reflections on Catholicism and Prospective Reflections on Islam," *Social Research* 68 (Winter 2001): 1041–80; and Vali Nasr, "The Rise of 'Muslim Democracy'?" *Journal of Democracy* 16 (April 2005): 13–27. For a data-based examination of why support for Islam in politics is compatible with support for democracy, see Amaney Jamal, "Reassessing Support for Democracy and Islam in the Arab World: Evidence from Egypt and Jordan," *World Affairs* 169 (Fall 2006): 51–63.

10. Samuel P. Huntington, *The Clash of Civilizations and the Remaking of the World Order* (New York: Simon and Schuster, 1996), 135–39. See also his article "Will More Countries Become Democratic?" *Political Science Quarterly* 99 (Summer 1984): 193–218.

11. Francis Fukuyama, *The End of History and the Last Man* (New York: Avon, 1992), 45–46.

12. See, for example, Daniel Pipes, "Debate: Islam and Democracy," *PBS "Wide Angle,"* 15 July 2003, *www.danielpipes.org/article/1167.* See also Bernard Lewis, *The Shaping of the Modern Middle East* (New York: Oxford University Press, 1994); and Elie Kedourie, *Democracy and Arab Political Culture* (Washington, D.C.: Washington Institute for Near East Policy, 1992).

13. We used factor analysis to assess the consistency among a number of survey items designed to measure judgments pertaining to political Islam. Many of these items loaded highly on a common factor, offering evidence of reliability and increasing confidence in validity. The item asking whether men of religion should have influence over government decisions was the best single indicator of this dimension, and for purposes of clarity and parsimony it is used in the present analysis as a measure of support for political Islam.

14. Our regression tables may be found at *www.journalofdemocracy.org/articles/gratis/TesslerGraphics-19-1.pdf.*

15. The regression table in question may be found at *www.journalofdemocracy.org/articles/gratis/TesslerGraphics-19-1.pdf.*

11

HOW MUSLIMS IN CENTRAL ASIA VIEW DEMOCRACY

Richard Rose

Richard Rose *is director of the Centre for the Study of Public Policy at the University of Aberdeen, Scotland, and creator of the New Europe Barometer surveys of mass response to transformation in postcommunist countries. His latest book, coauthored with William Mishler and Neil Munro, is* Understanding Transformation: From Unstable to Stable European States *(2009). This essay originally appeared in the October 2002 issue of the* Journal of Democracy.

The Arabic word "Islam" refers to submission to the will of God, but there is much disagreement within Islam about what that will is. Since September 11, 2001, there has been much debate in the West about whether Islamic and Western values are inherently in conflict, and especially whether Islam is inherently hostile to democracy. Nor are Americans and West Europeans alone in worrying about religious conflict. Recurrent conflicts in Chechnya have encouraged Islamophobia in Russia, where about 10 percent of the population is Muslim.

In *The Clash of Civilizations and the Remaking of World Order,* Samuel P. Huntington adopts an "essentialist" position: "Whatever their political or religious opinions," he writes, "Muslims agree that a basic difference exists between their culture and Western culture." Huntington also seems to suggest that this "basic difference" will lead to a violent clash with Western civilization: "The underlying problem for the West is not Islamic fundamentalism. It is Islam."[1]

The implications of a civilizational conflict between the West and Islam are profoundly disturbing, since the world's Muslim population is an estimated one billion, and states where the majority of the population is Muslim extend from Indonesia and Pakistan through the Middle East to the Atlantic shores of Africa. Moreover, several hundred million Muslims compose sizeable minorities in multicultural states from India and China through the Russian Federation and Israel to France, Britain and, increasingly, the United States.

Muslims have never agreed about the essence of their religion, and political and religious differences in the contemporary Muslim world demonstrate that Muslims do *not* think alike: "To say that someone is Muslim," Daniel Brumberg writes, "tells us little regarding that person's views on politics."[2]

Most of the Muslim world has been resistant to public opinion surveys, the standard way of finding out what people think about politics. In some countries, such surveys are forbidden, and in more traditional Muslim societies the status of women makes it very difficult to interview half the population. This essay draws on sample surveys of public opinion in two predominantly Muslim countries of Central Asia, Kazakhstan and Kyrgyzstan. These post-Soviet countries have distinctive histories that make them different from Muslim countries in the Middle East or South Asia. But since predominantly Muslim societies are very diverse, no single one of them—whether Turkey or Indonesia or Saudi Arabia—can represent the whole of Islam.

Kazakhstan and Kyrgyzstan are thousands of miles east of the fault line that Huntington draws between Western and Orthodox Christianity. Each is geographically much closer to Afghanistan than to Mecca or to Moscow. The historical roots of Kazakhstan go back half a millennium to the settlement of previously nomadic hordes in territory between China and Russia. The contemporary Kazakh state has been described as "an accidental country" in which clan networks remain the only semi-effective institutions.[3] The territory now known as Kyrgyzstan was occupied by nomadic tribes up until the arrival of Soviet institutions. Mountains divide it into distinct regions connected with neighboring areas in Kazakhstan, Uzbekistan, and northwestern China, respectively. Kazakhstan is rich in energy resources and fertile land, while Kyrgyzstan is not.

The object of this essay is to determine, first, what proportion of Muslims in Central Asia are in fact strongly committed to their faith; second, whether Muslims are more or less pro- or anti-democratic in their attitudes than the Russian Orthodox citizens of Kazakhstan and Kyrgyzstan; and finally, whether the differences among them tend to reflect their degree of religious commitment or, alternatively, such social and economic factors as income, education, and age.

Modernization Soviet-Style

Formal integration into the USSR brought to the historic populations of Kazakhstan and Kyrgyzstan Soviet-style modernization. This included the ideological and administrative apparatus of a communist party-state, plus a big rise in education. A consequence of Soviet rule was the introduction of a new secular faith that Huntington ignores—that is, the displacement of both Islam and Orthodox Christianity by belief in science and material progress.

Soviet economic development policies attracted Russians to the region. In the last Soviet census of 1989, Kazakhs constituted only two-fifths of Kazakhstan's population, with ethnic Russians roughly matching them in number. In the last Soviet census in Kyrgyzstan, the titular nationality constituted just over half the population, Russians one-fifth, and Uzbeks (the third-largest group) one-eighth of Kyrgyzstan's residents. At the time of the break-up of the Soviet Union in 1991, surveys of Russians in the two countries found little evidence of ethnic friction or fear. Less than a fifth said they felt alien in Kyrgyzstan; only a tenth felt so in Kazakhstan. Both Russians and people belonging to the respective titular nationalities worried that the dissolution of the Soviet Union would reduce living standards.[4]

When the Soviet Union was breaking up, Kazakh and Kyrgyz politicians rushed to take power as leaders of independent states. The result was the establishment of a Kazakh regime in which president Nursultan Nazarbayev was able to win 80 percent of the vote in a ballot that the OSCE described as free but unfair and a Kyrgyz regime in which President Askar Akayev was able to win 74 percent of the vote in an election that the OSCE described as subject to undue government influence. Both countries are categorized as Not Free by Freedom House.[5] The Perception of Corruption Index of Transparency International (TI) places Kazakhstan in the most corrupt quarter of the countries that it rates *(www.transparency.org)*. TI does not give a rating to Kyrgyzstan, but Kyrgyz politics is similarly characterized by clientelism and favoritism. The European Bank for Reconstruction and Development classifies both countries as having introduced more market institutions than the three neighboring "stans" of Central Asia. In each, GDP is officially calculated to have contracted by about a third since the introduction of market institutions. The energy resources of Kazakhstan give it a real GDP per capita almost double that of Kyrgyzstan, but a third less than that of the Russian Federation.[6]

Secularization and the breakdown of Soviet controls have made it possible to ask people in Kazakhstan and Kyrgyzstan questions about religion and democratic and undemocratic values.[7] Since both countries are mixed in ethnicity and religion, we can compare groups to see whether Muslims are more or less antidemocratic than Russians from the Orthodox tradition. Equally important, the surveys discriminate between people who are very committed and those who are not so committed to the practices of their nominal religion. The evidence suggests that religion and ethnicity make less difference to political values than do more "modern" influences such as education and economic well-being.

Religious Commitment

Where religion divides the population, it is not necessary to be a fervent believer to be treated as either Muslim or Orthodox. If one's ancestors were Muslim or Orthodox, that is enough to define one's place in society. As a consequence of in-migration, in Kazakhstan today there is no majority religion. When people are asked their religious denomination, 40 percent say Muslim; 38 percent, Russian Orthodox; 16 percent, none; and the remainder are scattered among a number of other denominations. In Kyrgyzstan, 75 percent say they are Muslims; 16 percent, Orthodox; only 4 percent, none; and the rest are scattered.

Nominal identification with a religion is not evidence of commitment to its beliefs and practices. Since mosque attendance is not an appropriate measure of the degree to which one follows the precepts of Islam, people were asked whether they observed the ceremonies and rules prescribed by their religion, wording that is particularly relevant to political action. In both countries, only one-fifth of Muslims say they constantly try to follow religious rules; a substantial majority—61 percent in Kazakhstan and 63 percent in Kyrgyzstan—say they sometimes adhere to religious practices; and one-sixth do not engage in religious practices at all.

Since people can and often do say one thing but do another, questions were also asked about drinking alcohol, which is not done by strict Muslims. In Kazakhstan total abstainers are in the minority. Two-thirds of Kazakh Muslims admit to taking a drink on occasion, and the minority that completely abstains from drinking is only nine percentage points more than the minority of Russians who are total abstainers. Those who describe themselves as "very committed" to Islam are twice as likely as semi-observant or non-observant Muslims to abstain from drinking. In Kyrgyzstan there is a stronger tendency to respect the proscription on alcohol: 51 percent of Muslims say they never drink, including a majority of those who say they do not practice their religion. The relatively small number of teetotallers among Muslims in the region emphasizes that generalizations about people based on religious texts full of "thou shalt nots" should be treated with caution.

People of Russian Orthodox backgrounds are more selective in following or ignoring religious precepts. In Kazakhstan, of those who are nominally Orthodox 37 percent ignore religious rules, while 56 percent try to follow religious precepts some of the time, and a very small group try to do so constantly. In Kyrgyzstan, 24 percent of the nominally Orthodox are indifferent to religious precepts, 64 percent say they sometimes follow these religious precepts, and 12 percent try to do so all the time.

Broadbrush generalizations that place Kazakhstan and Kyrgyzstan in a single "civilizational" category ignore the fact that neither country is homogeneous in terms of either religious or ethnic traditions. When people in Kazahkstan are asked about their nationality, 38 percent say Kazakh and 6 percent name another Central Asian nationality, while 49 percent report they are Russian or another Slavic nationality (such as Belarusian). The remainder is enormously heterogeneous. While ethnicity and nominal religious identification are closely correlated, ethnicity is not a good guide to religious commitment. Among those who say they are Kazakhs, only one-sixth are very observant Muslims. Among Russians, the link between ethnicity and religious commitment is even weaker. In Kyrgyzstan, 70 percent identify with the titular nationality and eight percent with another Central Asian nationality, while only 19 percent identify with a Slavic nationality. There too, most people who see themselves as Kyrgyz are only intermittently observant Muslims.

In Central Asia, religion is only one identity among many, starting with the family, extending to clan and regional loyalties and to the new state, as well as to transnational belief systems. Just as residents were not committed to Marxist-Leninist doctrines under Soviet rule, so today most are not strict Muslims. People usually select the religious precepts they follow and those they do not, and this is true of both Muslims and Orthodox Christians. The selectivity that people use in regard to religious precepts is a caution against assuming that abstract theological doctrines influence the behavior of nominal adherents.

Democratic Values and Religion

To speak of democratization in Central Asia is to misunderstand the intent of political leaders there. Like many rulers in non-Muslim countries, their first priorities are to maintain multiethnic states and to hold on to power for themselves. Nursultan Nazarbayev and Askar Akayev have succeeded in doing so by means less blatant than the Turkmenbashi of Turkmenistan.

Even if a country is ruled autocratically, those ruled may nevertheless hold democratic values. The fall of the Berlin Wall has shown that citizens of Central and Eastern Europe held values that were suppressed rather than expressed by communist rule. A standard way of ascertaining commitment to democratic values is to ask whether people think that democracy is better than any other form of government. In both Kazakhstan and Kyrgyzstan, 61 percent agree with this statement. Moreover, one-third to one-half of those who do not endorse democracy outright are "don't knows" rather than actively antidemocratic (see Table 1 on p. 148). These figures are much the same as in Latin America, Africa, Taiwan, and Korea, and higher than in the Russian Federation.[8]

In both Kazakhstan and Kyrgyzstan, there is very little difference between Muslims, the Orthodox, and nonbelievers. Even more strikingly, the most observant Muslims are almost as prodemocratic as those who are nonobservant. Furthermore, an absolute majority in each category of observance endorses democracy (see Table 1). In short, neither nominal religion nor the degree of religious observance has much influence on democratic values.

Barometer surveys have also developed a battery of questions measuring the extent to which people who have long lived under an un-

TABLE 1—RELIGIOUS OBSERVANCE AND SUPPORT FOR DEMOCRACY*
(IN PERCENTAGES)

	KAZAKHSTAN			KYRGYZSTAN		
	YES	No	DON'T KNOW	YES	No	DON'T KNOW
MUSLIMS						
Very observant	56	15	29	57	20	13
Sometimes observant	65	17	18	64	24	12
Not observant	66	16	18	62	23	15
Difference	10	1	11	5	3	2
ORTHODOX						
Observant	57	21	22	54	30	16
Not observant	64	25	11	66	17	17
Difference	7	4	11	12	13	1
NO RELIGION	60	29	11	62	25	13
Totals	61	21	18	61	25	14

* "Democracy may have its faults, but it's better than any other form of government."
Source: Nationwide sample surveys: 1,890 interviews in Kazakhstan between 26 October and 3 December 2001, and 1,964 interviews in Kyrgyzstan between 16 October and 27 November 2001.

democratic regime prefer it to a democratic alternative.[9] In Central Asia, asking people if they would like to return to communist rule generates confusion, because the question refers not only to one-party rule but to a period when there was greater economic prosperity than today. The percentage endorsing reversion to the former communist regime—38 percent in Kazakhstan and 64 percent in Kyrgyzstan—is higher than in the Russian Federation and far higher than in Central and Eastern Europe.

While military rule is found in many Muslim countries, it does not occur in successor states of the Soviet Union. When asked whether life would be better if the army governed the country, 24 percent in Kyrgyzstan and 10 percent in Kazakhstan endorsed the idea. These figures are similar to that in the Russian Federation (15 percent), though a larger minority than in Central and Eastern Europe (5 percent).

Dictatorial leadership is common in countries with Muslim majorities, and in this respect Kazakhstan and Kyrgyzstan are no exceptions. While both countries have parliaments, they are weak relative to the executive and they enjoy little public trust. Nevertheless, these parliaments are forums in which diverse opinions can be presented and criticism of corruption and the abuse of power can be voiced. The parliament of Kyrgyzstan is credited with making it "one of the least authoritarian regimes in Central Asia."[10]

When people in Kazakhstan are asked whether it would be better to have a leader govern without parliament, a plurality is against dictatorship. In Kyrgyzstan, public opinion is evenly divided on the issue, and the median person is a "don't know" (see Table 2). Although the minor-

TABLE 2—RELIGIOUS OBSERVANCE AND SUPPORT FOR
DICTATORSHIP* (IN PERCENTAGES)

	KAZAKHSTAN			KYRGYZSTAN		
	YES	No	DON'T KNOW	YES	No	DON'T KNOW
MUSLIMS						
Very observant	25	40	35	44	46	11
Sometimes observant	30	51	19	44	45	11
Not observant	41	43	15	46	38	15
Difference	16	3	20	2	8	4
ORTHODOX						
Observant	34	49	17	44	37	17
Not observant	37	53	10	45	38	17
Difference	3	4	7	1	1	0
NO RELIGION	39	48	13	44	43	13
Totals	34	49	17	44	43	13

* "We could live better if the parliament would be dissolved, free elections would be abolished, and a strong leader was in power."
Source: See Table 1.

ity favoring a dictator is quite large, it is similar to that in the Russian Federation.[11] In Kyrgyzstan, differences of opinion about dictatorial governance are completely unrelated to religion. In Kazakhstan, there is a small difference among nominal religious groups: 31 percent of Muslims endorse the idea of a dictator compared to 36 percent of those who are Orthodox and 39 percent of those with no stated religion. In Kazakhstan, Muslims who are least observant in religion are most ready to favor dictatorship, while in Kyrgyzstan no such relationship holds. Nonetheless, across all religious categories—including that of nonbelievers—less than half endorse dictatorship.

The weak correlation between religion and political attitudes in Central Asia is consistent with evidence from European communist countries, where increases in education, urbanization, and income in the post–World War II period likewise encouraged an increase in religious indifference. In Central and Eastern Europe today, differences in nominal religious commitment have little or no influence on political values. And on the basis of data from Mediterranean parts of the Muslim world, Mark Tessler concludes, "Religion influences political orientations more frequently and consistently in the West than in the Arab world."[12]

What Influences Political Values?

Whereas Max Weber thought the Protestant ethic was a major cause of the rise of capitalism, today European sociologists do not expect religious

TABLE 3—SOCIOECONOMIC INFLUENCES ON SUPPORT FOR DEMOCRACY
(PERCENTAGE RESPONDING THAT DEMOCRACY IS PREFERABLE)

	KAZAKHSTAN	KYRGYZSTAN
EDUCATION		
Minimum	48	53
Intermediate	60	59
Higher	70	69
Difference	22	16
AGE		
18–29	67	63
30–59	63	63
60+	48	52
Difference	19	11
STATE OF NATIONAL ECONOMY		
Good	71	72
So-so	68	66
Poor	61	63
Very bad	45	56
Difference	26	16
ETHNICITY		
Kazakh/Kyrgyz	63	62
Russian	59	56
Difference	4	6

Source: See Table 1.

beliefs to have political relevance and treat evidence of links between religion and politics in the United States as an indication of American exceptionalism. In Central Asia, social divisions are the chief influence on support for democracy as an ideal (see Table 3).[13] The difference in support for democracy between the most educated and the least educated Kazakhs is 22 percentage points; among Kyrgyz, the difference is 16 percentage points. There are similarly large differences between young and old. Ethnicity has limited influence; Kazakhs and Kyrgyz are slightly readier than Russians to support democracy as an ideal. Moreover, women are as likely to support democracy as are men.

Across the postcommunist world, economic transformation has turned command economies into market economies of sorts. When asked to evaluate the current state of the new economy, only a sixth of Kazakhs and less than a tenth of Kyrgyz say it is "good." The median Kazakh views the national economy as "so-so," and one-third think it is "very bad." In Kyrgyzstan the median person views the economy as being in poor

TABLE 4—SOCIOECONOMIC INFLUENCES ON
SUPPORT FOR DICTATORSHIP
(PERCENTAGE RESPONDING THAT DICTATORSHIP IS PREFERABLE)

	KAZAKHSTAN	KYRGYZSTAN
EDUCATION		
Minimum	39	42
Intermediate	33	45
Higher	34	43
Difference	5	1
STATE OF NATIONAL ECONOMY		
Good	32	39
So-so	35	41
Poor	35	41
Very bad	40	52
Difference	8	13
ETHNICITY		
Kazakh/Kyrgyz	32	47
Russian	35	43
Difference	3	4

Source: See Table 1.

shape, and more than a quarter regard it as being "very bad." The worse the perceived condition of the national economy, the less likely people are to be positive about democracy (see Table 3). But this difference in degree does not lead to the rejection of democracy. A clear majority of Kyrgyz who see conditions as very bad nonetheless endorse the idea of democracy, as do almost half of economically miserable Kazakhs.

Social differences have less influence on the evaluation of dictatorship (see Table 4). In both Central Asian countries, the worse people's view of the national economy, the more likely they are to endorse dictatorship, but the effect is less than the positive effect of views of the national economy on support for democracy. Education has a limited influence on attitudes toward dictatorship in Kazakhstan but none in Kyrgyzstan. Ethnicity, too, makes very little difference in attitudes toward dictatorship, and age and gender are completely insignificant.

In post-Soviet countries, the civilization that matters is not Islam; it is, rather, one based on secular values, a belief system that has flourished in democratic and undemocratic parts of Europe for more than a century. In Russia, secular values come before religious ones among the great mass of a nominally Orthodox population. More than half never go to church, and less than 10 percent attend an Orthodox service at least once a month. Muslims in Russia have been socialized into a culture offering material and social incentives to conform to secular norms, and enjoy higher living standards than their coreligionists in neighboring countries. The fragmentation of Muslims in post-Soviet societies among more than three dozen different nationality groups is an obstacle to the creation of a single pan-Muslim identity. Moreover, any Muslims who attempted to mobilize political opposition to the government of the Russian Federation on religious grounds would not only invite repression by the state but also risk alienating Russia's secular Muslims. Nor could they count on support from Central Asian countries, whose leaders have multiple incentives to maintain friendly relations with Moscow.[14]

Muslims, like postcommunist Christians and secularists, are divided among themselves in their political views. As with all major world religions, Islam gathers under its tent people who interpret the will of God in different ways. Evidence from Kazakhstan and Kyrgyzstan, countries that are geographically close to centers of Islamic fundamentalism, shows that being a Muslim does not make a person more likely either to reject democracy or to endorse dictatorship.

NOTES

1. Samuel P. Huntington, *The Clash of Civilizations and the Remaking of World Order* (New York: Simon & Schuster, 1996), 214, 217.

2 Daniel Brumberg, "Islamists and the Politics of Consensus," *Journal of Democracy* 13 (July 2002): 109.

3. Martha Brill Olcott, "Democratization and the Growth of Political Participation in Kazakhstan," in Karen Dawisha and Bruce Parrott, eds., *Conflict, Cleavage and Chance in Central Asia and the Caucasus* (Baltimore: Johns Hopkins University Press, 1997), 201.

4. See *Russians Outside Russia: A 1991 VCIOM Survey* (Glasgow: University of Strathclyde Studies in Public Policy No. 283, 1997), 6ff. Interviewing was conducted in August–September 1991.

5. The rating of each country is 5.5 on a 7-point scale, where 7 means "least free." For detailed discussions, see Bhavna Dave, "Kazakhstan," and Rafis F. Abazov, "Kyrgyzstan," in *Nations in Transit 2002* (New York: Transaction Publishers).

6. See *Transition Report 2001: Energy in Transition* (London: European Bank for Reconstruction and Development, 2001), 19; *World Bank Atlas 2001* (Washington, D.C.: World Bank), 47f.

7. These results are based on 1,890 interviews in Kazakhstan between 26 October and 3 December 2001 and 1,964 interviews in Kyrgyzstan between 16 October and 27 November 2001. The surveys were part of an eight-nation study of living conditions in successor states of the Soviet Union directed by Dr. Christian Haerpfer.

8. See Marta Lagos, "Between Stability and Crisis in Latin America," Table 1; Michael Bratton and Robert Mattes, "Africans' Surprising Universalism," Table 1; Yun-han Chu, Larry Diamond, and Doh Chull Shin, "Halting Progress in Korea and Taiwan," *Journal of Democracy* 12 (January 2001): 122–36. Richard Rose and Neil Munro, *Elections without Order* (New York: Cambridge University Press, 2002), Figure 10.6.

9. See Richard Rose, William Mishler, and Christian Haerpfer, *Democracy and Its Alternatives: Understanding Post-Communist Societies* (Baltimore: Johns Hopkins University Press, 1998), ch. 5.

10. Rafis F. Abazov, "Kyrgyz Republic," 1.

11. For details, see Richard Rose, *A Bottom-Up Evaluation of Enlargement Countries: New Europe Barometer 1* (Glasgow: University of Strathclyde Studies in Public Policy No. 364 [2002]).

12. See the report of surveys in Morocco, Algeria, Egypt, and the West Bank and Gaza by Mark Tessler, "Islam and Democracy in the Middle East," *Comparative Politics* 34 (2002): 350.

13. Introducing religious commitment or nominal religion as independent variables in a multiple regression equation adds almost nothing to the variance explained by socioeconomic influences in support for democracy and undemocratic alternatives.

14. See Dmitri Glinski, "Russia and Its Muslims: The Politics of Identity at the International-Domestic Frontier," *East European Constitutional Review* 11 (Winter–Spring 2002): esp. 81ff.

INDEX